The
Roman Cookery
of APICIUS

The
Roman Cookery
of APICIUS

Translated and Adapted for the
Modern Kitchen

BY

John Edwards

London Sydney Auckland Johannesburg

A Century Paperback published in Great Britain by
Random House Ltd, 20 Vauxhall Bridge Road,
London SW1V 2SA

Random House Australia (Pty) Ltd
20 Alfred Street, Milsons Point, Sydney 2061,
Australia

Random House New Zealand Ltd
18 Poland Road, Glenfield, Auckland 10,
New Zealand

Random House South Africa (Pty) Ltd
PO Box 337, Bergvlei 2012, South Africa

First published in Great Britain under the Rider imprint 1985
This edition 1988
Reprinted 1988, 1989, 1990, 1991, 1992, 1993

Printed and bound in Great Britain by
Mackays of Chatham PLC, Chatham, Kent

British Library Cataloguing in Publication Data

Edwards, John
The Roman cookery of Apicius.
1. Food: Aphrodisiacs—Recipes
I. Title   II. Apicius. De re cocuinaria
641.5937

ISBN 0–7126–2556–9

*I dedicate this book
to the memory of my father and mentor,
Newton Edwards.*

ACKNOWLEDGEMENTS

Of the various existing texts, I wish to express my admiration for the one edited by Mary Ella Milham, published in the Teubner collection, Leipzig, 1969. Her *De Re Coquinaria*, together with the alternate readings she supplies, have been enormously valuable to me as the foundation and touchstone upon which I built a practical translation and commentary for use in the modern kitchen.

André's Latin-French dual text, *L'Art Culinaire* (1965) supplies a clear French translation of Apicius and Vinidarius, and has been helpful to me as an example of comparative translation. Many of André's Latin readings were later confirmed by Milham. In some instances I chose André's reading over Milham's.

The Latin-English text, *The Roman Cookery Book* (1958), by Flower and Rosenbaum, uses the Giarratano-Vollmer text and contains a number of interesting speculations upon the nature of classical Roman cookery.

Vehling's *Cookery and Dining in Imperial Rome* (republished in 1977) is a fascinating and personal treatment of the *De Re Coquinaria*. Vehling refers frequently and in lively language to earlier students of Apicius. His translation is based upon texts by Torinus, Humelbergius, Lister, and Giarratano-Vollmer. Unfortunately, numerous interpolations and bracketed words make his text very difficult to read. However, his commentary contains valuable insights for the practical use of the *De Re Coquinaria*.

I also wish to acknowledge the encouragement of my mother, Betty Edwards, and the enormous support of my wife, Gillian, both in the kitchen and out of it, and the late Professor Edith Wightman, in whose house I first tasted an Apician meal.

SO THE MEALS
OF APICIUS
BEGIN:

CONTENTS

INTRODUCTION

THE COOKERY AND IDENTITY OF APICIUS

The Roman Cookery of Apicius (or, in Latin, *De Re Coquinaria*) is nothing less than a compilation of the secrets of Roman and classical Greek cookery during the reigns of the Caesars. Largely overlooked by scholars and cooks for most of the last fifteen hundred years, it describes the delicious meals eaten across civilized Europe during the centuries of Roman domination. The chapters which follow constitute the foundations of western cookery, shorn of food additives and artificial preservatives. Indeed, the title itself, *De Re Coquinaria*, means simply "On Cookery."

Who was Apicius and what is known about him? The two manuscripts which are ascribed to him are written in the Latin of the late fourth and early fifth century A.D. This was the period of Roman decline, redolent of the barbarian invasions of Goth and Vandal, and full of nostalgia for the golden age of the Roman peace that followed the accession of the great Augustus Caesar four hundred years before. The Latin of the *Coquinaria* may be imperfect and the spelling eccentric, but the spirit of the book is confident, joyous, and rich. A book composed not for the sour and unflinching stoic but for the epicurean, perhaps even the hedonist, with the culinary resources of an empire to command. It is worth noting that the spices and herbs used in the *Coquinaria* have, with only a few exceptions, a familiar sound. This is because Apicius had access through Greek and Roman traders to the spice markets of southern Asia. Pepper, cinnamon, ginger, nutmeg, and cloves were transported by ship from India, Ceylon, the Bay of Bengal, the Spice Islands in the Banda Sea, and China with a frequency that was not to be matched until

A page from a ninth century Latin transcription of De Re Coquinaria. *This is the recipe for* Extraordinary Spiced Wine (CONDITUM PARADOXUM) *which is translated on page 2. Photo courtesy New York Academy of Medicine.*

the voyages of the Portuguese caravels in the sixteenth century. In addition, the resources of North Africa, the Near East, the rivers and coasts of the Black Sea, and the waters and farms of central and western Europe all made their contributions to the recipes of Apicius. The citizens of Rome were as emancipated from the particular foods and seasonings of the Italian peninsula as today are the people of New York from the products of only the Atlantic seaboard.

Of Apicius, the man, confusion abounds. Three gastrophiles bore this name in Imperial Rome. The first lived during the meteoric rise of Julius Caesar (d. 44 B.C.). The second taught *haute cuisine* under Augustus and Tiberius (27 B.C.–37 A.D.), and enjoyed the reputation of a wealthy and decadent gourmet. The third Apicius lived during the reign of Trajan (98–117 A.D.).

> *When the Emperor Trajan was in Parthia, a journey of many days*
> *from the sea, Apicius arranged to have fresh oysters sent to him,*
> *preserved by his own skill.*
>
> Athenaeus, *The Deipnosophists*, 1.7.

It is recorded that so great was Apicius' love of food that he poisoned himself for fear of dying of hunger.

> *After you'd spent 60 million on your stomach, Apicius,*
> *10 million still remained,*
> *An embarrassment, you said, fit only to satisfy*
> *Mere hunger and thirst:*
> *So your last and most expensive meal was poison. . . .*
> *Apicius, you never were more a glutton than at the end.*
>
> Martial, *Epigrams*, 3.22.

In fact, by the end of the first century A.D., the name "Apicius" had already become a cliché for wealth.

> *What greater joke tickles the ear of the people than the sight of a*
> *poor Apicius?*
>
> Juvenal, *Satires*, 11.2–3.

We may amuse ourselves with the image of a man with this name delighting in his role as the arbiter of cuisine in the villas and palaces of Rome at the zenith of her wealth and power.

> *The great Apicius was pleased to go out to dine:*
> *Even gourmets grow depressed at home.*
>
> Martial, 2.69.

And perhaps this was so; but no individual personality emerges from the pages of Apicius' *Cookery*. Only twice does the mask of the impersonal momentarily slip. On one occasion he concludes a recipe by saying enthusiastically, "You'll be amazed." On the other he ironically comments on a recipe for anchovy stew made without anchovies, *Ad mensam nemo agnoscet quid manducet.* (At the table nobody will know what he's eating.) In short, "Apicius" is best regarded as a proverbial name for the greatest and most notorious of the Roman writers on cookery. Stories of his legendary wealth and excesses abounded and he passed into history as a kind of Croesus of the kitchen.

> *There lived in the reign of Tiberius a man named Apicius, a*
> *voluptuary of extraordinary wealth, who gave his name to many*
> *kinds of cakes. Apicius lavished countless sums of money on his*
> *stomach in Minturnae, a city in Campania. There he passed his*
> *time for the most part eating the very costly prawns of the region,*
> *which grow larger than the biggest prawns of Smyrna or the*
> *lobsters of Alexandria. He happened to hear that prawns also grew*
> *to an enormous size off the coasts of Libya and accordingly set sail*
> *from Italy without the delay of even a single day. After suffering*
> *from storms during the voyage across the open sea he drew near*
> *land. The Libyan fishermen sailed towards him before he had set*
> *out from his ship, for the report of his arrival had already spread,*
> *and they brought him their best prawns. Seeing these he inquired*
> *as to whether they had any that were larger. But when they replied*
> *that none grew larger than those they had offered him, Apicius*

suddenly remembered the prawns of his own Minturnae and commanded his helmsman to sail back to Italy by the same route they had taken to Libya, without making any further approach to land.

Athenaeus, 1.7.

In spite of the reputed deficiencies of his character his name gave legitimacy to successful and admired recipes, whether or not Apicius had been the first to create them, and his book captured for all time the essence of what was best in the art of Roman cooking. However, the credit for the book's survival must go to the anonymous Roman who transcribed 470 of Apicius' recipes into late fourth century A.D. Latin, and to Vinidarius who contributed his thirty-two extracts in the early years of the fifth century A.D.* In the fourth century, even as they were doing so, the frontiers of the Empire were crumbling, the sea trade routes to the Orient were dwindling, and the pages of Apicius' *Coquinaria* were passing into history as the barbarity of early mediaeval Europe began.

In a very real sense, we have come full circle since the book was inscribed on parchment in the shadow of universal ruin. We, too, draw upon the resources of the world to stock our kitchens; we, too, nostalgically recall past ages in which peace seemed secure. And now, as then, the art of cooking can comfort the spirit as well as the stomach.

*   *   *   *

The Roman Cookery of Apicius is divided into eleven chapters ("Books") and its composition does not differ greatly from a comprehensive modern cookbook. The chapters have such familiar titles as "The Gardener," "Of Birds," and "The Sea." It is in the choice of herbs, spices, and sauces, and in the methods of preparation that Apicius' recipes excel, and well may we say with him, *"Miraberis"* ("You'll be amazed") after tasting *Roast Suckling Kid Crowned with Laurel, Peas or Beans Vitellian,* or *Gourds Alexandrine.*

*A ninth century Latin transcription of the book now resides in the library of the New York Academy of Medicine. (See facsimile p. x.)

ROME AND THE SPICE TRADE WITH THE ORIENT

The *Coquinaria* contains a multitude of references to spices and herbs which are not indigenous to the Mediterranean. These include pepper, cinnamon, ginger, Indian spikenard, cardamom, Indian costum, and, indirectly, nutmeg and cloves. The source of these rare and expensive condiments was the Orient. In the first and second centuries of the Christian era, and to a lesser extent after the death of Marcus Aurelius in 180 A.D., trade flourished between Rome and the Indian peninsula, China, and, through intermediaries, with the Spice Islands. In addition to herbs and spices, the Romans sought perfumes, precious stones, ivory, and pearls from India, and silk from China. To pay for these luxuries the Empire exported linen, glass, and coral; but by far the most significant export was gold and silver coin. The drain upon the Imperial treasury was alarming, especially to conservatives like Pliny the Elder who viewed the situation with distaste.

> *At the lowest computation, India, China, and the Peninsula* [of Arabia] *carry off 100,000,000 sesterces a year from our Empire — such is the bill for our pleasures and our women.*
>
> Pliny, *Natural History*, 12.41.

Pliny wrote these words circa 70 A.D. when Rome had attained the zenith of her power. At first glance, the presence in Italy of Arabian perfumes, Indian spices, and Chinese silks might be taken as evidence for the extraordinary ability of the Roman upper classes to reach to the ends of the earth to satisfy their whims. In fact, trade links had existed between the Orient and the West for over three hundred years. The recipes appear to be much older than the Latin in which they are written, and their origins can be traced not only to the peoples of ancient Greece and Egypt, but also to the Orient.

ROMAN EATING HABITS AND COOKING UTENSILS

Under the Caesars, Romans customarily took three meals a day. The *ientaculum* (breakfast), was eaten immediately after sunrise. This was a very light meal consisting of a little bread and fruit. The *prandium* (midday meal) was a collation of some fish, eggs, cold meats, vegetables, and bread. It was thought vulgar to consume a large lunch. The philosopher Seneca, for example, boasted that he required only a little bread and some figs to sustain himself at the *prandium* (*Ad Lucilium Epistulae Morales*, 84, 87). These modest habits, however, were forgotten at the *cena* (dinner) which began at the ninth hour of the Roman day (about four o'clock) and continued into the evening, or even into the night. Readers of Petronius' *Satyricon* will recall that it was midnight before Encolpius and Ascyltos could escape from the dining room of the glutton Trimalchio, whose menu can be perused on pages 17–19. The *cena* had three parts: the *gustatio* (hors d'oeuvres), the *fercula* which means, literally, "dishes which are carried" (from the kitchen) and the *mensae secundae* (the dessert courses). The *fercula* were at least three in number and could increase to five, seven, or more courses according to the purse of the master of the house. Included in the *fercula* were fish and shellfish dishes, poultry, feathered game, joints of meat, and stuffed animals cooked whole. Of course the variety and size of Roman dinners were nearly infinite. Then, as now, people ate and drank in moderation or to excess in a manner consistent with their desires, their prosperity, and their luck.

In the first two hundred years of the Christian era and to a lesser extent in the third century and in parts of the fourth, a prosperous Roman citizen could choose from an enormous variety of foodstuffs from the lands and seas of the Empire, prepared with many exotic, imported herbs and spices. There were, however, some obvious omissions. Since there was no apparent intercourse between Rome and the Americas, the ancients were unaware of the tomato and the potato, two staple commodities which few in the West would now do without. Tropical fruits like the banana were imperfectly known. In spite of their trade connections with India, Ceylon, and China, the Romans did not develop a taste for tea and seem to have drunk herbal infusions only as medicines. Of course, there was no coffee or tobacco; honey and boiled (reduced) wines took the place of sugar.

Other differences were matters of preference, not geography. Instead of butter, Romans cooked with olive oil. Milk was obtained from the goat rather than from the cow. Unlike the peoples of the Near East and northern Europe, the Greeks and Romans did not brew beer. Wine was their staple drink, their primary food coloring, and often their preservative. As Trimalchio said in the *Satyricon,* "Wine is life!" They did not know how to distill liquor.

Judging from the space given to each in Apicius' *Cookery,* Romans of the time preferred hare and pork over all other meats. Next in importance came wild boar, kid, and lamb. After venison, beef and veal ranked last, with wild sheep and goat. It is possible, however, that this apparent "unpopularity" of beef was due largely to the scarcity of large grazing areas in the Italian Peninsula in 100 A.D. In the poems of Homer composed over 1,000 years earlier, sacrifices of 100 oxen were offered to Zeus, then eaten with obvious enjoyment by the Achaian Greeks. Of domestic and game birds, poultry was by far the most popular. Apicius recorded fifteen different ways of cooking chicken. Chickens were followed by domestic geese and ducks, and such game birds as pheasants, partridges, wood pigeons, wild ducks, and doves. The wealthy regaled themselves with crane, flamingo, and even ostrich. Other rare animals were also eaten occasionally—for the sake of ostentation, rather than the succulence of the viands. Thus Scissa served bear meat at her memorial dinner for a dead slave. (See p. 18 for the menu.) In addition, the Romans were in the habit of eating a wide variety of small birds, especially *beccaficos* (figpeckers), ortolans (garden buntings), and thrushes, which were raised in great numbers in aviaries.

As a rule, poultry, game, and domestic animals were first stuffed then stewed in cooking pots, or roasted or braised in pans in the oven. Some specialty meats like fattened liver and pork cutlets were cooked on a gridiron. Apicius made no mention of the spit. Clay cooking pots were called *clibani,* while those made of fine Cumaean clay were singled out by Apicius and called *cumanae.* Frying pans for meats, vegetables, and fish were either oval or round in shape and called *fretales* or *sartagines.* The *sartago* also served as a baking pan. Stews, ragouts, and casserole dishes were made in shallow pans called *patinae.* However, Apicius used this and other terms for cooking vessels very loosely, and *patina* and *caccabus* appear interchangeably in his directions. Kitchen ovens were made of brick and generally heated with wood and charcoal. The *thermospodium* was a portable bronze stove placed in the dining room, which burned charcoal and could be used either to cook dishes or to keep them warm before serving. Apicius also referred to the *angularis,* a square pot or pan, the *boletarium,* a dish used for cooking and eating mushrooms, and the *lanx*, a serving platter. Pots, pans, and dishes were made of iron, clay, or bronze, while silver was affected by the upper classes. Romans ate with knives and spoons, but rarely with forks. The dining room was usually upstairs and furnished with a *triclinium* (three couches). Guests were served at portable tables which were changed at the end of the different courses.

MENUS OF FAMOUS DINNERS

I

The Poet Martial's Dinner for His Friend Toranius

Gustatio (Hors d'oeuvres)
   Honeyed wine
   Lettuce and leeks
   Tunnyfish pieces in sliced egg

Fercula (Prepared dishes)
   Fresh boiled broccoli
   Sausage on white pulse pudding
   Pale beans and bacon

   Served with wine that *tu facies bonum bibendo* — by your drinking
      you will make good

Mensae secundae (Dessert)
   Grapes
   Pears
   Roasted chestnuts

II

The Millionaire Scissa's Funeral Feast for Her Dead Slave

Gustatio (Hors d'oeuvres)
  Olives
  Lettuce
  Seafood forcemeats and pheasant sausages
  Peacocks' eggs
  Honeyed wine

Fercula (Prepared dishes)
  Roast suckling pig stuffed with pastry and honey, served with
    chicken livers well done, beets, and wholemeal bread
  Cold elderberry tart with warm honey and Spanish wine
  Bear cuts with chick-peas and lupines

Mensae secundae (Dessert)
  Nuts and apples
  Cheese seasoned in must
  Snails
  Eggs
  Pickled olives

Petronius, *Satyricon.*

III

Trimalchio's Feast

Gustatio (Hors d'oeuvres)

White and black olives
Dormice sprinkled with
  honey and poppy seeds
Grilled sausages

Damsons and pomegranate
  seeds
Beccaficos in spiced egg yolk
Honeyed wine

Fercula (Prepared dishes)

Foods of the Zodiac served on a round plate (on the sign of the
Ram, chick-peas; on the Bull, beef; on the Twins, kidneys; on the
Crab, a crown of myrtle; on the Lion, African figs; on the Virgin,
a sterile sow's womb; on the Balance, scales supporting tarts and
honey cakes; on the Scorpion, a scorpion fish; on the Archer, an
eyefish; on the Goat's horns, a lobster; on the Waterbearer, a
goose; on the Fishes, two red mullets) served with bread and sur-
rounding:

Roasted fattened fowls, sow bellies, and hare

Roast whole wild boar with dates, suckled by piglets made of cakes
and stuffed with live thrushes

Boiled whole pig stuffed with sausage and black puddings

The *fercula* served with Falernian wine 100 years old

Mensae secundae (Dessert)

Fruits and cakes
Boned, fattened chickens and
  goose eggs
Pastries stuffed with raisins
  and nuts

Quince-apples and pork
  disguised as fowls and fish
Oysters and scallops
Snails

Petronius, *Satyricon*.

SEASONINGS AND SAUCES

Seasonings were of enormous importance to Roman cookery. In the preparation of his dishes, Apicius frequently used ten or more condiments, the sources of which included not only the provinces of the vast Roman Empire in the first century A.D., but also Arabia, Parthia (Iran), the Indian subcontinent and Ceylon, Southeast Asia, the Spiceries (the Banda and Molucca island groups), and China. Indeed, I would speculate that the prices paid by the Roman upper classes for foreign herbs and spices were so great and continued for so long a period (four centuries) that the drain upon Rome's gold and silver resources contributed to a hitherto unrecognized degree to the economic decline of the West. The primary evidence for this is Apicius' *Coquinaria* itself: over ninety percent of the five hundred recipes call for costly imported spices, particularly pepper. Moreover, it is safe to assume that Apicius represented the model for fine cookery from the reign of Augustus (27 B.C.) to the decline and final extinction of Roman power in the western Mediterranean in the fourth and early fifth centuries A.D. Pliny, Petronius, Martial, Juvenal, and Athenaeus supported this view in classical times, while the late Latin used in the "Excerpts of Vinidarius" (Book XI) suggests that Apicius' influence continued to be strong as late as the fourth century A.D. Further evidence is provided by the highly developed sea trade network which linked Rome with the Asian spice markets from the time of Augustus.

The discovery of Asian seasonings by the peoples of the Empire revolutionized Western cookery forever—a discovery immortalized by Apicius. The continuing interest in "The Indies" after the fall of Rome can be largely explained by the European desire to continue seasoning and preserving foods with Indian pepper, Chinese cinnamon, and cloves and nutmeg from the distant Spiceries. Western cookery has not changed substantially since Apicius lived. Our modern technology can prolong the life, but can do little to improve the flavor, of foods seasoned in the classical manner.

Of seasonings, the first in importance to Apicius was pepper. Romans had traditionally depended upon the native myrtle berry as their prime seasoning, but the discovery of pepper supplanted the milder myrtle berry. It was remembered in certain old-fashioned Roman dishes such as *isicia omentata* (forcemeat sausages), and even there it was accompanied by the ubiquitous peppercorn. It survived also as the basis for a wine called *myrtidanum*. Significantly, Apicius nearly always gave pepper as the first ingredient in his sauces; indeed, so dominant was pepper in the minds of Roman cooks that the word was used in an extended sense to include cinnamon, cardamon, and nutmeg. For Apicius, pepper performed the modern functions of both pepper and salt: it was used in the kitchen preparations of almost all meats, vegetables, and fish, and it was also sprinkled over cooked dishes that were ready to be served at the tables.

Second in importance was, lovage, a native green herb related to celery, whose seeds, roots, and leaves were used by Apicius almost as frequently as pepper. In the twentieth century, lovage is more often found in herbals than in cookery books, which is a pity since its distinctive taste, once acquired, is delightful and improves the flavor of almost every kind of food. Celery seed, or dried celery leaves, can be substituted for lovage, but the classical cook can easily grow this herb in a garden.

Another green herb which has unaccountably fallen from grace in modern times is rue. Added in small quantities to many of Apicius' sauces, it imparted a bitter taste balanced by the presence of honey and sweet raisin wines.

Other European herbs and spices which were frequently employed by Roman cooks were, in descending order of importance, coriander, cumin, oregano, celery seed, parsley seed, bay leaf, aniseed, fennel, mint, caraway, mustard seed, wormwood, chervil, colewort (rocket), saxifrage (sweet cicely), thyme, sage, pennyroyal, pellitory, elecampane, saffron, and mastic. Lesser used condiments can be found in Book XI, on page 282. Imported spices were dominated by pepper, followed by ginger, Indian spikenard, cinnamon, cardamon, nutmeg, cloves, and Indian costum. Finally, laser was imported from the countries of the Near East and Iran, safflower from Egypt, and expensive varieties of fish-pickle were shipped from Spain.

Apicius customarily half stewed his meats and game in seasoned water or stock and then finished them in a sauce whose ingredients invariably included pepper, lovage, wine, stock, and olive oil. To this was added, as was appropriate, green herbs, cumin, coriander, and imported seasonings. In many cases the cooked food was served in a second sauce which complemented the first. Vinegar and honey appeared in many sauces. Gravies were thickened with starch or flour. Ragouts (*minutal*) and stews were thickened with eggs and pieces of soft bread or pastry. Sausages and stuffings were bound with eggs, starch, or flour. Almost everything was served with a sprinkling of pepper. Salt was mainly used in marinades with ground cumin, and as a preservative for meats and fish. Other preservatives were honey, must (new wine), and vinegar. Dishes were sweetened either with boiled wines, sweet raisin wine, or honey. Vinegar was the foundation for dressings and sweet and sour dishes.

Apicius cooked his dishes slowly, in the classical manner, to allow the sauces to penetrate the vegetables, meats, and fish. Many cooked dishes were finished in a second sauce, incorporating the reduced, seasoned stock from the first. Chives, leeks, onions, and squills (or other bulbs) were often cooked with meats. Sauces, casseroles, puddings, stews, and stuffings frequently used varieties of nuts (pine nuts, hazelnuts, chestnuts, almonds, pistachios) and fruits (raisins, dates, damsons, quinces), in addition to dried onions or shallots.

The base for an Apician sauce is a mixture of wine, stock, and olive oil, seasoned with ground herbs and spices, brought to a boil, and then simmered. Honey and vinegar are added to taste. Nuts are chopped and roasted, and dried fruits steeped in water or wine, before they are mixed with the other ingredients.

The secret of classical cookery is time. Art of any kind cannot be hurried.

RARE OR UNCOMMON SEASONINGS

Roman fish-pickle

In the first century A.D., fish-pickle was of two general kinds: *liquamen* * or *garum* made from the entrails of mackerel, and *muria*, an inferior product derived from the Mediterranean tunnyfish. The term *garum* was related to the Greek word for shrimp, no doubt the base for an earlier kind of marine sauce. The preparation of *garum* began with the gills, intestines, and blood of

---

* The term *liquamen* was also used by Apicius in recipes requiring a liquid rather than a condiment. In those recipes, it has been translated as "stock," or more specifically "fish stock."

the mackerel. This was put in an open jar and saturated with salt. Vinegar, parsley, wine, and sweet herbs were added. The mixture was then exposed to the sun until the fish parts liquefied (*liquamen*), resulting in a thick sauce. After two or three months the sauce was bottled and used.

A faster method was employed to produce inferior fish-pickles or *muriae*. The parts of less expensive fish were mixed with a very thick brine seasoned with oregano. The sauce was then cooked over a fire until the fish parts dissolved. Boiled, reduced wine was added. The sauce was cooled, strained, and served when clear.

During the first century A.D., some extremely expensive fish-pickles were devised. The most extravagant was invented by Apicius himself. It used the livers of red mullet, bought at the height of this fish's inflated market prices (before the imposition of a sumptuary tax ordered by Tiberius Caesar). The moralistic Pliny called this fish-pickle *garum sociorum*. *Socies* had many meanings, one of which was "companion."

> *Marcus Apicius, who was born with a genius for every kind of extravagance, considered it an excellent practice for mullets to be killed in a sauce made from their companions, hence the name garum sociorum.*

> Pliny, 9.30.

The Romans were inordinately fond of this redolent and costly condiment and used it to season seafood dishes and meats, and as a dressing with salads. It was used with great restraint because of its strong taste and its costliness.

> *Take this costly gift, the proud sauce*
> *That's made from the first blood*
> *Of a still breathing mackerel.*

> Martial, 13.102.

Laser (or silphium)

Laser — among the most extraordinary of nature's gifts.

Pliny, 22.102.

This seasoning was probably derived from the *Ferula tingitana* plant, a species of giant fennel which flourished, but only in a wild state, in North Africa. It was gathered with such zeal by the Egyptians, Greeks, and Romans that by the first century A.D. the plant was extinct on the southern coast of the Mediterranean and had to be imported from what are now Syria, Iraq, and Iran. Apicius did mention Cyrenaic laser (Libyan assafoetida), but I believe this was based on an earlier Greek or Egyptian version of a recipe for laser relish. In modern times, the *Ferula tingitana* has returned to North Africa where it grows to heights of between six and eight feet.

The Egyptians, Greeks, and Romans extracted juice from incisions in the stalk and root, which Apicius called "laser," though occasionally he referred to it by its Greek name, "silphium." In modern Europe, assafoetida is used medicinally in combination with valerian for hysteria. It is extracted for this purpose from the root of the *Ferula fetida*, and is not to be confused with the fennel extract used as a condiment by Apicius.

"The number of uses of compounds made with laser is immeasurable," said Pliny. Among them were the following: diuretic, healing ointment for sores, antidote for wounds caused by poison-tipped weapons, snakebites, and scorpion stings, for shrinking corns and carbuncles, healing dog bites, soothing chilblains, alleviating coughing and wheezing, and as a cure for gout, cramps, pleurisy, and tetanus.

As a seasoning, laser was no less versatile. Apicius specified its use with relishes, turnips, sausages, gourds, peas, barley soup, chicken, pigeons, doves, flamingo, sow's womb, crackling, and knuckles, and with a multitude of seafood dishes.

Laser is perhaps the only major ancient seasoning which we in the West are no longer in the habit of using. In the modern versions of Apicius' recipes I have replaced it with ginger in some cases, and in others with fennel. In India, however, laser continues to be used in sauces under the name of "heeng."

Rue

Among our principal medical plants is rue.

Pliny, 20.51.

Rue (*Ruta graveolens*) was known to Apicius as garden rue (*hortensis*) and wild rue (*sylvestris*). This herb has strongly scented leaves and an exceedingly bitter taste. Apicius no doubt used the less harsh garden variety. In large doses rue is narcotic; its juice is a local irritant, and contact with its leaves may cause dermatitis. Obviously, this herb, like laser, was used with moderation. It can be omitted altogether if unavailable. A dash of rosemary is an effective substitute. Apicius used rue typically as one of a list of ingredients in sauces, either as a ground leaf or, less often, as a ground seed. Other Roman writers considered its application as principally medical, although the poet Martial mentioned rue leaves used as wrappings for sweetmeats and for eggs. Pliny recommended it for a host of complaints: as antidote for poisonous mushrooms, snakebites, insect stings, for improving eyesight, relief from chest pains, coughs, kidney complaints, indigestion, the prevention of hangovers, as an anti-diuretic, and more. The reputation of rue was so great that it was believed even animals knew of it.

In a similar way rue is an antidote for snakebite, since when weasels are about to fight with snakes they first fortify themselves by eating rue.

Pliny, 20.51.

One final testament to the reputation of this herb is the story of King Mithridates VI of Pontus, an enemy of Rome in the first century B.C. He consumed rue and other poisonous plants in vast quantities so as to become immune to the poisoning he feared daily. Unfortunately, he was defeated by Pompey and subsequently tried to commit suicide by swallowing yet more poison. This proved ineffective and Mithridates was forced to kill himself by falling on the sword of one of his guards.

Colewort

Colewort, or rocket (*Eruca sativa*), in modern times has been used as a salad herb, similar to watercress. In older herbals one finds the practice of mixing the seed with honey to remove freckles. Apicius used the seed as an ingredient in sauces. Where unavailable, mustard seed may be substituted. The Greeks enjoyed the flavor of colewort seed to such a degree that they called it "EUZOMON" (good sauce) and added it to meat and fish. In the ancient world there was another, less pleasant, use made of this plant:

> *They say that those who are about to submit to flogging drink it in wine to induce insensibility to pain.*

Pliny, 20.49.

Elecampane

This plant is among the list of dry seasonings at the beginning of Book XI. Elecampane (*Inula helenium*) is a hardy herbaceous perennial which grows wild or in cultivation from England to Tibet. Elecampane produces large egg-shaped tubers on its roots which, when dried and ground, yield a bitter seasoning and a camphor-like smell. It is still used to flavor sweetmeats. The leaves are similarly fragrant. The southern European variety, *Inula ensifolia* (inula with sword-shaped leaves) bears yellow flowers in August and grows to a height of ten inches. In *You make Liburnian oil this way*, (Book I), the herb helenium is specified instead of elecampane. *Inula helenium* may grow as tall as eight feet throughout Europe in the summer months. Apicius used only the leaves of this species of elecampane, but both leaves and roots of *Inula ensifolia* are edible. In the absence of either kind of elecampane, a sprinkling of aniseed will evoke the spirit of Apicius.

As for the cultivation of elecampane, Columella recommended planting *"circa Calendas Apriles"* (at the beginning of April). (*De Re Rustica*, 11.3.)

ROMAN COOKING WINES

Apicius was concerned with the kitchen, not the wine cellar, and his are principally cooking wines, with the exception of certain spiced and honeyed varieties served at the beginning of the Roman dinner.

Passum (raisin wine) was made from the musk-flavored psythian or muscatel grapes. These were left on the vine and not picked until they had shrivelled to half their weight. Alternatively, the grapes were aged more rapidly through being picked when ripe, then spread out on trays under the sun, or else they were immersed in boiling olive oil. The raisins were then soaked in a superior wine until they became swollen. At this stage they were crushed underfoot and pressed. *Passum* of the second rank was obtained by adding water to the grapes for another pressing. The Romans of Apicius' day valued Cretan *passum* most highly, followed by varieties from Cilicia (a Roman province in Asia Minor facing Cyprus), Africa (Libya), and lastly Italy. Apicius used raisin wine to color, sweeten, and flavor meats, vegetables, and fish. *Passum* invariably appears in the ingredients for sweet sauces. The modern descendants oj *passum* are Italian passito wines, and the vins de paille of France.

Boiled Wines

The drier the grapes the stronger the *passum*.

A Roman proverb

The "wines" used by Apicius to flavor, color, and sweeten his dishes were not wines so much as processes, since little fermentation was involved.

Defrutum was made from the must or juice obtained from crushed and pressed grapes. This was boiled and continuously stirred until the liquid was reduced to half its volume. (This is Pliny's method, but Varro and Columella, who were not cooks, disagreed and recorded a reduction to one third.)

Carenum was made in the same manner, except that the must was reduced by only one third.

Sapa was obtained by reducing two thirds of its initial volume. *Sapa* was very thick and sweet, with the consistency of honey.

All three boiled wines are present in nearly every kind of recipe in Apicius' book, usually accompanied by a true wine, honey, and a variety of seasonings. This suggests that classical cookery was, in general, sweet and highly spiced. The rare occasions when Apicius included measurements for the sweet wines and condiments for his recipes bear this out.

Sweet boiled wines had other uses for Apicius. In Book I, blackberries are preserved in a mixture of *sapa* and juice. This is related to the ancient practice of adding *defrutum* and *carenum* to wines in order to give them a longer life. Wines the Romans (who preferred strong wines) considered lacking in body were sometimes strengthened by adding these boiled-down musts. Those who enjoyed a very sweet wine even went so far as to mix *defrutum* and *carenum* with honey.

Mulsum (honey wine) was another sweet wine used by Apicius in cooking, and was wine mixed with honey according to taste. *Hydromeli* was a true mead, a product of rainwater and fermented honey.

Myrtle berry wine also appeared occasionally as a flavoring in Apicius' sauces. It was made by boiling the myrtle berries in must seasoned with salt. These berries were then pressed, their juice mixed with simple must, and finally reduced in volume through being boiled a second time.

Lastly, Apicius cooked with true fermented red and white wines, *vinum*. These were usually diluted with water. Occasionally, pure wine was used in the preparation of sauces, in which case Apicius called it *merum*.

A NOTE ON THE RECIPES

I have cooked and recorded alternative "modern" recipes containing measures, substitutions, and directions for cooking to accompany the originals in the *Coquinaria*. Apicius himself wrote in a plain, sometimes laconic, style. His book was intended as a practical treatise on cookery for use by professional cooks accustomed to exercizing their own judgement.

The Romans of the first century A.D. enjoyed foods which were very sweet and highly spiced. I have followed the rule of moderation in my use of the herbs and spices, but *The Roman Cookery of Apicius* lends itself to experimentation and no one version of each recipe can do justice to the wonderful combination of flavors. What I have done is only the beginning.

Apicius' recipes are not arranged in the groupings usually found in modern cookbooks. For example, one may find recipes for the same meat or fish in two or three different "Books" of the text, instead of all in one place, as might be expected. For this reason, the index provides the best way to find a dish. Of course, simply browsing through the book is another, very pleasant way to discover the recipes.

Note that the original, unadapted recipes always appear on boxed-in pages, with their identifying numbers in the margin. To find a corresponding adapted recipe, look for the matching number in the margin beside the modern recipe. (All the adapted recipes are on unboxed pages.)

The paragraphs which begin with the symbol ℂ identify my own explanatory commentaries. The quotations from such classical witers as Pliny were also not part of the original text.

A table showing the values of weights and measures used by Apicius is printed in Appendix I, p. 303.

Appendix II contains a list of substitutes for hard to find ingredients which will not do violence to Apicius' original recipes.

Appendix III contains directions for making the boiled wine, wine sauce, and fish-pickle, which occur as ingredients in various recipes.

Enjoy these meals: *Cenabis bene*—You'll dine well.

The Careful Cook

*When you've drunk deep into the night you promise me
everything. But in the morning you offer nothing.
Pollio, drink in the morning.*

Martial, *Epigrams,* 12.12.

CONDITUM PARADOXUM *Extraordinary Spiced Wine* Put fifteen pounds of honey into a bronze vessel, having previously poured in two pints of wine. In this way, the wine shall be boiled off in the melting honey. The mixture is heated by a slow fire of dry wood and stirred, while boiling, with a wooden rod. If it begins to boil over, pour more wine over it. After the fire has been withdrawn, the remaining mixture will settle. When it has grown cold, another fire is kindled beneath. This second fire is followed by a third and only then can the mixture be moved away from the hearth. On the following day it is skimmed. Then add four ounces of ground pepper, three scruples of mastic, a single handful each of saffron leaves and spikenard, and five dried date stones, the dates having previously been softened in wine of the right quantity and quality to produce a soft mixture. When all this has been done, pour eighteen pints of mild wine into the vessel. [Hot] coals are added to the finished product.

❡ Mastic is the gum or resin which exudes from the mastic tree or pistachio nut tree (*Pistaica lentiscus*), and was used by Apicius as a flavoring for the spiced, honeyed wine customarily offered to dinner guests at the beginning of the meal. Today mastic resin is still used in Turkey and Greece to flavor liquors.

Apicius used the word "folum" (leaf), by which he meant the fragrant leaves or shoots of Indian spikenard (*Valeriana phu*). This herb was used in cooking much as we treat laurel (bay leaf), and was also used as a flavoring for wines. Because of the cost of commodities imported from India, Mediterranean varieties of spikenard were often used—the Syrian, Gallic, and Cretan spikenards.

Spiced Wine Apicius

1 c. white wine
1 lb. honey
1 t. ground pepper
pinch of saffron
1 crushed bay leaf
(or spikenard)
1 t. cinnamon
(or mastic)
2 dates
3½ quarts white wine

Served hot, this spiced wine is an excellent drink for a winter's evening. As a dinner wine, Apicius' Conditum Paradoxum should be served at room temperature with the hors d'oeuvres or at the "gustatio" (light first course of the Roman meal).

For a party of ten, use the following adapted recipe, which reduces approximately by half in cooking.

In a saucepan, combine one cup of white wine and a pound of honey. Heat and dissolve, stirring continuously. Then pour the honeyed wine into a deep pot. Add the pepper, saffron, bay leaf (or spikenard), and cinnamon (or mastic). Steep two dates in white wine, then chop them finely, and add them to the pot. Now pour the 3½ quarts of white wine into the honey and spice mixture. Simmer for one hour over low heat, stirring from time to time with a wooden spoon or spatula.

To complement an evening of pleasant conversation, strain and serve the mulled spiced wine hot. Allow the wine to cool if it is to begin a dinner in the Roman style.

Prepared in this way, the spiced wine will have a subtle taste that hints of lemon.

II   CONDITUM MELIZOMUM VIATORIUM *Spiced Honey Wine for a Journey* This is the recipe for everlasting honey wine, which may be served while travelling along foreign roads. Put ground pepper with skimmed honey into a small cask, as for spiced wine. According to the quantity of wine required at the time, pour out a suitable measure of honey and mix with the wine. If you have a cask, first add a little wine to the honey and pepper mixture so that the honey may be poured more freely from the cask.

III   ABSINTHIUM ROMANUM *Roman Wormwood Wine* [1] Just like the recipe for Camerian spiced wine, if wormwood is unavailable, use one ounce of purified ground wormwood from Pontica or Thebes, three scruples of mastic and spikenard, six scruples of costmary, and three scruples of saffron. [Then mix this with] eighteen pints of an appropriate kind of wine. This bitter [wine] does not require any coals.

❡ A liter of indifferent *vin ordinaire* can be transformed into a stimulating spiced wine with the addition of a dash of each of the following ingredients: wormwood, mastic (if unavailable use cinnamon), spikenard (or ground bay leaf), costmary (or mint), and saffron. Simmer gently and serve on a cold winter's day or cool to room temperature and use as a apertif. In modern times wormwood, or absinthe, has become infamous because of its use in the preparation of the absinthe liqueur.

Costmary (*Tanacetum balsamita*) is a hardy perennial herb native to southern Europe. Its aromatic leaves are used in England to flavor puddings and to garnish dishes for the table. Apicius recommends it here as one of the ingredients of his excellent Roman absinthe. In the nineteenth century, brewers of ales used it to add an aromatic flavor to their liquors and knew it as alecost. Although such traditional elements have been largely ignored by the industry in this modern age, cottage ale brewers can still enjoy its delightful and stimulating presence in their tankards.

ROSATUM ET VIOLACIUM *Rose Wine and Violet Wine* First,   IV-1
remove the white sepals, then put the petals [which remain] into a linen
cloth and sew them together. Immerse as many as possible of the rose
petals in wine for seven days. At the end of seven days lift out the rose
petals from the wine. Then, in the same manner, put other freshly
sewn rose petals [into it]. Let these rest in the wine for seven days also,
and then take them out. Then repeat a third time and remove these
petals [accordingly]. Filter the wine. And when you wish to drink [a
portion of] the rose wine, finish the preparation with the mixing of a
portion of honey. Take great care to select the best rose petals, with the
dew dried off them. Use fresh roses. In the same manner make violet
wine. Similarly, mingle the wine with honey [before drinking].

ROSATUM SINE ROSA SIC FACIES *Rose Wine without Roses*   IV-2
Put green leaves of the citron tree in a small basket made of palm
branches and place this in a wide-mouthed jar of fresh wine before fermentation has taken place. After forty days lift out [the basket of citron
leaves]. When it is needed, mix the wine with honey and use instead of
rose wine.

OLEUM LIBURNICUM SIC FACIES *You Make Liburnian Oil*   V
This Way In Spanish oil, put elecampane, cyperus,[2] and fresh laurel
leaves. First pound all the ingredients [in a mortar] and then pass them

through a sieve. Reduce to a very light powder and add salt that has been rubbed and ground. For three days or more blend carefully. Let it sit for some time and all judge it to be Liburnian.

ꟼLiburnia (now in Yugoslavia) was a region on the northeast coast of the Adriatic Sea in the Roman province of Illyria. The Liburnians were famous for the quality of their olive oil. In this recipe an artificial kind, from Spain , is "doctored" and presented at the table as genuine Liburnian, through the addition of the four ingredients used by the oil exporters of Liburnia.

VI VINUM EX ATRO CANDIDUM FACIES *You Can Make Badly Muddied White Wine Clear* [Put the wine into] a flagon and add bean meal or the whites of three eggs. Stir for a considerable time. On the next day the wine will be clear. The ashes of the white vines will have the same effect.

VII DE LIQUAMINE EMENDANDO *On Reviving Fish-pickle* If the sauce should have acquired a stale odor, first fill an empty upturned vessel with laurel and cypress smoke. Then pour the sauce which was previously exposed to the air into the jar. If your fish-pickle should be too salty, mix in a pint of honey and a little spikenard to correct it. But new must does the same thing excellently [when added to the sauce].

UT CARNES SINE SALE QUOVIS TEMPORE RECENTES SINT   VIII
How Unsalted Meat May Be Kept Fresh   Cover whatever fresh meat
you wish to preserve with a layer of honey. The vessel [containing the
meat] should be suspended in the air and used whenever you wish.
This [method] is best in winter; in the summer [the meat] will last only
a few days. In the same way you can make cooked meat [last].

⟨ The Romans and Greeks customarily preserved foods and wines
in "amphorae," two-handled clay jars whose official measure was
six gallons, seven pints. The length of time the preserving process was expected to work can be deduced from Cato:

If you would keep must [grape juice] *for a year, pour it into an
amphora and seal the cork with pitch. Immerse the amphora in
cold water for thirty days. Then remove it and the must will be
preserved for one year.*

"De Agri Cultura," 120.

Of course, wines which had been matured in "dolia" (large storage jars) and then carefully bottled in amphorae could be expected to last considerably longer. Petronius' Trimalchio served
his guests a century old Falernian in the *Satyricon* (34), and in 30
B.C., Horace cheerfully drank a wine that was bottled thirty-six
years before in the consulship of L. Volcatius Tullus (*Odes*, 3.8).

Unlike wines, foodstuffs were not expected to improve through
being kept in the amphorae. It was merely hoped that they
would remain edible until fresh supplies could be bought in the
market or harvested on the farm. Certain costly foods were preserved because of their scarcity. This was the case with truffles
and the prized "boleti" mushrooms. Some treasured foods had to
travel long distances from their points of origin. The highest
quality fish-pickle came by sea from Spain, and oysters were
brought to Rome from as far away as the English Channel.

IX   CALLUM PORCINUM VEL BUBULUM ET UNGUELLAE COCTAE
UT DIU DURENT   *How to Preserve Skin of Pork or Beef and Boiled Trotters*   Add salt and honey to mustard prepared with vinegar. Completely cover [the skin or trotters] and use when you wish. You'll be amazed.

X   UT CARNEM SALSAM DULCEM FACIAS   *How Salted Meat Can Be Made Sweet*   You can make salted meat sweet if you cook it first in milk and afterwards in water.

XI   UT PISCES FRICTI DIU DURENT   *How to Preserve Fried Fish*   At the very moment that they are taken from the frying pan, sprinkle them with hot vinegar.

XII   OSTREA UT DIU DURENT   *How to Preserve Oysters*   Wash [the oysters] in vinegar, or wash a vase [coated] with pitch with vinegar, and lay the oysters [inside].

⌖ It is likely that the pitch made the vase or jar air tight, and that the vinegar purified it.

XIII   UT UNCIA LASERIS TOTO TEMPORE UTARIS   *How You Can Always Have an Ounce of Laser*   Put the laser into a small but ample glass cask; count out and add about twenty pine nuts. When laser is required for a recipe, grind the nuts. You will be amazed at the flavors [the pine meal] will give to food. Replace the ground nuts by putting a similar number of whole ones within the cask [to receive the seasoning of the laser].

⌖ Laser (also called "silphium" by Apicius) was probably the juice extracted by the Egyptians, Greeks, and Romans from the stalk or root of the *Ferula tingitana*, a species of giant fennel. This juice had a multitude of medical and culinary uses in the ancient world (see Introd., p. xxiv), but has since been replaced, in the kitchen at least, by ginger and fennel. In ancient Rome, the cost of laser increased with its scarcity, hence the method of conservation described above.

UT DULCIA MELLE DIU DURENT *How to Keep Honey Cakes Sweet* Take what the Greeks call safflower. Make flour from it and mix with honey when you are making honey cakes. XIV

⟨The safflower, which in the Latin text is called "cnecos" (pale yellow) refers to the *Carthamus tinctorius*, a plant which was originally cultivated in Egypt. We also know it today as the distaff thistle. The Egyptians made an oil out of its seeds and, it appears from the recipe above, used it as a sweetener and preservative. This is one of the passages in *The Roman Cookery of Apicius* which points to the Egyptian influence upon the Greek manuals which were translated into Latin by the Romans.

UT MEL MALUM BONUM FACIAS *How to Make the Best of Poor Honey* You can make poor honey good enough to sell if you mix together one part of the poor honey with two parts of the superior kind. XV

MEL CORRUPTUM UT PROBES *How to Test for Spoiled Honey* Put a lamp wick into the honey and light it. If it is unspoiled, it burns. XVI

UVAE UT DIU SERVENTUR *How to Store Grapes* Take grapes undamaged from the vine, and then take rainwater and boil it off to one-third its volume. Put the rainwater into the vessel in which you have stored the grapes and seal it with gypsum and pitch. Place the grape jar in a cool place, one to which the sun has no means of access, and, when you wish, you will discover the grapes still to be fresh. Use the same water as honey-water administered to those who are feeble. Cover the grapes with barley, and you will discover them to be fresh in this way too. XVII

UT MALA ET MALA GRANATA DIU DURENT *How to Preserve Apples and Pomegranates* Plunge them into boiling water, and instantly lift them out and suspend them. XVIII

UT MALA CYDONIA DIU SERVENTUR *How to Preserve Quince-apples* Select only unblemished quinces with their stalks and leaves, and put them all together in a vessel. Pour honey and boiled wine over them. They will be preserved for a long time. XIX

XX FICUM RECENTEM MALA PRUNA PIRA CERASIA UT DIU SERVES *How to Preserve Fresh Figs, Apples, Plums, Pears, and Cherries* Collect all of these fruits carefully with their stalks and cover them with honey, taking care that they do not touch each other.

XXI CITRIA UT DIU DURENT *How to Preserve Citrons* Put the citron into a jar, seal it with gypsum, and hang.

The fruit of the citron or the seed is to be drunk in wine as an antidote to poison. Citrons make the breath sweet when the mouth has been rinsed with their decoction or their extract. Their seeds are given to pregnant women to eat for relief from nausea; and the fruit of the citron is indeed effective for strengthening a weak stomach, but it will not be eaten very easily without vinegar.

Pliny, *Natural History*, 23.105.

XXII MORA UT DIU DURENT *How to Preserve Blackberries* Extract juice from blackberries and mix it with sapa. Put [this mixture] with whole blackberries into a glass vessel; they will remain unspoiled for a long time.

⟨ Sapa was obtained by boiling must (wort) from crushed grapes until only one-third of the original volume remained. It was very thick and sweet and had the consistency of honey. (See Introd., pp. xxvii–xxviii)

XXIII HOLERA UT DIU SERVENTUR *How to Preserve Garden Vegetables* Choose vegetables that are not quite ripe and place them in a jar and seal with pitch.

XXIV-1 RAPAE UT DIU SERVENTUR *How to Preserve Turnips* Sprinkle with myrtle berries and with honey and vinegar, turnips that have previously been arranged and cleaned.

XXIV-2 ALITER [*Preserving Turnips*] Add mustard, vinegar, and salt to honey. Pour over the turnips that have previously been arranged.

TUBERA UT DIU SERVENTUR *How to Preserve Truffles* Truffles which the rains have not damaged can be put into a vessel in layers which are covered and separated by sawdust. Seal the jar with gypsum and store in a cool place.

xxv

DURACINA PERSICA UT DIU DURENT *How to Preserve Hard-skinned Peaches* Select the very best, and put them in brine. On the following day draw them out and carefully wipe them off with a sponge. Arrange them in a suitable vessel. Pour in salt, vinegar, and savory.

xxvi

SALES CONDITOS AD MULTA *Of the Many Uses of Spiced Salts* Spiced salts are good for the digestion, for promoting regularity, and for averting all sorts of sicknesses and plagues and chills. Moreover, they are more agreeable to the taste than you might expect. Take one pound of common ground salt, two pounds of ground Libyan salt [sal-ammoniac], three ounces of white pepper, two ounces of ginger, one and one-half ounces of cumin, one and one-half ounces of thyme, one and one-half ounces of celery seed. If you do not want to take celery seed, take three ounces of parsley. Three ounces of oregano, one and one-half ounces of colewort seed, three ounces of black pepper, one ounce of saffron, two ounces of Cretan hyssop, two ounces of spikenard, two ounces of parsley, two ounces of aniseed.

xxvii

OLIVAS VIRIDES SERVARE UT QUOVIS TEMPORE OLEUM FACIAS *How to Preserve Green Olives for the Preparation of Oil* Put olives [just] taken from the tree in oil and they will appear, for any length of time, just to have been taken from the tree. From these you can make fresh oil if you wish.

xxviii

ꟼAccording to Pliny (15.4), choice olives should be preserved or imported in salt and kept either in the lees of crushed olives or in boiled must.

XIX-1 CUMINATUM IN OSTREA ET CONCHYLIA *Cumin Sauce for Oysters and Other Shellfish* [Mix] pepper, lovage, parsley, dried mint, and a larger amount of cumin. [Blend with] honey, vinegar, and [shellfish] stock.

XIX-2 CUMINATUM IN OSTREA ET CONCHYLIA *Cumin Sauce for Oysters and Other Shellfish* [Mix] pepper, lovage, parsley, dried mint, and a larger amount of cumin. [Blend with] honey, vinegar, and [shellfish] stock.

XXX-1 LASERATUM *Laser Sauce* Dissolve Cyrenaic or Parthian laser in lukewarm water, [and afterwards] mix with vinegar and stock. Or [prepare with] pepper, parsley, dried mint, laser root, honey, vinegar, and stock.

XX-2 ALITER [*Laser Sauce*] [Mix] pepper, caraway, aniseed, parsley, dried mint, silphium, bay leaf, cinnamon, spikenard, a little costmary, honey, vinegar, and stock.

XXI-1 OENOGARUM IN TUBERA *Truffles in Wine Sauce* Take pepper, lovage, coriander, rue, stock, honey, and a little olive oil. [Combine these ingredients with wine and add the truffles.]

Cumin-Cinnamon Sauce for Oysters

¼ t. pepper
1 t. celery seed (or lovage)
¼ t. cumin
2 t. parsley
½ t. mint
pinch of cinnamon
1 t. honey
1 t. white wine vinegar or
cider vinegar
1 c. shellfish stock

In a mortar, grind pepper, celery seed (or lovage), parsley, mint, cumin, and cinnamon. Add to honey, vinegar, and shellfish stock. Bring to a boil, then gently simmer for 20 minutes to reduce.

This is a sharp sauce to be used as a court bouillon in which to cook oysters and other shellfish.

xxix-1

Cumin Sauce for Oysters and Other Shellfish

Follow the preceding recipe, omitting the cinnamon.

xxix-2

Fennel Sauce for Fish

⅛ t. fennel
¼ t. ground pepper
2 t. parsley
½ t. mint
1 t. honey
1 t. white wine vinegar or
cider vinegar
1 c. fish stock

Combine fennel with pepper, parsley, mint, honey, vinegar, and stock. Bring to a boil, then gently simmer for 20 minutes to reduce.

xxx-1

Fennel Sauce for Meats

xxx-2

¼ t. pepper
1 pinch of caraway
pinch of aniseed
2 t. parsley
½ t. mint
⅛ t. fennel
pinch of cinnamon
pinch of costmary (or mint)
1 bay leaf, whole
1 t. honey
1 t. white wine vinegar or
cider vinegar
1 c. beef or chicken stock

In a mortar, grind pepper. Add to caraway, aniseed, parsley, mint, fennel, cinnamon, costmary (or mint), and bay leaf. Combine with honey, vinegar, and stock. Bring to a boil, then simmer to reduce for 25 minutes.

Truffles in Coriander Wine Sauce

xxxi-1

peeled truffles (or mushrooms)
¼ t. ground pepper
1 t. celery seed (or lovage)
½ t. coriander
pinch of rosemary (or rue)
½ c. beef stock
½ c. red wine
2 t. olive oil or butter

In a mortar, grind together pepper, celery seed (or lovage), coriander, and rosemary (or rue). Blend with stock, wine, and olive oil or butter. Bring to a boil, then simmer over low heat.

Lightly cook whole truffles or mushrooms in this sauce, and serve together.

Truffles in Savory-Thyme Sauce

xxxi-2

peeled truffles (or mushrooms)
¼ t. thyme
¼ t. savory
¼ t. ground pepper
¼ t. celery seed (or lovage)
1 t. honey
½ c. beef stock
½ c. red wine
2 t. olive oil or butter

In a mortar, grind together thyme, savory, pepper, and celery seed (or lovage). Combine with honey, stock, and olive oil or butter. Mix with wine, and simmer to reduce for 25 minutes.

Lightly cook whole truffles or mushrooms in this sauce, and serve together.

Condiment Sauce with Grated Cheese

¼ t. pepper
1 t. celery seed (or lovage)
½ t. mint
¼ c. pine nuts or finely chopped almonds
2 T. raisins
2 T. dates, finely chopped
1 t. honey
1 t. wine vinegar
1 c. beef or chicken stock
¼ c. white wine
2 T. butter
flour
½ c. mild white cheese, grated

In a mortar, grind pepper, and celery seed (or lovage). Add to mint, nuts, raisins, and dates. Mix with honey, vinegar, stock, wine, and butter. Bring to a boil, then simmer for 20 minutes and thicken with flour.

Sprinkle grated cheese over the sauce and serve.

This sauce is excellent with roasted game birds and fowls.

xxxi

Country Mint Sauce

1 T. chopped fresh mint
½ t. coriander
pinch of fennel
1 t. celery seed (or lovage)
⅛ t. ground pepper
2 T. honey
1 c. beef or chicken stock
1 t. wine vinegar

Mix fresh mint with coriander, fennel, celery seed (or lovage), and pepper. Blend with honey and stock. Add vinegar to taste. Bring to a boil, then simmer gently to reduce for 25 minutes.

This sauce complements the flavors of roast lamb or suckling kid.

xxxv

ALITER [*Truffles in Wine Sauce*] [Mix] thyme, savory, pepper, lovage, honey, stock, and olive oil.

OXYPORUM *Digestive* [Mix] two ounces of cumin, one ounce of ginger, one ounce of fresh rue, six scruples of soda, twelve scruples of the best dates, one ounce of pepper, and nine ounces of honey. Use cumin either from Ethiopia or Syria or Libya. Pour vinegar [over the spice, then] drain and pound [it in a mortar]. Combine all of the seasonings with honey. When the necessity arises, use [this preparation as an aid to digestion] with vinegar and garum sauce.

HYPOTRIMMA *Condiment Sauce* [Mix] pepper, lovage, dried mint, pine nuts, raisins, dates, sweet cheese, honey, vinegar, stock, wine, olive oil, and wine boiled down one-third and wine boiled down one-half.

OXYGARUM DIGESTIBILEM *Vinegar and Fish-pickle, A Digestive* Take one half ounce of pepper, three scruples of French saxifrage, six scruples of cardamon, and six of cumin, one of spikenard, and six of dried mint. Bruise and sift [these spices] and combine them with honey into a paste. When the need arises, add fish-pickle and vinegar.

ALITER [*Vinegar and Fish-pickle*] Grind one ounce of pepper with one ounce each of parsley, caraway, and lovage. Combine with honey. When the need arises, add fish-pickle and vinegar.

MORETARIA *Country Sauce* [Mix] mint, rue, coriander, and fennel, taking care that these herbs are fresh. Add lovage, pepper, honey, and stock. If there is need, add vinegar.

Why, Tucca, do you delight
In mixing cheap must with noble Falernian?
What harm has a vintage even done you?
We your guests may deserve a poisoning
But never a great wine like this.

Martial, 1.18.

— THE BOOK IS ENDED —

Chopped Meats

FORCEMEATS

I-I [UNTITLED] [*Forcemeats*] Seafood forcemeats are made from prawns and crabs, from squids and cuttlefish, and from lobsters. Season with pepper, lovage, cumin, and laser root.

I-2 ISICIA DE LOLLIGINE *Squid Forcemeats* [Prepare the squid by] removing the tentacles. Pound on the chopping board as usual. Then put the flesh into a mortar and diligently grind it with fish-pickle. After that, the forcemeat dumplings are formed.

I-3 ISICIA DE SCILLIS VEL DE CAMMARIS *Forcemeats Made from Prawns or Lobsters* Remove the shells from the prawns or from the lobsters and grind the meat in a mortar with pepper and the best fish-pickle. Mold the flesh into forcemeat dumplings.

I-4 OMENTATA ITA FIUNT *How to Make Sausages* Broil the liver of a pig and remove the membranes. Mix pepper, rue, and stock beforehand. This, pour over the liver and pound and mix well as if you were making sausages. [Stuff the forcemeat in skins.] Roll laurel leaves around each sausage and suspend in smoke for as long as you wish. When you are ready to eat, remove them from the smoke and broil a second time.

Forcemeats are finely chopped or ground shellfish, or meats, with the addition of spices and seasonings. They may then be stuffed into sausage casings, rolled into meatballs, or used to stuff fowls or other animals.

Mussel Forcemeat Sausage for Two

¼ lb. minced mussel or oyster meats
½ t. ground pepper
2 t. celery seed (or lovage)
1 t. cumin
⅛ t. fennel
1 raw egg
1 c. bread crumbs
casings; 2 T. olive oil

In a mortar, grind together pepper, celery seed (or lovage), cumin, and fennel. Mix with the minced shellfish meats. Bind with well beaten egg and bread crumbs. Stuff this mixture into sausage casings and sauté over low heat for 20 minutes in olive oil, in a covered pan.

This forcemeat mixture may also be used as a stuffing.

1-1

Prawn or Lobster Forcemeats

½ lb. minced prawn or lobster meats
½ t. pepper
2 T. fish pickle (see p. 305)
1 raw egg; 1 c. bread crumbs
casings; 2 T. olive oil

Season prawn or lobster forcemeats with the pepper and fish-pickle. Bind with well beaten egg and bread crumbs. Stuff into sausage casings and sauté over low heat in olive oil for 20 minutes in a covered pan.

1-3

Spiced Pork Liver Sausage

¼ lb. pork (or beef) liver
2 T. olive oil
½ t. pepper
½ t. rosemary (or rue)
3 cloves or 6 juniper berries
casings
1 raw egg
1 c. bread crumbs

Remove membranes from liver, slice thinly, and sauté in olive oil for 3–4 minutes on each side, then chop finely.

In a mortar, grind together coriander, pepper, rosemary, and juniper berries or cloves. Add the seasonings to the liver forcemeat, and bind with well beaten egg and bread crumbs. Stuff the mixture into sausage casings, and sauté over low heat in olive oil for 20 minutes, in a covered pan.

1-4

1-5   ISICIUM *Forcemeat* Into a mortar, put pepper, lovage, and oregano. Grind these seasonings. Moisten with stock and add some cooked brains. Grind diligently so that the mixture is smooth. Add five eggs and dissolve carefully to make one mixture. Blend with stock and empty the preparation into a bronze pan and cook. After cooking, turn out onto a clean board and cut into small cubes. Now grind pepper, lovage, and oregano in the mortar. Add stock. Pour into a pan and heat [a second time]. Break pastry [into the pan], thicken and stir, and empty into a serving dish. Sprinkle with pepper and serve.

1-6   ISICIA EX SPHONDYLIS *Mussel Forcemeats* Take mussels, boil them, and remove the membranes. Pound [the pulp] with boiled spelt,* eggs, pepper, and stock. Make forcemeats from this with nuts and pepper. Roast in skins. Moisten with wine sauce and serve like forcemeats.

1-7   ISICIA OMENTATA *Forcemeat Sausages* Chop meat finely and pound in a mortar with soft bread without crusts [previously] steeped in wine. Then add pepper, stock, and, if you like, myrtle berry with the seed removed. Insert nuts and peppercorns and form into small balls of forcemeat. Wrap each one in skin and roast a little in boiled new wine.

*German wheat yielding a fine flour.

Calf's Brains and Egg Dumplings

1 lb. calf's brains
½ t. pepper
1½ t. celery seed (or lovage)
1 t. oregano
5 raw eggs

In a mortar, grind the pepper, celery seed (or lovage), and oregano. Add to chopped, cooked calf's brains, and combine with well beaten eggs. Empty the mixture into a baking pan, and cook in a 325° F oven for 30 minutes. Remove from heat and cut into cubes.

Sauce:
½ t. pepper
1 t. celery seed (or lovage)
½ t. oregano
1 c. meat stock; flour

For the sauce, grind together pepper, celery seed (or lovage), and oregano. Add to stock, bring to a boil, then simmer and thicken with flour. Reheat the brain dumplings in this thick sauce, and serve with a sprinkling of pepper.

1-5

Shellfish Forcemeats or Sausage

¼ lb. minced shellfish meats
½ t. ground pepper
1 t. celery seed (or lovage)
¼ c. grated almonds or pine nuts
1 raw egg
1 c. bread crumbs
casings; 2 T. olive oil
wine sauce (see p. 306)

In a mortar, grind together pepper and celery seed (or lovage). Mix with the shellfish meats and nuts. Bind with well beaten egg and bread crumbs. Then stuff into sausage casings, and sauté gently in olive oil in a covered pan for 20 minutes.

When cooked and lightly browned, season with wine sauce, and serve.

1-6

Pepper (Myrtle) Sausages

½ lb. choice pork
1 c. fresh bread
¼ c. wine
½ t. ground pepper
a few peppercorns (or myrtle berries, if available)
(meat stock)
½ c. almonds or pine nuts
¼ c. boiled wine; casings

Finely grind pork, and then pound it in a mortar with bread moistened with wine. Add pepper and roughly ground peppercorns (or crushed myrtle berries), and stock, if too dry. Mix with finely chopped nuts. Stuff into casings, or form into balls and wrap in casings. Sauté in boiled wine.

1-7

FISH–PICKLE AND WATER SAUCE, APOTHERMUM, AND THICK SAUCE

II-I   ISICIA PLENA   *Pheasant Forcemeats*   Take the fat of freshly killed pheasants, brown and slice into cubes. [Mix these] with pepper, stock, and boiled wine. Shape each one into a dumpling. Poach in fish-pickle mixed with water and serve.

II-2   HYDROGARATA ISICIA SIC FACIES   *Forcemeats with Fish-pickle and Water*   Grind pepper, lovage, a very small amount of pellitory, and pour a little stock [over these seasonings]. Add cistern water and empty into a saucepan. Add the forcemeats and place the pan on the heat of the fire to cook. Serve. To be eaten just as it is.

II-3   IN ISICIATO PULLO   *For Chicken Forcemeats*   Make with 1 pound of the best oil, ¼ pint of stock, and ½ ounce of pepper.

II-4   ALITER DE PULLO   *For Chicken*   Grind thirty-one peppercorns, put in a cup of the best quality stock, as much of boiled wine, and eleven cups of water. Put it on the heat to cook.

II-5   ISICIUM SIMPLEX   *Plain Forcemeats*   Mix a quarter cup of fish-pickle with one and three-quarter cups of water, some green celery, and a spoonful of ground pepper. Cook the forcemeat dumplings [in this mixture]. This recipe will promote regularity. The lees of spiced wine can be added to the fish-pickle and water.

II-6   [UNTITLED]   [*Forcemeats*]   Peacock forcemeats are the best if the hard skin is first fried and so softened. Pheasants are the second choice, rabbits come third, chickens fourth, and the flesh of tender piglets, fifth.

II-7   ISICIA AMULATA A BALINEO SIC FACIES   *Forcemeats with Starch from a Vat*   Grind pepper, lovage, oregano, a small quantity of silphium, and the least ginger. Mix with measures of a little honey and stock, and pour over the forcemeats. Bring to the boil, and then thicken the gravy with starch. Serve it to be sipped.

Seasoned Fowl Forcemeat Dumplings

½ lb. cooked pheasant, or
fowl meats, chopped
¾ t. ground pepper
1 T. boiled white wine
1 raw egg
fowl stock
water
1 T. fish-pickle (see p. 305)

Take cooked, browned meat and dice into small   II-I
cubes. Season with the pepper and boiled wine. Add
well beaten egg and just enough stock to bind.
Shape into balls and poach gently for 30 minutes, or
until done, in water seasoned with fish-pickle.

Meat Dumplings Cooked in Fish-pickle Sauce

½ lb. uncooked forcemeats
(see Seasoned Fowl
Forcemeats above)
Sauce:
½ t. ground pepper
½ t. celery seed (or lovage)
pinch of chamomile (or
pellitory)
1 T. fish-pickle (see p. 305)
1 c. water

In a mortar, grind pepper, celery seed (or lovage),   II-2
and a dash of chamomile (or pellitory). Add fish-
pickle, and blend with water. Mix and pour into a
pan. Poach the dumplings in this sauce, adding a
little more water if necessary. Serve when the liquid
has been evaporated by the heat.

Chicken Dumplings

½ lb. chicken forcemeats
(see ms. 50)
¼ c. chicken stock
1 raw egg
½ t. ground pepper
1 T. olive oil

Bind the dumplings with stock and well beaten egg,   II-3
and season with pepper. Prepare the fish-pickle
sauce from the preceding recipe. Pour into a pan
and poach uncooked dumplings in this sauce, adding a little more water if necessary. Serve when
liquid has evaporated.

Roman Chicken Broth

II-4

1 stewing chicken
10 peppercorns
½ c. reduced vegetable stock
½ c. boiled white wine
water

In a mortar, grind peppercorns. Mix with reduced stock, boiled white wine, and water to cover. Add the chicken cut in pieces, and cook gently over low heat until the fowl is done.

Simple Seafood Dumplings

II-5

½ lb. mussel forcemeats
(see p. 19)
1 T. fish-pickle (see p. 305)
1 c. water
½ c. finely chopped celery
1 t. ground pepper
spiced wine sediments

Mix fish-pickle with water, chopped celery, and pepper. Bring to a boil, then simmer over very low heat. Add seafood dumplings to the mixture and cook till done. The sediments from spiced wine can be added while cooking for a richer flavor.

Seafood Forcemeats with Gingered Gravy

II-7

½ lb. mussel forcemeats
(see p. 19)
½ t. ground pepper
1 t. celery seed (or lovage)
1 t. oregano
¼ t. ginger
1 t. honey
1½ c. shellfish stock
flour

In a mortar, grind pepper, celery seed (or lovage), oregano, and ginger. Combine with honey and stock. Pour into a pan and add the seafood forcemeats. Cover and cook over very low heat until done. Thicken the gravy with flour, and serve.

◖ Apicius frequently used "amulum" (starch) as a binding and thickening agent. The Roman recipe for amulum is found in "De Agri Cultura" by Cato (234–149 B.C.), the oldest surviving Latin prose work.

Clean white wheat diligently, then put it in a deep vessel and add water to it twice a day. Drain off the water on the tenth day. Carefully squeeze out the liquid and knead the wheat well in a clean tray. Do this until it has the appearance of sediment in a wine jar. Pour [some of] this in a clean linen [bag], press out the pap into a fresh pan or mixing bowl. Do the same thing with all of it and then knead a second time. Put the pan into the sun to dry. When the starch is dry, put it in a new pan and cook it with milk.

Cato, 87.

AMULATUM ALITER [*Thick Sauce*] The day before, grind peppercorns and immediately pour in enough stock so that the resultant pepper sauce is well mixed and has a muddy yellow appearance. To this, add boiled new quince-apple wine that has been reduced to the essence of honey through the action of a burning sun. But if this cannot be done, put in unfermented dried fig wine, which the Romans term coloring. Finally, add flour-and-water or rice flour and heat over a slow fire.   II-8

AMULATUM ALITER [*Thick Sauce*] Make a broth from the small bones of fowls. Pour this into a saucepan with chives, aniseed, and salt. When cooked, add pepper and celery seed, rice flour, stock, raisin wine, or boiled wine. Mix all of the ingredients well and serve with the forcemeats.   II-9

APOTHERMUM SIC FACIES *Apothermum* Boil spelt with small nuts and skinned almonds. The almonds should previously have been soaked in water mixed with the chalk that is used to polish silver, so that they are brought to an equal whiteness. To this, add raisins and boiled wine or raisin wine. Sprinkle with ground pepper. [Cool and] serve in the dish [with the prepared forcemeats].   II-10

SOW'S WOMB; SMALL SAUSAGE

III-1   VULVULAE ISICIATAE SIC FIUNT *Forcemeats for Sow's Womb*
Take ground pepper and cumin, the heads of two small leeks made
supple by rinsing, rue, and stock. Thoroughly rub and grind the
forcemeat [and mix it with the other ingredients]. Then pound and
grind a second time so that all blends well. Then add peppercorns and
small nuts. Wash the womb scrupulously and press [in the stuffing].
Cook in water, olive oil, and stock, and with a bouquet of leeks and
aniseed.

> *That blood sausage I sent you at midwinter*
> *Arrived at my house before the seven days of Saturn.*
>
> Martial, 14.72.

III-2   BOTELLUM SIC FACIES *Small Sausage* Take the yolks of six
hard-boiled eggs, chopped pine nuts, onion, and sliced leeks, and mix
with blood [and forcemeats]. Add ground pepper and fill the intestine
with the stuffing. Cook in stock and wine.

LUCANIAN SAUSAGES

IV   LUCANICAE *Lucanian Sausages* Lucanian sausages [are made according to a recipe] similar to that written above: grind pepper, cumin,
savory, rue, parsley, herbs, and laurel berries. Add stock. Thoroughly
grind the forcemeats and mix [with these ingredients]. Then grind a second time so that all blends well. Add [more] stock. Now add peppercorns and plenty of fat and small nuts. Put all this into the intestine,
extending it thinly as much as possible, and suspend in smoke.

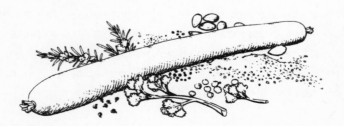

Thick Sauce for Meat Dumplings

2 c. chicken broth
1 T. chives
pinch of aniseed
salt to taste
½ t. ground pepper
1 t. celery seed
¼ c. sweet white wine or
muscatel
flour

Pour broth into a saucepan with chives, aniseed, and salt. Bring to a boil, then gently simmer for 25 minutes. Add ground pepper, celery seed, and wine. Stir in flour, to thicken, and serve over dumplings or rissoles.

II-9

Pork Almond Sausage with Leeks

1 lb. finely ground pork
½ t. ground pepper
1 t. cumin
pinch of rosemary
1 c. bread crumbs
½ c. almonds, grated
1 raw egg
casings
1 c. pork or vegetable stock
leeks
aniseed

In a mortar, grind together pepper, cumin, and rosemary. Add to bread crumbs, and almonds, and mix with the pork. Bind with well beaten egg and moisten as needed with stock. Stuff into sausage casings, then poach the sausages in equal parts of water and stock for 30 minutes.

Serve with leeks cooked in water seasoned with aniseed.

III-1

Small Black Pork Pudding

III-2

6 hard-boiled egg yolks
¼ c. almonds, grated
1 chopped onion
½ c. thinly sliced leeks
blood
½ lb. ground pork or beef
1 raw egg
½ c. bread crumbs
½ t. pepper
casings
1 c. meat or vegetable stock
½ c. red wine

Mix the chopped yolks of hard-boiled eggs, nuts, onion, leeks, and sufficient blood to moisten. Combine with ground beef or pork. Season with pepper and bind with well beaten egg and bread crumbs. Then stuff all into sausage casings. Put stock and red wine in a pan with the sausages, cover, bring to a boil, then cook over low heat for 30 minutes.

Lucanian Sausage

IV

½ t. pepper
½ t. cumin
1 t. savory
1 T. parsley
pinch of rosemary (or rue)
6 cloves or juniper berries (or laurel berries)
1 lb. finely ground beef or pork
¼ c. almonds, grated
1 c. bread crumbs
¼ c. beef stock
1 raw egg
casings
2 T. olive oil

In a mortar, grind together pepper, cumin, savory, parsley, rosemary (or rue), and cloves or juniper berries. Combine with meat, and add nuts and bread crumbs. Moisten with stock, and bind with well beaten egg. Stuff into sausage casing, and sauté in olive oil in a covered pan, over low heat for 30 minutes.

This sausage is also used as an ingredient in other recipes.

Calf's Brain and Almond Sausage

1 lb. cooked calf's or pork brains
¼ c. almonds, grated
1 t. pepper
½ t. ginger
1 c. bread crumbs
1 c. beef or pork stock
1 raw egg
casings

Finely chop the brains and mix with grated almonds. Season with pepper and ginger. Add bread crumbs, and stock to moisten. Bind with well beaten egg and stuff into sausage casings. Cook in a little water, over low heat, in a covered pan for 20 minutes. Then brown in the oven and serve.

v-1

Pork, Barley, and Bacon Sausage

1 lb. ground pork
½ c. cooked pearl barley (or 1 c. bread crumbs)
2 leeks, finely chopped
½ c. cooked bacon, chopped
¼ c. almonds, grated
1 t. pepper
2 t. celery seed (or lovage)
pork or beef stock
1 raw egg
casings

Mix cooked barley or bread crumbs with leeks, bacon, almonds, and meat. Season with pepper, celery seed (or lovage). Moisten with stock as needed, and bind with well beaten egg. Stuff into sausage casings.

Cook in a little water, in a covered pan, for 30 minutes, then brown in the oven.

v-3

Sausage in a Ring with Thick Wine Sauce

1 lb. Lucanian sausage meat (see p. 28)
casing
2 T. olive oil
1 c. wine sauce (see p. 306)
flour

Prepare the sausage meat and stuff into a 1 foot sausage casing. Tie in a circle and sauté in a hot frying pan with olive oil. Cover and cook over low heat for 30 minutes.

Serve in hot wine sauce thickened with flour.

v-4

❡This sausage was originally made by the people of Lucania, a district of southern Italy.

A little sausage lying on snowy pottage.

Martial, 5.78.

SAUSAGES

V-1 [UNTITLED] [*Sausage*] Grind eggs and brains, pine nuts, pepper, stock, and a little laser. Fill the intestine with this preparation. Boil and then afterwards roast [the sausage] and serve.

V-2 ALITER [*Sausage*] Take cooked, ground spelt and mix with chopped pork meats, pepper, stock, and small nuts. Stuff the intestine and boil. Then salt [the sausage] and roast it. Serve with mustard. Or, if you like, slice [the boiled sausage and serve] on a dish that is shaped like a ring.

V-3 ALITER [*Sausage*] Rinse spelt. Boil the wheat with stock and the finely chopped white of a leek. Remove this mixture when it has boiled. Chop fat and small pieces of forcemeat. Mix all together. Now combine in a mortar, pepper, lovage, and three eggs with small nuts and peppercorns. Add these ingredients to the wheat. Moisten with stock. Fill up the intestine, boil, and then roast a little, or if you prefer, only boil. Serve.

V-4 ALITER CIRCELLOS ISICIATOS *Forcemeats in a Ring* Fill an intestine with seasoned forcemeats and form it into a circle. Smoke it. When it has turned cinnabar red, roast it a little. Arrange attractively on a serving dish. Last, pour wine sauce for pheasant dumplings over it, but [remember to] add cumin.

**BOOK II,
CHOPPED MEATS,
—— IS ENDED ——**

The Gardener

OF GARDEN VEGETABLES

I-I   UT OMNE HOLUS SMARAGDINUM FIAT *How to Make All Vegetables the Color of Emeralds* They should be cooked with soda.

BROTH TO BE USED AS A LAXATIVE

II-I   [UNTITLED] [*Beets with Leeks*] Boil young beets and stored leeks and put them in a stew pan. [In a mortar] grind pepper and cumin. Pour stock [over these seasonings]. Add raisin wine until it is somewhat sweet. Bring to the boil. When it has boiled [pour the sauce over the vegetables and] serve.

SIMILITER [*Polypody Root*] Put [the roots of] polypody fern in lukewarm water. When tender, grate it, and season with ground pepper and cumin. Put in a boiling pan and use.

II-2   ℭ Apicius was referring to the *Polypodium vulgare,* or "polypody of the oak," so named because it grows not only on stone but also on stumps of oak, willow, etc. In herbal medicine, polypody root, dried, ground, and mixed with honey, is a traditional cure for nasal polypus; but according to Theophrastus the polypody needed only to be worn to be effective.

The Greeks and Romans considered the root of the polypody to be palatable when prepared with beets, and were correct to recommend it as a gentle laxative.

II-3   ALITER AD VENTREM [*Polypody Root and Beetroots*] Clean a bunch of beetroots by wiping [them with a cloth]. Do not wash them. Sprinkle soda over the middle of them and bind them into separate bouquets. Boil them in water and then arrange them in a stew pan. Add some raisin wine or boiled wine, and sprinkle with cumin, pepper, and a little olive oil. When it has boiled, grind polypody [root] and chopped nuts, [and mix with] stock. Pour [this sauce] into the hot pan. Cover, remove [from the heat] immediately, and serve.

Beets with Leeks in Wine

½ lb. young whole beets
3 thinly sliced leeks
½ t. ground pepper
½ t. cumin
1 c. beet stock
½ c. sweet raisin wine or
muscatel

Cook beets, drain, reserve liquid, and slice. Put them in a saucepan with leeks. In a mortar, grind pepper and cumin. Add to the leeks and beets. Then add stock and sweet wine. Pour this sauce over the vegetables, bring to a boil, then simmer till leeks are cooked.

I-I

Fern Roots and Beets with Almonds

3–4 medium sized beets
water
¼ c. boiled red wine
¼ t. pepper
¼ t. cumin
2 T. olive oil
¼ c. almonds, finely chopped
1 c. roasted polypody, deer
fern, lady fern, or bracken
fern roots
½ c. beet stock

Put beets in a saucepan, cover with water, and cook until tender. Drain, reserve liquid, slice, and sauté lightly in a mixture of boiled wine, pepper, cumin, and olive oil.

Meanwhile, combine chopped almonds and chopped fern root with stock. Pour this over the sautéed beets, cover, reheat, and remove from heat.

II-3

II-4   ALITER BETACIOS VARRONES *Varro's Recipe for Beetroot* According to Varro, take beetroots, but only the black variety, whose roots have been cleaned and cooked with honey wine and a little salt and oil, or cooked with salt, water, and oil. Cook and serve. The broth may be drunk. The broth will be even better if a chicken is cooked in it.

❡ Marcus Terentius Varro (116–27 B.C.) was a Roman of immense learning who wrote over 600 volumes on poetry, history, law, grammar, biography, and science. In his recipe for black beetroots, Apicius was recalling Varro's treatise on agriculture, *De Re Rustica*, in which the author tried to revive the ideals of country life after the horrors of the civil war that had laid waste much of the Italian Peninsula and had marked both the end of the Roman Republic and the rise of the Caesars.

The Greeks and Romans cultivated two kinds of beets and called them the white and the black according to the color of their leaves. Theophrastus wrote, "the white variety has a better taste than the black and gives fewer seeds. Certain people call the white beet the 'Sicilian'" (*Inquiry into Plants*, 7.4).

II-5   ALITER AD VENTREM *Another Laxative* Wash [fresh] green celery stalks with their roots and dry them in the sun. In a fresh saucepan, boil together the [tender] white parts and the heads of leeks until the water has boiled away to the third part, that is to say, of three parts water one remains. Afterwards grind pepper, and blend with stock and liquid honey. Strain boiled celery-water into the mortar. Pour over the leeks. When they have cooked together, serve. If you like, throw in the celery, too.

ASPARAGUS

III   ASPARAGOS *Asparagus* Dry the asparagus, put them again in hot water, you will restore the hard flesh.

Varro's Recipe for Beets with Chicken

10 small beets
¼ c. mead, or sweet white wine
salt
1 T. olive oil
½ lb. part cooked chicken pieces

Put whole, small beets, into a saucepan. Add mead or sweet wine, salt to taste, olive oil, and enough water to cover. Bring to a boil, add chicken pieces, and cook till done.

II-4

Leeks with Celery

1 bunch fresh celery
4 leeks

Sauce:
½ t. ground pepper
¼ c. vegetable stock
2 c. celery stock
1 t. honey

Put pieces of celery in water, bring to a boil, then simmer for 15 minutes. Drain and reserve celery stock. In a fresh saucepan, cook the heads and tender parts of leeks until ⅓ of the water has boiled away.

For the sauce, combine pepper, stock, and honey, and add to strained celery stock. Bring to a boil and simmer for 25 minutes to reduce. Put the cooked leeks into a new saucepan and pour the sauce over them. Heat the sauce with the leeks and serve.

The celery stalks may be added, if you wish.

II-5

Squash with Herbs and Spices

1 medium sized squash, zucchini, or pumpkin

Sauce:
½ t. ground pepper
¼ t. cumin
¼ t. ginger
pinch of rosemary (or rue)
1 t. cider vinegar
2 T. boiled red wine
½ c. squash stock

Peel and cut the squash, gourd, or pumpkin, into pieces, put in a pan with water, and cook till done. Press the water out of the cooked squash, and reserve liquid. Put the squash into a fresh pan.

For the sauce, in a mortar, grind together pepper, cumin, ginger, and rosemary (or rue). Add vinegar, wine, and stock. Pour this sauce over the squash and simmer till well cooked.

Serve with a sprinkling of pepper.

IV-1

GOURDS

◖Apicius used the word "cucurbita" for this division of his recipes for garden vegetables and, indeed, many fruits of the order cucurbitaceae are delicious when prepared classically. This would include gourd, pumpkin, squash, zucchini, or vegetable marrow.

IV-1

GUSTUM DE CUCURBITIS *Gourd Antepast* Squeeze out the water from the cooked gourds and put them into a shallow pan. In a mortar, add pepper, cumin, a little silphium, that is laser root, a little rue, and blend with stock and vinegar. Put in a little boiled wine for color. Pour the sauce into the pan. When [the gourd antepast is] boiled a second and third time, remove [from the heat] and sprinkle over it a very small quantity of pepper.

IV-2

ALITER CUCURBITAS IURE COLOCASIORUM *Gourds in Broad Bean Broth* Cook the gourds in water as you would broad beans. [Meanwhile] mix pepper, cumin, rue, and sprinkle with vinegar and stock. Simmer in a pan. Add to this a little olive oil. Put into the pan the chopped and drained gourds. Heat. Thicken with starch, sprinkle with pepper, and serve.

IV-3

CUCURBITAS MORE ALEXANDRINO *Gourds Alexandrine* Boil the gourds and squeeze them [to extract the water]. Sprinkle them with salt and put them in a saucepan. Now grind pepper, cumin, coriander seed, fresh mint, and laser root. Pour vinegar over [these seasonings]. Then toss in some dates and nuts, and grind. Blend with honey, vinegar, stock, boiled wine, and olive oil. Pour this over the gourds. When [the dish] has been brought to the boil, sprinkle with pepper and serve.

◖This recipe, named after Alexandria, in Egypt, is evidence of the influence of Egyptian cooking upon *The Roman Cookery of Apicius*.

IV-4

ALITER CUCURBITAS ELIXATAS *Stewed Gourds* [Cook] in stock, oil, and unmixed wine.

Squash in Bean Broth with Rosemary Sauce

*1 medium squash, gourd,
zucchini, or pumpkin
bean stock*

Take a whole squash and steam it in bean broth.   IV-2
When done, slice open the cooked squash, cut out
the flesh, and press out moisture.

*Sauce:
½ t. ground pepper
¼ t. cumin
pinch of rosemary (or rue)
1 t. cider vinegar
1 c. gourd or vegetable stock
1 T. olive oil or butter
flour*

Meanwhile, in a mortar, grind together pepper,
cumin, and rosemary (or rue). Add to vinegar and
stock. Heat this sauce in a pan with butter or olive
oil. Add the cooked squash to the sauce, and simmer
for 10 minutes over low heat. Thicken with flour,
and serve with a sprinkling of pepper.

Alexandrine Squash

*1 medium squash, gourd,
zucchini, or pumpkin
water
salt*

Cut squash in pieces, and steam in water till cooked.   IV-3
Press the water out of the cooked flesh, add salt to
taste, and put into a cooking pot.

*Sauce:
½ t. ground pepper
¼ t. cumin
½ t. coriander
½ t. mint
¼ t. ginger
1 t. cider vinegar
¼ c. dates, finely chopped
¼ c. almonds, finely chopped
1 t. honey
¼ c. boiled white wine
½ c. squash or vegetable stock
1 T. olive oil or butter*

For the sauce, in a mortar, grind pepper, cumin, coriander, mint, and ginger. Combine with vinegar,
chopped dates and almonds, honey, boiled wine,
stock, and olive oil or butter. Pour this sauce over
the squash, bring gently to a boil, and simmer briefly
to blend flavors. Sprinkle with pepper, and serve.

IV-5   ALITER CUCURBITAS FRICTAS *Fried Gourds* [Prepare] in a plain wine sauce with pepper.

IV-6   ALITER CUCURBITAS ELIXATAS ET FRICTAS *Gourds, Stewed and Fried* Put [the boiled gourds] in a pan. Sprinkle cumin [over them] with a little olive oil added on top. Cook and serve.

IV-7   ALITER CUCURBITAS FRICTAS TRITAS *Gourds, Fried and Sliced* [Season with] pepper, lovage, cumin, oregano, onion, wine, stock, and olive oil. Add starch to the pan to thicken and serve.

IV-8   ALITER CUCURBITAS CUM GALLINA *Gourds with Chicken* [Put the gourds and a fowl into a stew pan and add] apricots, truffles, pepper, caraway, cumin, silphium, fresh herbs, mint, celery, coriander and pennyroyal, dates, honey, wine, stock, olive oil, and vinegar.

CITRON

V   CITRIUM *Citron* [Serve with] mountain saxifrage, silphium, dried mint, vinegar, and stock.

¶Two thousand years ago it was the custom to eat citron raw, with an herb and vinegar dressing.

CUCUMBERS

VI-1   CUCUMERES RASOS *Peeled Cucumbers* [Peel the cucumbers and cook them] in stock or in wine sauce. The cucumbers will be tender and not [cause] flatulence or heaviness.

VI-2   ALITER CUCUMERES RASOS *Peeled Cucumbers* Scrape the cucumbers and boil them along with a small quantity of cooked brains, cumin, a moderate portion of honey, celery seed, stock, and olive oil. Thicken with eggs, sprinkle with pepper, and serve.

VI-3   ALITER CUCUMERES *Cucumbers* [Make with] pepper, pennyroyal, honey or raisin wine, stock, and vinegar. Occasionally silphium is added as well.

Squash Cooked in Wine

*1 medium squash, gourd,
zucchini, or pumpkin*
½ c. squash or vegetable stock
1 T. olive oil or butter
¼ c. white wine

Peel and slice the zucchini, squash, or gourd. Put the slices into a shallow pan, and add stock, olive oil or butter, and white wine. Cover, bring to a boil, and simmer gently until done. Serve with a sprinkling of pepper.

IV-4

Squash in Oregano Wine Sauce

*1 medium squash, gourd,
zucchini, or pumpkin*
1 c. wine sauce (see p. 306)
1 t. celery seed (or lovage)
1 t. oregano
¼ t. cumin
ground pepper

Gently simmer the sliced squash in wine sauce seasoned with celery seed (or lovage), oregano, and cumin. When cooked, serve the squash in the sauce, with pepper, to taste.

IV-5

Steamed Squash Sautéed with Cumin

*1 medium squash, gourd,
zucchini, or pumpkin*
water
1 T. olive oil or butter
¼ t. cumin
ground pepper

Peel and slice the squash, gourd, or zucchini, and steam with water until tender. Drain and put into a hot frying pan greased with olive oil or butter. Season with cumin. Sauté lightly, and serve with a sprinkling of pepper.

IV-6

Sautéed Squash in Herb Sauce

IV-7

1 medium onion, thinly sliced
1 T. olive oil
¼ t. ground pepper
¼ t. celery seed (or lovage)
¼ t. oregano
dash of cumin
3 c. diced squash or gourds
½ c. squash or vegetable stock
¼ c. white wine
1 t. olive oil
(flour)

Sauté sliced onion in olive oil. In a mortar, grind pepper, celery seed (or lovage), and oregano. Add to onions, with a dash of cumin. Stir. Then add diced squash. Add stock, white wine, and olive oil. Stir repeatedly over medium heat until the gourds are cooked. If you wish, thicken the liquid with flour, and serve.

Spiced Squash with Chicken and Apricots

IV-8

4 c. diced squash or gourd
3–4 lb. chicken
green olives
1 c. apricots, fresh or dried
mushrooms (or truffles), sliced
3 celery stalks, chopped
1 t. ground pepper
pinch of caraway seeds
¼ t. cumin
½ t. ginger
1 t. mint
½ t. coriander
¼ c. dates, finely chopped
1 T. honey
½ c. white wine
½ c. vegetable or chicken stock
1 T. olive oil or butter
1 t. white wine vinegar or cider vinegar

Put diced squash and a whole chicken stuffed with olives into a large cooking pot. To the pot add apricots, sliced mushrooms (or peeled truffles), and celery.

In a mortar, grind pepper, caraway, cumin, ginger, mint, and coriander. Combine with dates, honey, white wine, stock, olive oil or butter, and vinegar. Stir these ingredients to mix flavors and add to the pot. Cover, and cook slowly over low heat until the chicken is done.

Cucumbers Cooked with Wine Sauce

Peel and slice the cucumbers. Cover with stock or   VI-I
wine sauce (see p. 306). Bring to a boil, then simmer gently till cooked.

Cucumbers with Calf's Brains

4 cucumbers, sliced   Slice the cucumbers. Put into a cooking pot with   VI-2
1 c. cooked calf's brains,   calf's brains, veal stock, cumin, honey, celery seed,
chopped   and olive oil. Bring to a boil, then simmer till cu-
1 c. veal stock   cumbers are lightly cooked. Bind with well beaten
¼ t. cumin   yolks, and serve with a sprinkling of pepper.
1 t. honey
½ t. celery seed
2 t. olive oil
2 raw egg yolks
ground pepper

Cooked Cucumbers with Fennel

4 cucumbers, sliced   Slice the cucumbers into a pot. Season with pepper,   VI-3
½ t. ground pepper   mint (or pennyroyal), and honey or raisin wine.
½ t. mint (or pennyroyal)   Add stock and vinegar. Bring to a boil, then cover,
1 T. honey, or 2 T. sweet   and simmer gently. Sprinkle with fennel to taste,
raisin wine   and serve when cucumbers are lightly cooked.
½ c. veal or chicken stock
1 t. white wine vinegar
fennel

PUMPKINS AND MELONS

VII PEPONES ET MELONES *Pumpkins and Melons* [Prepare in] pepper, pennyroyal, honey or raisin wine, stock, and vinegar. Occasionally silphium is added as well.

MALLOWS

Have lettuce and gentle mallows for lunch, Phoebus,
*   You look constipated!*

Martial 3.89.

VIII MALVAS *Mallows* Serve smaller mallows with fish-pickle, olive oil, and vinegar. Larger-leaved mallows [are cooked] in wine sauce, pepper, fish-pickle, and boiled wine or raisin wine.

ℂApicius was referring to *Althaea officinalis*, the marshmallow, which Pliny also called "hibiscum" (20.14). The mallow leaves were eaten by the Greeks and Romans at the "gustatio," or appetizer course.

YOUNG CABBAGES AND STALKS

IX-I CYMAS *Cabbages* [Cook with] cumin, salt, aged wines, and olive oil. If you like, add pepper, lovage, mint, rue, coriander, and the leaves of young stalks, and [cook in] stock, wine, and oil.

You'll dine well at my house, Fabullus
If the gods protect you for a few more days
And if you bring along a fine expensive dinner
With your dazzling new young lady
And your wine and wit and laughter....
*   For Catullus*
Has a wallet that's bursting with cobwebs.

Catullus, *Carmina*, 13.

Pumpkins with Squash or Apples

3 c. diced pumpkin and squash, or apples
butter

Peel and dice the pumpkin and squash, and arrange in a buttered baking dish.

VII

Sauce:
¼ t. pepper
pinch of mint (or pennyroyal)
1 T. honey, or 2 T. sweet raisin wine
¼ c. squash or vegetable stock
dash of white wine vinegar
1 t. ginger

For the sauce, mix pepper, mint (or pennyroyal), honey or raisin wine, stock, and vinegar. Pour the sauce over the pumpkin. Bake in a 325° F oven for 30 minutes or until tender. Sprinkle with ginger as the dish is cooking.

The recipes which follow are adapted from "Young Cabbages and Stalks," to be used for all brassicas and other greens.

Cauliflower or Broccoli in Celery Mint Sauce

1 cauliflower, cabbage, or bunch of broccoli

Take cauliflower, cabbage, or broccoli, quarter them, and put in a saucepan.

IX-1

Sauce:
¼ t. cumin
pinch of salt
2 T. white wine
1 T. olive oil

For the first sauce, combine the cumin, salt, wine, olive oil, and enough water to steam the vegetable. Add to the vegetables, bring to a boil, then simmer gently till done.

Sauce:
¼ t. ground pepper
½ t. celery seed (or lovage)
½ t. mint
pinch of rosemary (or rue)
¼ t. coriander
½ c. vegetable stock
2 T. white wine vinegar
1 T. olive oil or butter

Meanwhile, in a mortar, grind pepper, celery seed (or lovage), mint, rosemary (or rue) and coriander. Add to stock, vinegar, and olive oil or butter. Bring to a boil, then simmer to reduce for 25 minutes. Serve over the cooked, strained vegetables.

(All three vegetables may be combined in this recipe).

Complaint of a boletaria*

Although boleti mushrooms gave me my noble name,
Enslaved by stalks now am I in shame.

Martial, 14.101.

IX-2   ALITER   [*Stalks*]   Cut boiled stalks in half and mix the most tender leaves with coriander, onion, cumin, pepper, raisin wine or boiled wine, and a little olive oil.

IX-3   ALITER   [*Stalks*]   Boil the stalks and put them in a saucepan [and season them] with stock, oil, unmixed wine, and cumin. Sprinkle with pepper, and chop chives, cumin, and green coriander over it.

IX-4   ALITER   [*Stalks*]   Prepare [and season] the stalks as above and cook with boiled leeks.

IX-5   ALITER   [*Stalks*]   [Prepare and] season as above, but mix with green olives and heat together.

IX-6   ALITER   [*Stalks*]   Having prepared and seasoned the stalks as above, pour over [the vegetable] boiled spelt mixed with nuts and raisins. Sprinkle with pepper [and serve].

*a particularly fine serving dish.

Broccoli and Cabbage in Coriander Wine Sauce

1 bunch of broccoli heads, or the tender leaves of a cabbage, parboiled

Take pre-cooked broccoli heads or cabbage leaves and simmer in the following sauce.

IX-2

Sauce:
½ t. coriander
1 medium onion, sliced
pinch of cumin
¼ t. ground pepper
¼ c. sweet raisin wine, or boiled white wine
2 T. olive oil

For the sauce, combine the coriander, onion rings, cumin, pepper, raisin wine or boiled wine, and olive oil or butter. Bring to a boil, then add vegetables, and simmer together gently for 10 minutes to combine flavors.

Spiced Broccoli, Cabbage, and Brussel Sprouts

1 bunch broccoli heads
½ medium cabbage
½ lb. brussel sprouts
¼ c. vegetable stock
2 T. olive oil
2 T. white wine
cumin
½ t. ground pepper
1 T. chives
1 t. roasted coriander seeds

Chop the cabbage into wedges and steam in water with the other vegetables. Drain, and reserve liquid. Put vegetables into a saucepan and simmer till tender in a mixture of the stock, olive oil, wine, and cumin to taste. Before serving, garnish with pepper, chives, and roasted coriander seeds.

IX-3

Chestnut Sauce for Greens

2 T. butter
2 T. white pastry flour
1 c. milk
¼ c. dark raisins
¼ c. roasted chestnuts or almonds, chopped
ground pepper

Over low heat, first melt butter and mix with flour. Stir in milk and cook gently. Add raisins and chopped roasted chestnuts, or almonds. Simmer to blend flavors, then pour over the greens. Sprinkle with pepper and serve.

IX-6

LEEKS

⟨Apicius did not distinguish between the capitate leek and the sectile chives. We, however, have inherited the standard Roman practice of cooking with leeks and seasoning with chives.

X-1   PORROS *Leeks*   Select leeks and cook them with a fistful of salt in water and olive oil. Remove [from the water] and serve with olive oil, fish-pickle, and unmixed wine.

X-2   ALITER PORROS *Leeks*   Cover the leeks with young cabbage leaves and steam them over hot coals. [Season] as above and serve.

X-3   ALITER PORROS *Leeks*   Cook in water, as above, and serve.

X-4   ALITER PORROS *Leeks*   If the leeks have been boiled, add a large quantity of unseasoned beans to the sauce in which you will eat them.

BEETS

XI-1   [UNTITLED]   [*Beets*]   Into a stewing pot, put sliced leeks, coriander, cumin, raisins, and flour. [Cook the beets in this sauce.] Thicken the sauce, and serve them with stock, oil, and vinegar.

XI-2   ALITER BETAS ELIXAS *Stewed Beets*   They are good served with mustard, a little olive oil, and vinegar.

To season the common beet for dinner
How often must the cook add wine and pepper?

Martial, 13.13.

Leeks with White Wine

2 leeks, sliced
½ t. salt
1 T. olive oil
water

Cut leeks into 1 inch slices. Add salt and olive oil. Add a little water, bring to a boil, and simmer until the leeks are tender. Drain.

X-1

Sauce:
1 t. olive oil
¼ c. chicken stock
¼ c. white wine

For the sauce, mix olive oil and stock. Add white wine. Heat and simmer gently for 15 minutes to reduce. Pour over the cooked leeks, and serve.

Beets and Leeks in Raisin Sauce

½ lb. young whole beets
3 or 4 sliced leeks
1 t. coriander
¼ t. cumin
¼ c. raisins
2 c. vegetable stock
flour
olive oil
white wine vinegar or
cider vinegar

In a mortar, grind together coriander and cumin. Add to raisins and stock. Bring to a boil, then add the beets and leeks. Simmer gently for 25 minutes to reduce the liquid or till vegetables are tender. Thicken with flour, and serve the vegetables in the sauce with a sprinkling of olive oil and vinegar.

XI-1

Pickled Beets

3–4 medium beets
2 T. mustard seed
water
1 c. white wine vinegar
1 c. unchlorinated water

Put whole beets into a saucepan and cover with water. Add mustard seed. Cook until the beets can be pricked easily with a fork. Drain and slice the beets into pint jars. Add mustard seed to each jar. In a saucepan, mix vinegar with water. Heat and then pour over the sliced beets. Seal. Yields two pints of pickled beets. Serve in oil and vinegar dressing.

XI-2

½ c. olive oil
2 T. white wine vinegar

Alternatively, cook the beets as above and slice them into a bowl. Add olive oil and vinegar. Stir well. Chill and serve. Use only tender beets.

HORSE PARSLEY

XII

HOLISERA *Horse Parsley Sauce* Collect and tie the horse parsley into small bouquets. They are good served uncooked with stock, oil, and unmixed wine, or with broiled fish.

⟨Apicius used the Latin word "holisera," a corruption of "holus-atrum" (black herb). Pliny also called it "hipposelinum" (horse parsley). Soyer, on the other hand, took this plant to be chervil. (*The Pantropheon, or A History of Food and Its Preparation in Ancient Times*, 84).

TURNIPS

XIII-1

[UNTITLED] [*Turnips*] Squeeze the liquid out of the boiled turnips [and put them in a saucepan]. Then grind a goodly quantity of cumin, less of rue, Parthian laser, honey, vinegar, stock, boiled wine, and a little olive oil. Heat and serve.

XIII-2

ALITER RAPAS SIVE NAPOS *Turnips* Boil [in water and] serve. Sprinkle drops of olive oil over [the turnips]. If you like, add vinegar.

RADISHES

XIV

RHAPHANOS *Radishes* [Serve] radishes with pepper sauce [made by] grinding pepper [and mixing with] fish-pickle.

⟨Among the many effects of eating radishes listed by Pliny, the most fascinating one is the following:

Democritus considers that radishes taken as food are an aphrodisiac, and probably for this reason others have related that radishes are harmful to the voice.

Pliny, 20.13.

Green Chervil Sauce

¼ t. coriander
1 T. chopped onion
2 sprigs fresh chervil, finely chopped
1 sprig lovage, finely chopped
1 fresh mint leaf
½ c. white wine
½ c. vegetable or chicken stock
1 t. white wine vinegar
1 t. honey
flour

In a saucepan, combine coriander and onion with XII fresh, chopped herbs. Combine with wine, stock, vinegar, and honey. Gently bring to a boil, then simmer over low heat for 10 minutes. Thicken with flour, and serve with fish or meat.

Care must be taken to assert the chervil's subtle flavor in the face of the other seasonings.

Turnips in Cumin Sauce

1 lb. turnips, cubed
water

Peel turnips, and cut into cubes. Steam in a little XIII-1 water till half-cooked, drain, and reserve liquid.

Sauce:
½ t. cumin
pinch of rosemary (or rue)
¼ t. ginger
1 t. honey
2 t. olive oil
¼ c. boiled white wine
1 c. turnip stock
flour

For the sauce, mix cumin, rosemary (or rue), ginger, honey, olive oil, boiled wine, and sufficient stock to cover. Add to the turnips and finish cooking them in the sauce. Thicken with flour, and serve with a sprinkling of pepper.

VEGETABLE PURÉES

XV-1
HOLUS MOLLE EX HOLISATRO *Vegetable Purée with Horse Pars-ley* Cook them in water mixed with soda. Press out the water and chop into little pieces. [For the sauce] mix pepper, lovage, dried savory, dried onions, stock, olive oil, and wine.

XV-2
ALITER HOLUS MOLLE *Vegetable Purée* Boil celery in water mixed with soda. Press and chop minutely. In a mortar, mix pepper, lovage, oregano, onion, wine, stock, and olive oil. Cook [these ingredients] in a saucepan and then mix with the celery [and serve].

XV-3
ALITER HOLUS MOLLE FOLIIS LACTUCARUM CUM CEPIS *Vegetable Purée with Lettuce Leaves and Onions* Boil [the lettuce and onion] in water mixed with soda. Press them and chop finely. In a mortar, grind pepper, lovage, celery seed, dried mint, onion, stock, olive oil, and vinegar. [Serve the vegetables in this sauce.]

XV-4
[UNTITLED] [*Vegetable Purée*] So that the young green garden vegetables will not wither, cut off the top leaves. Rinse the top leaves and moisten the stalks in water in which wormwood has been dissolved.

COUNTRY HERBS

XVI
HERBAE RUSTICAE *Country Herbs* Country herbs should be eaten as they come to hand as a salad in a dressing of fish-pickle, olive oil, and vinegar, or stewed with pepper, cumin, and berries of the mastic tree.

NETTLES

XVII
URTICAE *Nettles* When the sun is in the sign of the Ram, female nettles may be taken against sickness.

❡An explanation of this curious passage follows on page 52.

Pureed Greens in Lovage-Savory Sauce

½ large cabbage, sliced c. cauliflower, or 2 c. greens water

Use tender young cabbage, or cauliflower, (or broc-   XV-1 coli, brussel sprouts, or other early greens). Simmer them in a little water, drain, press, and chop very finely.

Sauce:
½ t. pepper
2 t. celery seed (or 1 T. fresh lovage)
½ t. savory
2 T. chopped onion
½ c. vegetable stock
flour
1 t. olive oil or butter
¼ c. white wine

For the sauce, blend the pepper, celery seed (or lovage), savory, onion, stock, olive oil or butter, and white wine. Bring to a boil, thicken with flour, and serve with pureed greens.

Pureed Celery in Lovage-Oregano Sauce

2 c. chopped celery

Place chopped celery in a pan, and simmer in water   XV-2 till tender. Drain, and press out the moisture from the vegetable.

Sauce:
¼ t. ground pepper
½ t. celery seed (or lovage)
½ t. oregano
2 t. chopped onion
¼ c. white wine
½ c. vegetable stock
1 t. olive oil
flour

For the sauce, grind together in a mortar, pepper, celery seed (or lovage), and oregano. Add to onion, white wine, stock, and olive oil, and heat. Finish cooking the celery in the sauce and thicken with flour. Serve with a sprinkling of pepper.

*There are a number of different kinds of nettles. There are wild
nettles which they call female, and also cultivated nettles. . . .
Indeed, the young female nettles are not disagreeable to the taste
when they are picked in the spring, and they are eaten faithfully
by many people to drive away diseases during the whole year to
come. And the root of the wild nettle will make any kind of
meat more tender when it is boiled with it.*

Pliny, 21.92–93.

ENDIVE AND LETTUCES*

XVIII-1

[UNTITLED] [*Endive*] Endive is served with [a dressing of] fish-
pickle, a little oil, and chopped onion. Endive may be used in place of
lettuce in winter, in a dressing or [with] honey and sharp vinegar.

*Endive is good whether raw or cooked for both the healthy and the
infirm, but raw endive is best eaten after drying for a day in the sun.*

Anthimus, 51.

XVIII-2

[UNTITLED] [*Lettuce*] Serve lettuce in [a dressing of] "oxyporum," vinegar, and a little fish-pickle.

XVIII-3

AD DIGESTIONEM ET INFLATIONEM ET NE LACTUCAE
LAEDANT *An Aid to Digestion and a Preventative of Flatulence So That
Lettuce Will Not Harm You* Two ounces of cumin, one ounce of ginger, one ounce of green rue, twelve scruples of plump dates, one ounce
of pepper, nine ounces of honey. The cumin should be either Ethio-
pian or Syrian or Libyan. Grind the cumin and then pour it into vinegar. [Strain and] when it has dried, combine all the ingredients with the
honey. When necessary, mix half a spoonful with vinegar and fish-
pickle and take half a spoonful after dinner.[1]

❡The point of this recipe seems to be to arm the stomach for the
onslaught of a rich Apician banquet, rather than enjoyment of
the lettuce salad.

*Eaten at the "gustatio," the light first course which began a formal Roman
meal.

Onion and Lettuce Puree in Lovage Mint Sauce

1 head of lettuce
1 onion
water

Place the vegetables in a pan with a little water and steam till tender. Drain, press, and chop very finely. xv-3

Sauce:
¼ t. ground pepper
1 T. lovage (or celery seed)
½ t. celery seed
sprig of mint, chopped
1 c. chicken stock
1 t. olive oil
ash of white wine vinegar or cider vinegar

For the sauce, in a mortar, grind the pepper, lovage (or celery seed), and celery seed. Add to mint, stock, olive oil, and vinegar. Bring to a boil, then simmer for 25 minutes to reduce. Pour over the vegetable puree and serve.

Watercress Salad

watercress
1 T. fish-pickle (see p. 305)
3 T. olive oil
1 T. cider vinegar
water
¼ t. ground pepper
pinch of cumin
2 T. pistachios nuts, chopped

Use fresh watercress and serve it as a salad in a dressing made by combining the fish-pickle, olive oil, and vinegar. xvi

Alternatively, put the watercress in a pan with a little water, season with pepper, cumin, and chopped pistachio nuts, and simmer gently for 2–3 minutes over low heat.

Endive in Dressing

endive
1 t. fish-pickle (see p. 305)
3 T. olive oil
1 T. onion, finely chopped
1 t. white wine vinegar
1 t. honey
3 T. olive oil
1 T. cider vinegar

Serve endive in a dressing made from fish-pickle, olive oil, chopped onion, and vinegar. xviii-1

Or serve in a dressing of honey, vinegar, and olive oil.

ARTICHOKES

The prickly artichoke is planted, welcome
To the drinking daughters of Bacchus.
But Phoebus denies his followers sweet songs
If they should deign to eat it.

Columella, *De Re Rustica*, 10.235–36.

❡Then, as now, people had ambiguous attitudes towards the artichoke, although the vegetable seems to have been in vogue in the first century A.D. and found its way into the pages of Apicius. The Romans called them "cardui" from which we derive the term cardoons. But the artichoke was also known by the name "cinara" in memory of a beautiful girl in obscure myth who was so unlucky as to offend a god on the island of Cinara (now Zinara) in the Aegean Sea. He spitefully turned her into the edible thistle we know as Cynara today. The bitter punishment received by the innocent maiden no doubt combined with the sweetness of her nature to produce the bland tasting artichoke of classical and modern times.

XIX-1   CARDUOS *Artichokes* [Serve] with fish-pickle, olive oil, and chopped egg.

XIX-2   ALITER CARDUOS *Artichokes* Grind rue, mint, coriander, and fennel. [Make certain that these herbs are] all fresh [and mix them well]. Add pepper, lovage, honey, stock, and oil.

XIX-3   ALITER CARDUOS ELIXOS *Steamed Artichokes* [Prepare with] pepper, cumin, stock, and olive oil.

The first two recipes below are dressings in which the boiled artichoke leaves are dipped and eaten. The last is a sauce in which the artichokes are boiled whole. After cooking in this manner, a dressing may be added according to taste.

Artichokes with Fish-pickle Dressing

3–4 artichokes
water
1 t. fish-pickle (see p. 305)
½ c. olive oil
hard-boiled eggs, very finely chopped

Cut off the artichoke stems, remove the tough bottom leaves and trim ½ inch from the tips of the remaining ones. Put in a covered pan with water, and steam for 45 minutes, or until tender. Chill.

For the dressing, combine fish-pickle, olive oil, and chopped egg. Serve cold with the chilled artichokes.

XIX-1

Artichokes with Hot Herb Dressing

3–4 artichokes
pinch of rosemary (or rue)
2 fresh mint leaves (or 1 t. dried)
¼ t. coriander
pinch of fennel
¼ t. ground pepper
½ t. celery seed (or lovage)
2 t. olive oil
1 c. vegetable stock or water
(2 t. honey)

Trim and steam the artichokes as in preceding recipe.

For the dressing, grind together rosemary (or rue), mint, coriander, fennel, pepper, and celery seed (or lovage). Add to olive oil and stock. (To make a sweet dressing, add honey.) Bring to a boil, then simmer gently for 10 minutes to blend flavors. Serve with the steamed artichokes.

XIX-2

Cumin Spiced Artichokes

3–4 artichokes
1 c. vegetable stock
½ t. pepper
1 t. cumin
2 t. olive oil

Steam artichokes in a covered pan in stock seasoned with pepper, cumin, and olive oil.

XIX-3

Coriander Parsnips Cooked in Wine

xx-2

6 whole parsnips
1 c. water
¼ t. salt
2 t. olive oil
¼ c. white wine
1 ½ t. coriander
a few peppercorns
2 t. olive oil or butter

Put cleaned parsnips in a pan. Add water seasoned with salt, olive oil, white wine, coriander, and peppercorns. Bring to a boil, then simmer gently for 10 minutes or until parsnips are tender. Drain and serve with olive oil or butter.

Celery Seed Sauce for Parsnips

xx-3

6 cooked parsnips, sliced
water
1 t. celery seed
pinch of rosemary (or rue)
½ t. ground pepper
1 t. honey
¼ c. white wine
1 c. vegetable stock
2 t. olive oil or butter
flour
ground pepper

To make the sauce, first grind celery seed, rosemary (or rue), and pepper together in a mortar. Blend with honey, white wine, stock, and olive oil or butter. Simmer for 10 minutes, and thicken with flour. Pour over the cooked parsnips, and serve with a sprinkling of pepper.

Parsnips in Coriander Chive Sauce

xx-4

6 parsnips, sliced
1 t. coriander
½ t. cumin
pinch of rosemary (or rue)
1 c. parsnip stock
¼ c. boiled white wine
2 t. olive oil
1 T. chopped chives
flour

Cook the parsnips in water, drain, and reserve liquid for stock.

For the sauce, grind together coriander, cumin, and rosemary (or rue). Blend with stock, boiled wine, and olive oil. Add chives. Bring to a boil, simmer gently for 10 minutes, and thicken with flour. Serve over the cooked parsnips.

Parsnips Cooked in Sweet Wine Sauce

6–8 parsnips
water

Slice parsnips lengthwise and half-cook them in
water. Drain and reserve liquid. Finish cooking
them in the following sauce.

xx-5

Sauce:
2 t. olive oil or butter
1½ c. parsnip stock
½ t. pepper
¼ c. sweet raisin wine or
muscatel
flour

Combine olive oil or butter, stock, pepper, and
sweet wine. Bring to a boil, add parsnips, then simmer together till parsnips are tender. Thicken sauce
with flour, and serve with parsnips.

Carrots Sautéed in Peppered Wine Sauce

8 medium carrots
½ c. white wine
½ c. vegetable stock
2 t. olive oil
½–1 t. pepper

Thinly slice carrots lengthwise, and sauté them in a
mixture of the wine, stock, olive oil, and pepper until done.
    Serve carrots with the sauce.

xxi-1

Carrots Cooked with Cumin

Slice carrots, cook in a little water, then drain. Add
olive oil and cumin, to taste, and reheat with the
carrots. Serve.

xxi-3

PARSNIPS²

xx-1   [UNTITLED]   [*Parsnips*]   Fried [and served] in a plain wine sauce.

xx-2   ALITER   [*Parsnips*]   Boil with salt, oil, unmixed wine, chopped fresh coriander, and whole peppercorns.

xx-3   ALITER   [*Parsnips*]   Pour over the boiled parsnips a thick sauce made from these ingredients: grind celery seed, rue, honey, pepper, raisin wine, stock, and a little olive oil. Thicken with starch, sprinkle with pepper, and serve.

xx-4   ALITER SPHONDYLOS   *Parsnips*   Grind cumin and rue. [Mix with] stock, some boiled wine, olive oil, fresh coriander, and chives. Serve the boiled parsnips in place of saltfish.

xx-5   ALITER   [*Parsnips*]   Take boiled parsnips, half cook and then stew in olive oil, stock, and pepper. Color them [with a little raisin wine], thicken [with starch] [and serve].

xx-6   ALITER   [*Parsnips*]   Cover the parsnips with olive oil and stock, or broil in olive oil and salt. Sprinkle with pepper and serve.

xx-7   ALITER   [*Stuffing*]   Take boiled parsnips and remove the fibers growing from them. Pound them and then mix the pulp with boiled spelt, eggs, pepper, and stock. Make a stuffing of this mixture by adding nuts and pepper. Roast the parsnip stuffing in skin and serve with wine sauce, as forcemeats.

CARROTS OR PARSNIPS

xxi-1   [UNTITLED]   [*Carrots or Parsnips*]   Fry the carrots and serve in wine sauce.

xxi-2   ALITER CAROETAS   *Carrots*   Serve [carrots] with salt, pure olive oil, and vinegar.

xxi-3   ALITER   [*Carrots or Parsnips*]   Boil the carrots. Chop them and simmer in a little olive oil seasoned with cumin. Make the cumin sauce as for young green stalks.

BOOK III OF APICIUS,
THE GARDENER,
——— IS ENDED ———

All Kinds of Dishes

POTTED SALADS

I-1   SALA CATTABIA *Potted Salad* [For the dressing, mix] pepper, mint, celery, dried pennyroyal, cheese, pine nuts, honey, vinegar, stock, egg yolks, and fresh water. In the pot, arrange layers of pressed bread previously soaked in vinegar and water, cheese made from cow's milk, and cucumbers. Strew nuts between the layers. Then add buds of the caper shrub, chopped up very finely, and a layer of little chicken livers. Pour the dressing on top. Chill in ice water and serve.

I-2   ALITER SALA CATTABIA APICIANA *Potted Salad Apicius* In a mortar, mix celery seed, dried pennyroyal, dried mint, ginger, green coriander, seedless raisins, honey, vinegar, olive oil, and wine. In the salad bowl, strew pieces of Picentian bread. Arrange the bread in alternate layers with pieces of chicken, goat-kid's glandules, Vestinian cheese, pine nuts, cucumbers, and dried onions chopped very finely. Pour the dressing made above over the potted salad. Strew snow around it until the dinner hour and serve.

I-3   ALITER SALA CATTABIA *Potted Salad* Hollow out an Alexandrine loaf[1] and soak the pieces in vinegar and water. Mix in a mortar, pepper, honey, mint, garlic, green coriander, cow's milk cheese seasoned with salt, water, and olive oil. Pack in snow and serve.

FISH, VEGETABLE, AND FRUIT DISHES

II-1   PATINA COTIDIANA *Everyday Dish* Grind cooked brains with pepper, cumin, and laser. Cook with fish-pickle, boiled wine, milk, and eggs over a gentle fire or in warm water. Steam gently.

II-2   ALITER PATINA VERSATILIS *Upside-down Dish* Take pine nuts and chopped nuts. Bake these and then grind [and mix] them with honey, pepper, fish-pickle, milk, and eggs. [Cook] in a little olive oil.

II-3   ALITER PATINA [*Vegetable Dish*] Pound lettuce stalks. [Mix] with pepper, stock, boiled wine, water, and olive oil. Cook and thicken with eggs. Sprinkle with pepper and serve.

Tart Potted Salad

(¼ lb. white bread)
(¼ c. mild white wine vinegar)
water
½ c. chopped walnuts or almonds
½ c. grated mozzarella (or other mild) cheese
½ medium cucumber, sliced
¼ c. pickled capers
½ lb. cooked chicken livers, chopped

Soak the bread in vinegar and water, press it, and use it to cover the bottom of a salad bowl. (One may prefer to omit the vinegar soaked bread, and serve this salad with rolls.) Sprinkle with some of the chopped nuts. Cover this with the grated cheese and sprinkle with more nuts. Make a third layer with cucumber slices, a fourth with pickled capers, and a fifth with cooked chicken livers, adding a sprinkling of nuts to each. Chill, and serve with the following dressing.

1-1

Dressing:
½ t. chopped fresh mint
dash of ground pepper
inch of pennyroyal (or mint)
1 t. honey
1 T. almonds, finely chopped
¼ c. white wine vinegar
1 c. olive oil
2 hard-boiled egg yolks
1 c. mild cheese, shredded

Combine chopped mint, pepper, and a pinch of pennyroyal, with honey, chopped nuts, vinegar, and olive oil. Blend with mashed egg yolks. Pour over the salad, and decorate it with shredded cheese. Chill and serve.

Potted Salad Apicius

I-2

3 c. fine white bread
1 c. cooked chicken meat, sliced
1 c. cooked sweetbreads, chopped
1 c. mild cheese, shredded
¼ c. pine nuts or almonds, chopped
½ medium cucumber, sliced
½ onion, finely chopped

Dressing:
1 t. celery seed (or ground lovage)
pinch of pennyroyal, if available
¼ t. mint; pinch of ginger
½ t. coriander
¼ c. dark raisins
1 t. honey
2 T. vinegar
1 c. olive oil
1 T. white wine

Cover the bottom of a large salad bowl with some of the white bread. Cover this with sliced chicken. Add a layer of bread. Complete the salad with layers of sweetbreads, shredded cheese, pine nuts or almonds, cucumber slices, and onions chopped very finely, alternating with a layer of bread, as in *Tart Potted Salad.* Chill, and serve with the following dressing.

Mix celery seed with pennyroyal, mint, ginger, coriander, raisins, honey, vinegar, olive oil, and white wine.Pour over the salad, and serve.

Bread Salad

1 lb. loaf fine white bread
3 t. mild vinegar
1 c. water
1 c. mild cheese, shredded
salt

Dressing:
dash of pepper
1 t. honey
½ t. mint
clove of garlic, crushed
¼ t. coriander
1 c. olive oil
2 T. mild white wine vinegar

Remove the crusts from the loaf of bread, slice, and moisten it with vinegar and water. Cover a shallow salad bowl with pieces of the prepared bread. On top of it, sprinkle a dash of salt, and a cup of shredded cheese. Chill.

To make the dressing combine the pepper, honey, mint, garlic, coriander, olive oil, and vinegar. Pour over the chilled bread, and serve at once.

"Everyday" Creamed Calf's Brains

1 lb. cooked calf's brains, chopped
½ t. ground pepper
¼ t. cumin
½ t. ginger
dash of fish-pickle (see p. 305)
½ c. boiled white wine
¾ c. milk
2 raw egg yolks

Season brains with pepper, cumin, and ginger. Put into a pan, and combine with fish-pickle, boiled wine, milk, and well beaten egg yolks. Bring to a boil, then simmer together gently until the "everyday" dish has thickened.

II-1

Nut Omelette

¼ c. roasted chestnuts or almonds, chopped
1 t. honey
pinch of ground pepper
dash of fish-pickle (see p. 305)
½ c. milk
5 raw eggs
2 t. butter or olive oil

Roast chestnuts or almonds for 20 minutes in a 350°F oven. Grind the nuts and mix with honey, pepper, fish-pickle, milk, and eggs. Heat a frying pan, and melt butter or olive oil. Add the omelette mixture. Cook till done.

Alternatively, bind the roasted, ground chestnuts with reduced veal stock and fold into the omelette.

II-2

Lettuce Puree

1 head of lettuce, finely chopped
dash of ground pepper
½ c. vegetable stock
¼ c. boiled white wine
2 t. olive oil or butter
2 raw egg yolks

Season fresh lettuce leaves with pepper, and combine with stock, boiled wine, and olive oil or butter. Bring to a boil, then simmer gently for a minute or two. Thicken with the well beaten egg yolks, and serve with a sprinkling of pepper.

II-3

II-4   ALITER PATINA FUSILUS [*Stew*] Take horse parsley, clean, wash, cook, [remove from heat,] cool, and drain. Take four calves' brains, remove the membranes, and cook them. Into a mortar, put six scruples of pepper. Pour in stock and blend. After this is done, add the brains and pound with the seasonings. Then add the cooked horse parsley and mix all of the ingredients together. Afterwards break eight eggs, one-twelfth of a pint of stock, one-twelfth of a pint of wine, and one-twelfth of a pint of raisin wine. Beat well and blend. Grease the pan [and pour the thick soup into it]. Place it on the thermospodium. When cooked, sprinkle with pepper and serve.

¶ The thermospodium was a charcoal-burning, portable bronze heater used to warm the dining room and heat dishes.

II-5   ALITER PATINA DE ASPARAGIS FRIGIDA *Cold Asparagus* Take cleaned asparagus, grind it in a mortar, and drench with [cold] water. Shake and strain through a colander. Then set aside meats prepared from beccafico birds.[2] Grind in a mortar, six scruples of peppercorns, moisten with stock, and blend. In a saucepan, heat this mixture with one-twelfth of a pint of wine, one-twelfth of a pint of raisin wine, and three ounces of olive oil. Then, into a greased dish, put six eggs seasoned with wine sauce and the asparagus puree. Place this on the hot ashes [in the thermospodium] and then put on this the mixture described above. Then mix in the beccafico meats. Cook. Sprinkle with pepper. [Chill] and serve.

II-6   ALITER PATINA DE ASPARAGIS *Asparagus* Take asparagus tips, which are usually thrown away. Throw them into a mortar, grind, and drench in wine. Strain through a colander. Mix pepper, lovage, green coriander, savory, onion, wine, stock, and olive oil. Grease the dish, and put the sauce and the prepared asparagus into it. As it cooks on the fire, you may wish to thicken the stew with eggs. [Before serving] sprinkle with finely ground pepper.

II-7   PATINAM EX RUSTICIS [*Watercress*] You make a dish of watercress or wild grape or green mustard or cucumber or cabbage leaves this way. If you wish, strew fish or chicken meats in the dish.

Celery and Brains with Egg Sauce

1 large bunch of celery,
chopped
1 lb. cooked calf's brains,
chopped
1 c. veal stock
½ t. ground pepper
¼ c. white wine
1 raw egg yolk

Trim, wash, steam, drain, and cool celery (or other   11-4
fresh greens). Then, in a mixing bowl, season veal
stock with pepper. Take the cooked brains, pound
them, and combine them with the stock. Now add
the celery and wine, and stir together. Pour the
celery and brains mixture into a greased cooking
pot, heat gently on top of the stove, add well beaten
yolk, and simmer till thickened. Serve with a sprinkling of pepper.

Asparagus Stewed in Wine

1 lb. asparagus, finely
chopped
1½ c. white wine
¼ t. ground pepper
1 t. celery seed (or lovage)
1 t. coriander
¼ t. savory
1 medium onion, chopped
2 t. chopped onion
1 c. vegetable stock
2 t. olive oil
1 raw egg yolk
ground pepper, to taste

Take chopped asparagus, pound in a mortar, and   11-6
steep in wine for about ½ hour. Strain through a
colander, reserve wine, and set aside. Now combine
pepper, celery seed (or lovage), coriander, savory,
onion, ¼ cup of the wine, stock, and olive oil. Pour
the asparagus puree and the sauce into a cooking pot, bring to a boil, then simmer gently for 15
minutes. Thicken with well beaten egg yolk. Serve
with a sprinkling of finely ground pepper.

Puree of Watercress or Other Green Vegetables

Puree of watercress (or grape leaves, green mustard   11-7
plant leaves, cucumber, young cabbage, or cauliflower) is made as in *Stewed Asparagus in Wine*,
above. You may wish to put cooked fish or chicken
in the dish before adding the prepared vegetable.

II-8 ALITER PATINA DE SABUCO CALIDA ET FRIGIDA *Hot or Cold Elderberries* Take Elderberries, clean them, cook in water, and drain in a colander. Grease a dish and arrange the elderberries with a small stick. Add six scruples of pepper, one-twelfth of a pint of stock, and the same of wine and of raisin wine. Blend, then put four ounces of olive oil into the [elderberry] stew. Place the dish on the thermospodium and heat. When the dish has cooked, break six eggs into it, stir, and so thicken. Sprinkle with pepper and serve [hot or chilled].

II-9 PATINAM DE ROSIS *Rose Hips* Take the rose hips and remove the leaves. Lift out the white part and put the hips into a mortar. Pour stock over them and pound. Afterwards, add one and one-half cyathi of stock and strain through a colander. Set aside. Take four brains and remove the membranes. Grind with eight scruples of pepper. Moisten the brains with rose hip liquor and mix. Then break eight eggs, and measure one and one-half cyathi of wine, one-twelfth of a pint of raisin wine, and a small quantity of olive oil. [Mix all with the rose hips and brains.] Afterwards, pour all the ingredients in a greased dish and place this on the hot ashes, and put in it the mixture described above. When it has cooked in the thermospodium, sprinkle finely ground pepper over it and serve.

II-10 PATINA DE CUCURBITIS *Gourds* Boil the gourds and then fry them. Put them in a dish. Sprinkle with cumin. Pour a little olive oil on top. Heat and serve.

II-11 PATINA DE APUA *Anchovies* Wash the anchovies, steep them in olive oil, and arrange them in a pan made of Cumaean clay. Add [more] olive oil, fish stock, and wine. Bind rue and oregano into bouquets and, from time to time during cooking, dip the bound herbs into [the anchovies]. When the dish is cooked, throw out the herbs, sprinkle [the anchovies] with pepper, and serve.

II-12 PATINA DE APUA SINE APUA *Anchovy Casserole without Anchovies* Finely chop enough baked or boiled fish to fill a casserole dish of the size you want to use. Grind pepper and a little rue, and mix with sufficient fish stock and some olive oil. Mix these seasonings with the fish pieces. Then add raw eggs and blend all until the texture is smooth.

Rose Hips and Calf's Brains Custard

2 c. young rose hips
¼ c. vegetable stock
1 lb. cooked calf's brains,
chopped
½ t. ground pepper
8 small raw eggs
¼ c. red wine
¼ c. sweet raisin wine or
muscatel
½ c. vegetable stock
2 t. olive oil or butter
ground cinnamon

Cook the rose hips for 5 minutes in a little water, II-9
drain them, and grind them to a pulp in a mortar.
Add stock and strain together through a very fine
sieve. (Alternatively, pick seeds out by hand.) Take
finely chopped brains and season with pepper.
Combine with rose hip juice. In a separate bowl,
combine well beaten eggs, wine, sweet wine, stock,
and olive oil or butter. Mix brains, seeded rose hips,
and the sauce together, and pour all into a greased
baking dish. Cook in a 350° F oven for 30 minutes or
until firm. Sprinkle with finely ground cinnamon
and serve.

Anchovies Cooked in Herbed Wine

20 fresh (or unsalted,
canned) anchovies
olive oil
½ c. white wine
½ c. fish stock
2 t. olive oil
½ t. rosemary
¼ t. oregano
ground pepper

Wash the anchovies and immerse them in olive oil II-11
for 2 hours (or use canned, oil packed, unsalted ones).
Then arrange them in a cooking pot with 2 t. of the
olive oil. Combine white wine and fish stock with
rosemary (or rue) and oregano to taste, add to pot
and cook over low heat till fish are done. During
cooking spoon the sauce over the fish. Serve with a
sprinkling of pepper.

Steamed Fish Custard

2 lbs. cooked fish fillets
½ t. ground pepper
pinch of rosemary (or
rue)
2 t. olive oil
2 c. fish stock
4 raw eggs
(sea anemones if available)

Steam fillets and reserve liquid. Chop them, and put II-12
them into a cooking pot. Mix pepper with ground
rosemary (or rue), olive oil, and fish stock. Stir this
sauce into the fish. Now add well beaten eggs and
stir the mixture until it has a smooth texture. (Finish
by gently placing sea anemones on top.) Cover and
steam over low heat till eggs are firm. Serve with a
sprinkling of pepper.

Next, gently place sea nettles on top, taking care to see that they do not mix with the eggs. Cook by steaming so that the sea nettles and the eggs may not mix. When they have become firm and dry, sprinkle it with ground pepper and serve. At the table no one will know what he is eating!

II-13 PATINAM EX LACTE *Milk Casserole* Steep nuts and dry them. Make sure you have freshly prepared sea urchins on hand. Take a dish, and in it put the ingredients written below into the casserole dish one by one: mallows and beetroots, ripe leeks, celery, freshly boiled greens and vegetable purée, chicken pieces cooked in their own juices, boiled brains, Lucanian sausages, hard-boiled eggs cut in half. Next, add pork sausages made with Terentine sauce, that have been cooked and sliced, chicken livers, fillets of fried codfish, sea nettles, pieces of oyster meat, and fresh cheese. Arrange these ingredients in layers, and then sprinkle each with small nuts and peppercorns. The sauce to be poured over [the dish] is made of these [ingredients]: pepper, lovage, celery seed, and silphium. [Blend these seasonings and] heat. After cooking, strain milk and into it mix raw eggs so that the sauce has a smooth texture. Pour it over the casserole. Cook. When it is cooked, set the fresh sea urchins on top. Sprinkle with pepper and serve.

Fruitless eggs, which we have termed "wind eggs," are conceived by the imagined passion of the females between themselves or through dust; not only by pigeons, but also by fowls, partridges, peacocks, geese, and Egyptian geese. They are, however, unfruitful, smaller, less pleasing to taste, and more liquid. Some people suspect they are begot by the wind, and for this reason call them "zephyr eggs"; but on the other hand these wind eggs are formed only in the spring when the hens have forsaken brooding. There are also eggs called "cynosura," wind eggs laid in the autumn. Eggs soaked in vinegar are softened to such a degree that they can pass through signet rings. Eggs should be preserved in bean meal or, in winter, in chopped bay and straw. In summer, bran is most beneficial. It is thought that eggs become utterly empty if they are preserved in salt.

Pliny, 10.80.

Milk Casserole

¼ c. almonds or pine nuts
1 t. coarsely ground pepper
6–10 green cabbage or grape
leaves (or mallow leaves),
parboiled
3–4 beets, sliced
1 c. leeks, sliced
½ c. celery, chopped
½ c. cooked peas or beans
½ lb. cooked chicken
½ c. cooked calf's brains,
chopped
Lucanian sausage (see
p. 28)
3 hard-boiled eggs
½ c. pork sausage slices
½ c. Terentine sauce (see
p. 194)
½ c. cooked chicken livers,
chopped
½ c. poached cod fillets
5 ozs. small raw oysters,
chopped
½ c. cottage cheese
5 sea urchins (the freshly
cooked meats, see p. 251)

Steep nuts in water for an hour, drain them, and II-13 season each layer of the casserole with some of them combined with ground pepper.

In a casserole, carefully arrange the following ingredients in layers: a few parboiled grape, cabbage (or mallow) leaves, beets, leeks, celery, and peas, or beans, or other cooked green vegetable. On these prepared vegetables, place slices of boned chicken cooked in their own juices, cooked calf's brains, and a few slices of Lucanian sausage. Add hard-boiled egg halves, a layer of sliced pork sausage mixed with the Terentine sauce, cooked chicken livers, poached cod fillets, and oysters. Finish with the cottage cheese.

Sauce:
pinch of ground pepper
¼ t. lovage (or celery seed)
½ t. celery seed
fennel
2 raw eggs
1 c. milk

To make the sauce, grind pepper with lovage (or celery seed) and celery seed in a mortar. Add fennel to taste. In a pan, combine with well beaten eggs and milk. Stir and heat. Pour this sauce over the casserole. Decorate with the sea urchins. Cook, covered, for 40 minutes to 1 hour in a 350°F oven until vegetables are done.

II-14 PATINAM APICIANAM SIC FACIES *Casserole Apicius* Take pieces of cooked sow's udder, fish fillets, chicken meats, figpecker birds or the cooked breasts of thrushes, and whatever else is best. Chop all [the meats] carefully except for pieces of figpecker meats. [Next, mix and] stir fresh eggs and olive oil. Grind pepper and lovage. Pour stock and wine and raisin wine [over the eggs and seasonings], and put [the mixture] into a saucepan and heat, and thicken with cornstarch. But first add all the chopped meats to the pan and boil. Then take a ladle and pour in layers [into a casserole dish] the meats in their own sauce, seasoned with peppercorns and with pine nuts. Pour each layer over a flat cake base of flour and olive oil. However many layers of cake you place in the casserole, that many ample ladlesful of stewed meats pour by turns over each. Pierce the last cake with a reed and set it atop the casserole. Sprinkle with pepper. Beforehand, however, you should crack eggs and thicken the meats and then put them into the saucepan along with the mixture. The bronze dish you ought to use is shown below.

❡ The last sentence of this recipe is the only one in the entire *Roman Cookery of Apicius* to refer to an illustrated book. Unfortunately, only the words have survived in the manuscript.

II-15 PATINA COTIDIANA *Everyday Casserole* Take pieces of cooked sow's udder, cooked fish fillets and cooked chicken meats. Chop all diligently. Set aside in a bronze casserole dish. Break eggs into a pan and beat them. Throw into a mortar, pepper and lovage. Grind and then pour some stock, wine, raisin wine, and a moderate quantity of olive oil [over these seasonings]. Empty this into the pan [with the eggs and] bring [the mixture] to the boil. Then thicken [the sauce] and put the chopped meats into it. Now put oil cakes in the bronze pan and a full ladleful of the meat. Sprinkle with olive oil. In the same way, place an oil cake on top. As many oil cakes as you put on, place the same number of ladlesful of mixture [into the pan]. Now pierce the last cake with a reed and set it atop the casserole. Flip onto a ring-shaped dish.[3] Sprinkle with pepper and serve.

Casserole Apicius with Meat or Fish

Pancakes:
3 eggs
½ c. flour
⅓ c. milk
⅓ c. water

1½ lbs. cooked fish fillets (sole,
halibut, turbot, or salmon)
or 2½ c. cooked pork, or
chicken, thinly sliced
3 raw eggs
2 T. olive oil
½ t. ground pepper
½ t. celery seed (or lovage)
2 c. beef or chicken stock
¼ c. white wine
¼ c. sweet raisin wine or
muscatel
flour
coarsely ground pepper
pine nuts or almonds

To make 6 pancakes beat 3 eggs, and add the flour, milk, and water to make a thin batter. Into a greased 8 inch frying pan, pour a little of the batter and allow it to spread evenly. Cook each pancake over high heat and flip over when it is lightly browned.

Prepare cooked meat or fish. Mix these with the eggs, olive oil, celery seed (or lovage), stock, white wine, and sweet wine. Heat the meats in this sauce, adding more liquid if required. Thicken sauce with flour.

Next, take a greased casserole dish and cover the bottom with a layer of meats or fish in their sauce. Sprinkle with coarsely ground pepper and with nuts. On this, place a pancake. Fill the dish with layers of the sauced meats, seasoned with pepper and nuts, each alternating with a pancake. Pierce a hole in the final pancake to allow steam to escape and cook uncovered in a 375° F oven for 20–25 minutes until the dish is uniformly heated. Serve with a sprinkling of pepper.

II-14

II-16   PATINA VERSATILIS VICE DULCI *A Sweet Upside-down Dish*
Take pine nuts and larger nuts that have been shelled and washed, and
roast them. Then mix them well with honey, pepper, fish-pickle, milk,
eggs, and unmixed wine and olive oil.

   ⟨Fish caught at a distance from Rome were salted before trans-
   port. Presumably Apicius soaked the salted fish in water before
   cooking it.

II-17   PATELLAM TYROTARICHAM EX QUOCUMQUE SALSO
VOLUERIS *A Dish of Cheese and Whatever Saltfish You Wish* Cook in
olive oil and remove the bones. In a casserole dish, heat these ingredients altogether: cooked brains, the prepared fish, chicken livers, hard-
boiled eggs, and cheese made supple by having been washed in warm
water. Then mix pepper, lovage, oregano, rue berry, wine, mead, and
oil. [Add this sauce] to the pan and simmer over a slow fire. [When
cooked] thicken with raw eggs. Sprinkle with finely ground cumin and
serve attractively.

   Of cheeses brought here from across the seas, the Bithynian
   [Turkish] *is justly famous. There is salt in pastures that produce
   cheese. This is perceived by the fact that all cheese becomes salty as it
   ages, although if old cheeses are steeped in vinegar and thyme it is
   certain the flavor of their youth will return. They say that
   Zoroaster lived in the desert for twenty years on cheese prepared in
   this way so as not to suffer from old age.*

                                                        Pliny, 2.97.

II-18   PATELLAM ISICIATAM ISICIA DE THURSIONE *A Dish Made
with Porpoise Forcemeats* [Make a quantity of] porpoise forcemeat.
Remove the sinews from the meat and chop finely. Grind pepper,
lovage, oregano, parsley, coriander, cumin, rue berry, dried mint, and
the porpoise forcemeat itself. Shape into dumplings. Cook in wine,
stock, and olive oil. Transfer the dumplings to a shallow dish. Make the
sauce from pepper, lovage, savory, onion, wine, stock, and olive oil.
Put it in a pan to cook. Thicken with eggs [and pour over the porpoise
dumplings]. Sprinkle with pepper and serve.

Fish with Meats in Seasoned Cheese Sauce

1 lb. fish fillets
olive oil
1 c. cooked calf's brains, chopped
1 c. chicken livers
4 hard-boiled eggs, chopped
1 c. melted mild white cheese

Lightly sauté fish fillets in olive oil, debone, and break the fillets into pieces. Heat these together with chopped calf's brains, chicken livers, hard-boiled eggs, and melted cheese. (The cheese may first be steeped in vinegar and thyme.)

II-17

Sauce:
dash of ground pepper
¼ t. celery seed (or lovage)
½ t. oregano
2 rue berries (or peppercorns)
1 t. honey (or mead)
¼ c. wine
2 t. olive oil
1 c. stock
2 raw egg yolks
butter
ground cumin

Meanwhile, grind together, in a mortar, pepper, celery seed (or lovage), oregano, and a couple of rue berries (or peppercorns). Combine with honey (or mead), wine, and olive oil. Thicken this sauce with well beaten yolks and add to the first dish. Cook in a buttered casserole for 20 to 30 minutes in a 375° F oven. Serve with a sprinkling of cumin (or sprinkle on top while cooking).

II-19   PATELLAM EX HOLISATRO *A Dish Made with Horse Parsley*
Boil horse parsley in water mixed with soda. [Then take it out of the water,] press, and put in a shallow dish. Next, mix pepper, lovage, coriander, savory, onion, wine, stock, vinegar, and oil. Transfer this sauce to the pan [with the boiled vegetable]. Cook and then thicken with starch. Sprinkle the dish with thyme and finely ground pepper. Whatever herb you please may be prepared in this way.

II-20   PATINA DE APUA FRICTA *Fried Anchovies* Wash the anchovies, crack eggs and mix with the anchovies. [Into a pan] add stock, wine, and olive oil. Heat, and when very hot, add the anchovies. Turn when the sauce has set. Give the dish color by adding a plain wine sauce. Sprinkle with pepper and serve.

II-21   PATINA EX LAGITIS ET CEREBELLIS *Brains and Lizard Fish*[4]
Fry eggs until hard, boil the brains and remove the membranes, and boil chicken giblets. Slice these ingredients, except for the fish, and mix together. Set this mixture in the stewing dish and then place the cooked salted fish in the middle. Mix pepper and lovage, and pour over [the seasonings some] raisin wine for sweetness. Add this pepper sauce to the dish and boil. When it has boiled, stir the dish with a sprig of rue and thicken with starch.

II-22   PATINA MULLORUM LOCO SALSI *Red Mullet in Place of Saltfish*
Scale red mullet and put them into a clean pan. Add a sufficient quantity of olive oil, place it among the saltfish, and heat. Add honey wine or raisin wine to the fish. Sprinkle with pepper and serve.

⊄This recipe is designed for salted red mullet, a fish of which the Romans in Apicius' day were extremely fond. The seasoning is plain and the honey wine is added to counter the saltiness of the preserved fish. For elaborate sauces designed for the receptive flesh of freshly caught mullets, see Book X.

II-23   PATINA PISCIUM LOCO SALSI *A Dish of Fish in Place of Saltfish*
Prepare fish of whatever kind and fry it. Add sufficient olive oil to the pan and put it in the middle of the fish. Heat. When the pan is hot, put honey-water into it and stir the gravy.

Stewed Green Vegetables with Pepper and Thyme

1 large bunch of celery,
1 medium cabbage,
2 large heads of broccoli

Take celery, cabbage, or other green vegetable, and steam in a little water till cooked. Spread the vegetable in a shallow pan.

II-19

Sauce:
dash of ground pepper
1–1½ t. celery seed (or lovage)
¼ t. coriander
pinch of savory
2 t. chopped onion
½ c. white wine
1 c. vegetable stock
1 t. white wine vinegar or
cider vinegar
2 t. olive oil
flour
ground thyme
ground pepper

For the sauce, grind the pepper, celery seed (or lovage), coriander, and savory together in a mortar. Add to the onion, wine, stock, vinegar, and olive oil. Pour this sauce over the green vegetable. Heat and simmer gently for 5 minutes, then thicken sauce with flour. Sprinkle the dish with thyme and pepper, and serve.

(Though Apicius added a dash of baking soda to restore the color of the greens, it is omitted here as some vitamins are destroyed in the process.)

Wine-Fried Anchovies

6 oz. fresh anchovies (or
unsalted, canned anchovies)
1 raw egg, lightly beaten
1 T. olive oil
¼ c. white wine
¼ c. fish stock

Wash and trim the anchovies and brush them with egg. In the frying pan, heat olive oil with wine and stock added. When the pan is very hot, add the anchovies and cook them lightly. Serve with a sprinkling of pepper.

II-20

Brains and Salted Fish

II-21 ½ lb. salted (or fresh) cod,
tuna, or sturgeon
4 hard-boiled eggs
1 c. cooked calf's brains
1 c. cooked chicken livers

(Soak the salted fish in water before using it in this dish.) Chop the hard-boiled eggs, brains, and chicken livers. Set this mixture in a stew pot, with the fish in the middle.

Sauce:
¼ t. ground pepper
¼ t. celery seed (or lovage)
½ c. sweet raisin wine
or muscatel
½ c. veal or chicken stock
pinch of rosemary (or rue),
or sage
flour

To make the sauce, mix the pepper, celery seed (or lovage), sweet wine, and stock. Add rosemary, rue, or sage. Bring to a boil and pour over the prepared meats. Simmer together over low heat until fish is tender. Thicken the sauce with flour, and serve.

Red Mullet Sautéed in Wine

II-22 1 lb. red mullet fillets
2 T. olive oil or butter
½ c. sweet raisin wine or
mead

Sauté the mullet fillets in olive oil or butter. While they are cooking, season each fillet with a tablespoon of mead or sweet wine. Serve with a sprinkling of pepper.

Fish Poached with Shallots

II-24 1 lb. fish fillets
6 shallots
1 c. fish stock
2 T. olive oil or butter
white wine vinegar or cider
vinegar
parsley

Put the fish on a bed of shallots in a pan. Add fish stock and olive oil or butter, sufficient to reach half way up the fish. Poach the fillets till done. Place the cooked fish in the middle of a platter, sprinkle with vinegar, decorate with parsley, and serve.

Fish with Sweet and Sour Onions Lucretius

6 shallots or sweet onions
1 c. fish stock
2 T. olive oil
water
1 lb. fish fillets (sole, cod, salmon)
1 t. honey
1 t. white wine vinegar or cider vinegar
1 t. boiled wine
fish pickle (see p. 305)
honey
parsley

Take shallots or sweet onions, discard the tops, and chop into a cooking pot. Moisten this bed of onions with stock, olive oil, and a little water. Place pieces of uncooked fish in the middle, bring to a boil, then cook gently over low heat, basting the fish from time to time. When nearly done, season with honey, vinegar, and boiled wine. (Taste and correct for blandness with fish-pickle and for saltiness with honey). Decorate the dish with parsley and serve.

II-25

Fish Fillets with Leeks and Coriander

2 lbs. raw fish fillets or steaks
1 c. fish stock
1 c. boiled white wine
1 T. olive oil
1 c. sliced leeks
1 t. coriander
½ t. ground pepper
½ t. celery seed (or lovage)
½ t. oregano
2 raw egg yolks

Take fish fillets, chop into pieces, and put into a pot. Add stock, boiled wine, olive oil, and leeks. Bring to a boil, then simmer over low heat. Meanwhile, grind together coriander, pepper, celery seed (or lovage), and oregano. Add these seasonings to the stew. Thicken the liquid by adding well beaten yolks little by little. Simmer for 10 minutes. Serve with a sprinkling of pepper.

II-27

II-24   PATINA PISCIUM *A Dish of Fish* Scale and prepare fish of whatever kind you like. Take dried shallots or another kind of onion and chop them into the cooking vessel and arrange the fish on top. Add fish stock and olive oil. Cook. Afterwards, put cooked saltfish in the middle [of the platter]. Sprinkle with vinegar and add a chaplet made from the oxtongue plant.

II-25   PATELLAM LUCRETIANAM *A Lucretian Dish* Wash onions. Throw out the green parts and slice [the onions which remain] into a cooking vessel. Add a little fish stock, olive oil, and water. While [the onions are] cooking, place raw saltfish in their midst. And when the [stewed onions and] fish are almost cooked, sprinkle a spoonful of honey and just a touch of vinegar and boiled wine. Taste. If the dish is bland, add a little fish-pickle. If it should be too salty, add a little honey [to temper it]. Sprinkle with the leaves of the oxtongue plant and simmer.

    ⟨This dish is named after Titus Lucretius Carus (99–55 B.C.), the greatest philosopher/poet to write in Latin. He believed in the philosophical system of the Greek Epicurus, who tried to replace religion with a doctrine of natural causes. Ethically, this led to the conclusion that pleasure was the only good, to be attained by the harmony between mind and body which resulted from moderation and virtue. But those devoted to sensual pleasures saw in Lucretius a justification for their behavior and this is the modern sense of the word "epicure." It is ironic that Apicius should name a dish after Lucretius, who would have heartily despised him.

II-26   PATINAM DE LAGITIS *Lizard Fish* Scale the lizard fish, clean it, and break raw eggs and mix them with the fish. Add stock, wine, and olive oil and cook. Afterwards, pour plain wine sauce [over the dish], sprinkle with pepper, and serve.[5]

II-27   PATINA ZOMOTEGANON *Fish Stew* Take whatever fish you have on hand and put it raw into a stewing dish. Add olive oil, fish stock, boiled wine, a bouquet of leeks and coriander. While these are cooking, grind pepper, lovage, and a bouquet of oregano. Bruise. Pour some of the elixir from the stew over [these seasonings]. Combine [this mixture] with raw eggs. Empty over the stewed fish and thicken. When the liquid is reduced in quantity [and the texture of the stew is firm], sprinkle the dish with pepper and serve.

PATINA SOLEARUM *Sole*   Beat the soles and then arrange them in a pan. Add olive oil, fish stock, and [white] wine. While [the soles are] cooking, grind and bruise pepper, lovage, and oregano. Pour broth from the pan [over these seasonings and] add raw eggs. Blend into a sauce and then pour over the soles. Cook over a slow fire. When it is firm, sprinkle with pepper and serve. II-28

PATINA DE PISCIBUS   *A Dish of Fish*   Use one ounce of pepper, half a pint of boiled wine, half a pint of spiced wine, two ounces of olive oil. II-29

II-30   PATINA DE PISCICULIS   *A Dish of Little Fish*   [Mix] raisins, pepper, lovage, oregano, onions, wine, fish stock, and olive oil. Transfer these ingredients into a stewing dish. When it has cooked, add cooked little fish. Thicken [the sauce] with starch and serve.

II-31   PATINA DE PISCIBUS DENTICE AURATA ET MUGILE   *A Dish of Fish Made with Dentex, Gilthead Bream, and Grey Mullet*   Take the fish, fillet them, and lightly bake. Chop up the flesh. Next, shuck a quantity of oysters. Put into a mortar, six scruples of pepper. Moisten with fish stock and blend. Add to this one-twelfth of a pint of fish stock and one-twelfth of a pint of wine. Put this and three ounces of olive oil and the oysters in a pan. Bring the wine sauce to the boil [with the oysters]. When it has boiled, grease a stewing dish and put the fish and oyster sauce described above into it. After cooking, break eleven eggs over the fish and oyster. When the sauce has thickened, sprinkle with pepper and serve.[6]

II-32   PATINA DE PISCE LUPO   *Wolf Fish*   Mix pepper, cumin, parsley, rue, onions, honey, fish stock, raisin wine, [and a few] drops of olive oil.

II-33   PATINA DE SORBIS CALIDA ET FRIGIDA   *Hot or Cold Serviceberries*   Take the serviceberries, wash them, pound them in a mortar, and strain them through a colander. Then take four cooked brains and remove the membranes. Next, put into a mortar eight scruples of pepper. Moisten with stock and pound. Add the serviceberries and combine. Break eight eggs into the mixture, beat them, and then add one-twelfth of a pint of stock. Pour [all ingredients] into a clean, greased dish and cook in the thermospodium, so that there are embers above and below. When the dish is ready, sprinkle with finely ground pepper and serve [hot or chilled].

> *There are four species of serviceberries: some of them have the round shape of an apple, others the spinning-top shape of the pear, and still others are ovate like certain species of apple. This ovate species is often sour to taste but the round serviceberries surpass the others in sweetness, and the rest have the flavor of wine.*[7]
>
> Pliny, 15.23.

Fillet of Sole with Wine and Oregano

1 lb. fresh fillets of sole
2 T. olive oil or butter
¼ c. fish stock
¼ c. white wine

Take fillets and arrange them in a pan with the olive oil or butter, fish stock, and white wine. Cook lightly.

II-28

Sauce:
dash of ground pepper
½ t. celery seed (or lovage)
¼ t. oregano
1 c. fish stock
2 raw egg yolks

Meanwhile, for the sauce, grind together pepper, celery seed (or lovage), and oregano. Add to stock and well beaten yolks. Stir and pour over the fish. Finish the fillets in the sauce over low heat, and serve with a sprinkling of pepper.

Fish Cooked with Raisins and Wine

½ lb. cooked fresh tuna, fresh sardines, or anchovies

For the sauce grind together in a mortar, pepper, celery seed (or lovage), and oregano. Add to onion, white wine, fish stock and olive oil. Pour the sauce into a pot, bring to a boil and simmer 20 minutes over low heat. Then add the cooked fish. Cook together for a few minutes more, then thicken sauce with flour and serve together.

II-30

Sauce:
¼ c. dark raisins
dash of ground pepper
½ t. celery seed (or lovage)
½ t. oregano
2 t. chopped onion
½ c. white wine
1 c. fish stock
2 T. olive oil
flour

Fish with Oysters in Wine Sauce

II-31

1 lb. poached fish fillets (bream, mullet, golden shiner)
½ c. oyster meats, chopped
¼ t. ground pepper
1 c. fish stock
½ c. white wine
3 T. olive oil or butter
1 raw egg yolk

Lightly poach fish fillets, cut in pieces and set aside. Shuck and chop enough raw oysters to yield ½ cup of meat. In a mortar, grind pepper and add to fish stock and white wine. Put this wine sauce into a pan with olive oil, bring to a boil, and simmer for 10 minutes to reduce. Add the oysters, and cook for 2–3 minutes in the sauce. Now put the fish and oysters into a cooking pot along with reduced sauce from the pan. Cook together gently over low heat for a few minutes more, thickening with well beaten yolk. Serve with a sprinkling of pepper.

Pike Fillets in Cumin Wine Sauce

II-32

1 lb. poached pike fillets
fish stock

Sauce:
dash of ground pepper
½ t. cumin
1 T. chopped parsley
pinch of rosemary (or rue)
2 t. chopped onion
1 t. honey
1 c. fish stock
¼ c. sweet white wine
1 t. olive oil

To make the sauce, in a mortar, grind pepper with cumin and rosemary (or rue). Add to parsley and onion. Blend with honey, stock, sweet wine, and olive oil. Bring to a boil, then simmer gently for 25 minutes to reduce.

Meanwhile, take pike fillets and poach them in fish stock. To serve, arrange fillets on a platter and pour the sauce over them.

Apples and Calf's Brains Casserole

2 lbs. apples (or
serviceberries)
½ lb. cooked calf's brains,
chopped
dash of ground pepper
½ c. beef or chicken stock
2 raw eggs
ginger or cinnamon
butter

Take serviceberries or apples, wash, peel and pound
the fruit in a mortar, and strain through a colander
(or put through a blender). Then season the brains
with pepper. Add the mashed fruit and combine,
binding the mixture together with well beaten eggs
and sufficient stock. Grease a casserole dish, place
the fruit and meat mixture in it, and cook for 30
minutes in a 375°F oven. Serve with a sprinkling of
ginger or cinnamon. Alternatively, chill and serve
cold.

II-33

Peaches Cooked with Cumin

Take early peaches, wash, cut them in quarters, and
remove pits. Steam in water until soft. Drain,
reserve liquid, and put them in a cooking pot with a
little of the peach liquid, a few drops of olive oil, and
cumin to taste. Simmer gently for a few minutes and
serve hot.

II-34

Pears Cooked with Cinnamon and Wine

1 lb. pears
water
1 t. cinnamon
pinch of cumin
2 T. honey
½ c. sweet white wine
1 T. olive oil or butter
1 c. pear liquid
2 egg yolks
nutmeg

Take pears, wash, peel, and steam in water till soft.
Drain and reserve liquid. Remove the pear cores,
and quarter them. Put the pieces into a pot, and
season with cinnamon, cumin, honey, sweet white
wine, olive oil or butter, and the pear liquid from
the steaming pan. Simmer gently for a few minutes.
Thicken liquid with well beaten yolks. Serve hot
with a sprinkling of nutmeg.

II-35

II-34   PATINA DE PERSICIS *A Dish of Peaches* Take peaches which have a firm texture and wash them. Cut them into pieces and stew. Put the peaches into a dish and sprinkle a few drops of olive oil over them. Season with cumin, and serve.

II-35   PATINA DE PIRIS *A Dish of Pears* Wash and boil the pears. Remove the centers. Mix [the pears] with pepper, cumin, honey, raisin wine, stock, and a little olive oil. Thicken the mixture with eggs. Sprinkle with pepper and serve.

II-36   PATINA URTICARUM CALIDA ET FRIGIDA *Hot or Cold Nettles* [8] Take the nettles, wash them, and drain in a colander. Dry them on a board and chop. Then grind [in a mortar] ten scruples of pepper, moisten with stock, and blend. Then add two cups of stock and six ounces of olive oil. Boil this sauce, remove, and cool it. Afterwards, grease a clean shallow pan, break eight eggs into it, and stir. Pour [the nettles and the sauce]. Cook in the thermospodium so that there are embers above and below. Sprinkle with ground pepper when cooked and serve [hot or chilled].

II-37   PATINA DE CYDONEIS *Quinces* Cook the quince-apples with leeks, honey, stock, olive oil, and boiled wine, and serve. The quinces can also be stewed, simply, in honey.

Hot or Cold Nettle Quiche

1 c. nettles
butter
2 c. fresh mushrooms, sliced
1 c. cheddar cheese, grated
1 medium onion, sliced in rings
½ c. flour
¼ t. salt
1 T. fish-pickle (see p. 305)
3 raw eggs
1½ c. cream
1 t. coriander
½ t. pepper, coarsely ground

Pick a basket of young spring nettles and steam in a covered pan for 30 minutes. Take 1 cup nettles, drain and chop. Arrange in a buttered quiche pan. Cover with layers of mushrooms, cheese, and onion. Now blend the flour, salt, fish-pickle, well beaten eggs, cream, coriander, and pepper. Pour the mixture over the dry ingredients in the quiche pan. Bake in a 400°F oven for 35 to 40 minutes, and serve hot with a sprinkling of pepper. Alternatively, chill and serve cold.

II-36

Quinces Stewed with Leeks

1 lb. quinces
water
½ c. leeks, sliced
2 T. honey
1 T. olive oil or butter
¼ c. boiled white wine
quince liquid

Take ripe quinces, quarter, peel them, put in a pot, cover with water, and cook for 45 minutes. Reserve the liquid, then put the quinces in another pot. Add sliced leeks, honey, olive oil or butter, boiled wine, and sufficient liquid from the first pan to cover the fruit. Cook gently, covered, over low heat for ½ hour or until done.

Alternatively, the quinces can be stewed simply in honey diluted with liquid from the boiling pan.

II-37

FISH AND FORCEMEAT RAGOUTS

❡ Apicius used the word "minutal," for which the French "ragout" is the closest modern translation. The minutal was typically a dish of chopped meat or fish stewed with vegetables and/or fruit, highly seasoned and thickened with flour or mixed with pieces of pastry or bread. The pastry was soft and able to absorb the liquid of the ragout — unlike the hard cakes imported by Romans from the island of Rhodes.

III-1   MINUTAL MARINUM   *Seafood Ragout*   Put the fish into a cooking pot. Add fish-pickle, olive oil, wine, and boiled stock. Finely chop leeks and their heads and coriander. Use the flesh of the chopped fish to make a number of small forcemeats. Cut up fillets of cooked fish, add a goodly quantity of well washed sea nettles, and cook. [In a mortar] grind pepper, lovage, and oregano. Moisten with gravy from the ragout. Empty the sauce into the cooking pot with the fish. When it boils, break pastry into the ragout and stir to give the dish a thicker texture. Sprinkle with pepper and serve.

III-2   MINUTAL TERENTINUM   *Ragout Terentine*   Into a [deep] dish, put finely chopped whites of leeks. Add olive oil, stock, gravy, and exceedingly small dumplings, and blend so as to make them soft. Make Terentine meatballs. You will find their preparation among the forcemeat [recipes].⁹ Make the sauce by bruising [in a mortar] pepper, lovage, and oregano. Moisten [these herbs] with stock and the gravy from the ragout. Blend with wine and raisin wine. Put into a saucepan. When it has boiled, break pastry [into the ragout to] thicken. Sprinkle with pepper and serve.

Spiced Seafood Dumplings

1 lb. fish fillets
2 T. olive oil
¼ c. white wine
1 c. reduced fish stock
heads of leeks, finely chopped
1 t. coriander
½ c. flour
¼ c. fish stock
dash of ground pepper
½ t. celery seed (or lovage)
½ t. oregano
(flour)

Place fish fillets in a pot and poach lightly in a mixture of olive oil, white wine, and reduced fish stock. Remove the fish, reserve liquid, and flake it. Mix with chopped leeks, coriander, flour, and fish stock, if needed. Shape into small balls of forcemeat. Put the fish dumplings into a buttered casserole, cover, and cook gently in a 325°F oven for 20 minutes.

Meanwhile, in a mortar, grind pepper, celery seed (or lovage), and oregano. Combine with liquid from the pan of cooked fish. Pour over the dumplings. Cook for a further 10 minutes, and then, if you wish thicken the liquid with flour. Serve with a sprinkling of pepper.

III-1

Meatball Ragout Terentine

lb. very small cooked beef or pork meatballs
4 heads of leeks, sliced
2 t. olive oil
½ c. reduced beef stock
1 c. vegetable stock

First cook small beef or pork meatballs in a pan in olive oil.

Into a casserole put leeks. Add olive oil, reduced stock, vegetable stock, and cooked meat balls. Cook with the following sauce.

III-2

Sauce:
¼ c. red wine
¼ c. sweet raisin wine or muscatel
pinch of ground pepper
1 t. celery seed (or lovage)
½ t. oregano
2 T. pastry flour
¼ c. water

To make the sauce, combine the red wine, sweet or raisin wine, pepper, celery seed (or lovage), and oregano. Pour over the ragout. Cover and cook in a 325°F oven for 30 to 40 minutes. Combine flour and water and add to the dish to thicken it. Serve with a sprinkling of pepper.

III-3   MINUTAL APICIANUM *Ragout Apicius* Take olive oil, stock, wine, leeks, heads and all, mint, small fish, small forcemeat dumplings, testicles of capon, and pork tidbits. Cook all these together. Grind pepper, lovage, green coriander or coriander seed. Moisten with stock. Add a moderate amount of honey and gravy [from the meats]. Blend with honey and wine. Heat the sauce [and pour into the dish]. Break pastry into the ragout to thicken the texture. Stir vigorously. Sprinkle with pepper and serve.

III-4   MINUTAL MATIANUM *Matius' Ragout* Into a cooking pot, put olive oil and stock, and reduced stock. Chop into it, leeks, coriander, and very small forcemeat dumplings. Now chop into cubes a leg of pork previously cooked, together with its rind. Cook [the pork and the dumplings] in the same pot. While cooking, of this, add some of the apples [named after the poet] Matius, having first washed them, removed the skins and the seeds, and cut them into cubes. While the ragout is cooking, bruise pepper, cumin, green coriander or coriander seed, mint, and laser root. Pour vinegar [into the mortar]. Add honey, stock, and a little boiled wine. Blend with gravy from the ragout, with a little vinegar. Bring to the boil. When it has boiled [add it to the ragout] and then break pastry into it to thicken. Sprinkle with pepper and serve.

III-5   MINUTAL DULCE EX CITRIIS *Sweet Citron Ragout* [10] In a [deep] dish, put olive oil and stock, reduced stock, and the head of a leek and coriander, both chopped finely. Add to this a leg of cooked pork, chopped, and small forcemeat dumplings. While this is cooking, grind pepper, cumin, green coriander or coriander seed, [green] rue, and laser root. Pour vinegar [over these seasonings and add some] boiled wine and gravy from the ragout. Blend with vinegar. Cook. [Add to the ragout]. Wash the citron, inside and out. Cut into cubes and boil them. Add them to the ragout and thicken with pastry. Sprinkle with pepper and serve.

❡The citron, *Citrus medica*, is related to the lemon but is larger, has a thicker rind, and is less acid. The citron was highly regarded by the ancients as an antidote to poison.

Ragout Apicius with Fishes and Meats

½ lb. fresh small fish (fresh
anchovies, sardines, etc.)
1 c. (uncooked) ground
pork dumplings
½ c. cooked chicken livers,
diced
1 pair sweetbreads, chopped
2 T. olive oil
1 c. meat stock
½ c. white wine
4 heads of leeks, chopped
1 t. of mint

In a casserole, put olive oil, stock, wine, leeks, mint, III-3 whole cleaned fish, pork dumplings, chicken livers, and sweetbreads. Cover and cook in a 350°F oven for an hour, adding stock if necessary.

Sauce:
¼ t. ground pepper
½ t. celery seed (or lovage)
½ t. coriander
1 T. honey
½ c. white wine
flour

Meanwhile, for the sauce, grind pepper, celery seed (or lovage), and coriander. Moisten with some gravy from the ragout. Blend with honey and white wine. Heat this sauce and pour it over the ragout. Continue cooking for a few minutes, then finish by thickening the liquid with flour. Sprinkle with pepper and serve.

Matius' Ragout with Ham and Apples

III-4

½ *lb. small (uncooked)*
ground pork dumplings
1 lb. cooked ham, diced
2 t. olive oil
1 c. beef or pork stock
½ c. reduced beef or
pork stock
2 leeks, sliced
½ t. coriander
2 c. apples, diced

In a deep casserole, put olive oil, stock, and reduced stock. To these ingredients add leeks, coriander, and pork meatballs. Dice the cooked ham and add to the ragout. Cook, covered, in a 350°F oven for 1 hour. After 45 minutes, add peeled, diced apples, and cook 15 minutes more.

Then make the following sauce and finish together.

Sauce:
pinch of ground pepper
¼ t. cumin
½ t. coriander
1 t. of mint
¼ t. ginger
1 t. wine vinegar or cider
vinegar
1 t. honey or sugar
½ c. beef or pork stock
¼ c. boiled wine
¼ c. casserole juices
flour

For the sauce, in a mortar grind pepper, cumin, coriander, mint, and ginger. Moisten these seasonings with vinegar. Combine with honey, stock, boiled wine, and liquid from the casserole. Bring this sauce to a boil, then pour it over the apples and pork. Continue cooking for a few minutes, then thicken with flour. Serve with a sprinkling of pepper.

Sweet Citron Ragout of Ham and Pork

1 lb. cooked ham, diced
½ lb. (uncooked) ground
pork
2 t. olive oil
1 c. beef or pork stock
½ c. reduced beef or
pork stock
2 heads of leeks, chopped
½ t. coriander

In a casserole, put olive oil, stock, reduced stock, leeks, coriander, cooked ham, and pork meatballs. Cook, covered, in a 350°F oven for 1 hour.

III-5

Sauce:
pinch of ground pepper
¼ t. cumin
½ t. coriander
pinch of rosemary (or rue)
¼ t. ginger
1 t. wine vinegar
¼ c. boiled wine
¼ c. casserole juices
½ c. beef or pork stock
½ c. diced lemon (or
citron) peel
honey
flour

For the sauce, in a mortar, grind pepper with cumin, coriander, rosemary (or rue), and ginger. Moisten with the vinegar. In a pan, add to boiled wine, liquid from the casserole, and stock. Bring the sauce to a boil, take diced lemon (or citron), add to sauce, and simmer for 20 minutes. Pour into the ragout and cook together 15 minutes more. (If lemon peel is used, add honey to taste.) To finish the dish thicken sauce with flour. Serve with a sprinkling of pepper.

III-6   MINUTAL EX PRAECOQUIS *Apricot Ragout* Into a cooking pot, put olive oil, stock, wine, dry chopped shallots, and a cooked leg of pork chopped into squares. When these are cooked, grind pepper, cumin, dried mint, and aniseed [in a mortar]. [Over these seasonings] pour honey, stock, raisin wine, a little vinegar, and liquid from the ragout. Blend. [Cook.] [Pour over the pork.] Add pitted apricots and heat until they are completely cooked. [Add them to the ragout.] Break pastry into the dish to thicken it. Sprinkle with pepper and serve.

III-7   MINUTAL EX IECINERIBUS ET PULMONIBUS LEPORIS *Hare's Liver and Lungs Ragout* You may find this formula among the recipes for hare [in Book VIII]. Into the [same] cooking pot, put stock, wine, olive oil, reduced stock, chopped leeks and coriander, small forcemeat dumplings, and diced, cooked leg of pork [and the chopped cooked liver and lungs of a hare]. While the ragout is cooking, grind pepper, lovage, and oregano. Mix with liquid from the ragout, wine, and raisin wine. Bring to the boil, [add to the liver and lungs of the hare and the diced ham], and cook. When it has boiled, thicken with pieces of pastry. Sprinkle with pepper and serve.

III-8   MINUTAL EX ROSIS *Rose Hip Ragout* [Cook] in the same manner as the recipe written above, but add more raisin wine.

HULLED BARLEY SOUPS

❡The two recipes in this section are derived from the ancient medical practice of administering "tisanes," barley waters, to the feeble. Apicius took a simple formula and embellished it with herbs and wine to make these unique barley soups.

IV-1   TISANAM SIC FACIES *Barley Soup* Soak the barley in water for one day, then rinse and hull it. Put [it in a saucepan] on a hot fire. Bring to the boil and add sufficient olive oil, a bouquet garni of anise, dry onion, savory, and a pig's knuckle to give flavor to the soup. Add green coriander and ground salt. When all has cooked thoroughly, remove the bouquet of anise and transfer the barley into another cooking vessel such that the barley is not scorched by the bottom of the pan.

Ham and Apricot Ragout

1 lb. cooked ham, diced
2 t. olive oil
1 c. pork stock
¼ c. white wine
¼ c. shallots, chopped

In a casserole, put ham, olive oil, stock, wine, and shallots. Cook, covered, in the oven for 1 hour.

III-6

Sauce:
pinch each of pepper and
cumin
1 sprig of mint
pinch of aniseed
1 T. honey
¼ c. pork stock
¼ c. sweet raisin wine or
muscatel
1 t. wine vinegar
¼ c. casserole liquid
10 fresh apricots (or dried,
pre-soaked in water)
flour
ground pepper

To make the sauce, in a mortar, grind pepper with cumin, mint, and aniseed. Combine with honey, stock, sweet wine, vinegar, and liquid from the casserole. Bring the sauce to a boil and add to the ragout for the last 15 minutes.

When ragout is nearly done, take the apricots, divide in half, and pit them. Add them to the casserole and cook together for 5 minutes. Finish by thickening with flour. Serve with a sprinkling of pepper.

Make the mixture smooth and strain the soup into a saucepan over the pig's knuckle. Then grind pepper, lovage, a little dried pennyroyal, cumin, and ground silphium. Pour vinegar over [these herbs], [add some] boiled wine and stock, and then pour the whole mixture evenly over the pig's knuckle. Cook over a slow fire.

IV-2   TISANAM *Barley Soup* [Into a pot] pour [dried] chick-peas, lentils, and peas. Grind the barley and then boil it with these vegetables. When they have boiled, add olive oil as required, and chop over the vegetables, leeks, coriander, aniseed, fennel, beets, mallows, and soft cabbage leaves. Put all of the finely chopped greens into the pot. [In a mortar] grind enough fennel seed, oregano, silphium, and lovage. Boil the cabbage. Moisten these seasonings with stock, and pour [the sauce along with boiled cabbage into the soup] over the vegetables [and barley]. Stir. Garnish with finely chopped cabbage leaves.

ANTEPASTS

V-I   GUSTUM VERSATILE *Upside-down Antepast* Take small white beets, stored leeks, celery, bulbs, poached snails, [cooked] chicken giblets, small bird meats, and forcemeat dumplings cooked in their own gravy. Grease a stewing dish and strew inside it mallow leaves, and then arrange the mixed green vegetables so that they have plenty of room. Add to these, the bulbs, which have previously been bruised [in a mortar], damsons, snails, forcemeats, Lucanian sausage sliced finely, stock, olive oil, wine, and vinegar. Put the stewing dish [on the fire] to cook. When it has cooked, grind pepper, lovage, ginger, a little pellitory [and wine]. Blend and pour [into the stewing dish]. Cook well. Now break a number of eggs and mix with the remaining sauce in the mortar, and use this to thicken the dish. While it is setting, make the wine sauce for it in this way: bruise pepper and lovage, mix and pour stock and wine [over these seasonings], and then blend in raisin wine or sweet wine. Blend [the sauce] in a pan, adding a little olive oil. Bring to the boil. Afterwards, thicken the sauce with starch. Now turn the antepast out onto a platter. Remove the mallow leaves, and pour the wine sauce. Sprinkle with pepper and serve.

Barley Soup with Meat

½ c. pearl barley or wheat berries
10 c. water
2 T. olive oil
1 t. aniseed (tied in cheesecloth)
½ t. savory
1 pig's knuckle (or 3 lbs. lamb or mutton bones)
½ t. coriander
¼ t. ground pepper
½ t. celery seed (or lovage)
pinch each of mint (or pennyroyal) and fennel
½ t. cumin
1 t. wine vinegar
½ c. boiled white wine

IV-1

Soak barley or wheat for 24 hours in water, then rinse. Put it in a pan and cook till tender together with water, olive oil, the small bouquet garni of aniseed, savory, and the knuckle or bones to flavor the broth. Add coriander, and salt to taste. Remove the bouquet garni of aniseed. In a mortar, grind pepper, celery seed (or lovage), mint (or pennyroyal), cumin, and fennel. Moisten with vinegar and combine with boiled white wine. Pour into the barley soup and simmer over very low heat for at least 2 hours more.

Vegetable and Lentil Soup

1 c. chick-peas
1 c. lentils
1 c. green peas
½ c. barley (pre-soaked)
10 c. water
2 T. olive oil
2 heads of leeks, finely chopped
½ t. coriander
pinch each of aniseed and fennel
½ c. beets, diced
grape (or mallow) leaves, chopped
½ c. cabbage leaves, chopped
½ t. oregano
pinch of fennel
pinch of celery seed (or lovage)
½ t. honey
¼ c. cabbage leaves, chopped

IV-2

Soak barley for 24 hours in water, then rinse. Into a pot, put chick-peas, lentils, and peas. Add drained barley to the legumes, together with water and olive oil. To this, add heads of leeks, coriander, aniseed, fennel, beets, grape (or mallow) leaves, and cabbage leaves. Cook gently over low heat for at least 3 hours. One half hour before the soup is cooked, grind together oregano, fennel, and celery seed (or lovage), and add to the soup. Stir. Simmer ½ hour and serve with a garnish of chopped raw cabbage leaves.

Upside-down Mixed Hors D'oeuvres

v-i   8 cabbage, grape (or mallow) leaves, parboiled
4 beets, diced
2 leeks, finely chopped
3 stalks celery, chopped
6 whole small onions
7 poached snails
½ c. chicken livers, chopped
½ c. cooked chicken breast (or bird meats), thinly sliced
10 damsons or plums
1 c. chicken dumplings (see p. 19)
½ c. Lucanian sausage (see p. 28), thinly sliced
olive oil or butter
¼ c. white wine
1 c. chicken stock
dash of wine vinegar

Take a deep casserole, and grease it with olive oil. Spread grape (or mallow) leaves on the bottom and along the sides. Arrange the green vegetables and the beets as a first layer. Allow a little room between the vegetables. Now bruise the onions in a mortar and add them to the green vegetables. Carefully place on this the prepared snails, halved and pitted damsons, the chicken dumplings, and thinly sliced sausage. Moisten with olive oil or butter, wine, and stock. Add vinegar to taste.

First sauce:
dash of ground pepper
½ t. celery seed (or lovage)
pinch of ginger & chamomile
½ c. white wine
3 raw egg yolks

To the casserole, add the following sauce, but reserve a little. Combine pepper, celery seed (or lovage), ginger, chamomile (or pellitory), and wine. Add well beaten egg yolks to the remaining sauce and pour this atop the antepast. Cook the covered casserole in a 350°F oven for 1 hour or until done.

Second sauce:
dash of ground pepper
¼ t. celery seed (or lovage)
½ c. chicken stock
½ c. white wine
¼ c. sweet raisin wine or muscatel
olive oil

Now make the second sauce by combining pepper, celery seed (or lovage), stock, wine, and sweet wine. Bring the wine sauce to a boil, adding a little olive oil. Thicken with flour. Turn the cooked antepast upside down onto a serving dish, remove the leaves, and pour some of the wine sauce over it. Serve with a sprinkling of pepper, and the rest of the sauce.

Liver, Chicken, and Onion Hors D'oeuvres

3 medium onions
1 c. chicken stock
2 T. olive oil
½ c. white wine
1 c. pork and chicken livers, sliced
cooked chicken breasts, sliced

In a deep pot, poach onions in stock, olive oil, and white wine till done. Combine with sliced livers and chicken (or meats from small birds). Put all in a casserole and cook for 1 hour in a 375°F oven. v-2

Sauce:
dash of pepper
½ t. celery seed (or lovage)
1 c. chicken stock
¼ c. white wine
flour

When the meats are almost cooked, combine pepper, celery seed (or lovage), stock, and white wine for the sauce. Add a little liquid from the casserole dish and bring the sauce to a boil. Take the onions out and pour the sauce over the meats. Bring to a boil, thicken with flour if you wish, and serve.

Sweet Apricot Hors D'oeuvres

1 lb. hard-ripe apricots

Take washed apricots, halve and pit them, and put them in a stew pot. v-4

Sauce:
1 t. mint
1 t. cinnamon
3 t. honey
½ c. sweet raisin wine or muscatel
½ c. white wine
1 t. white wine vinegar
1 T. olive oil
flour
cinnamon or nutmeg

For the sauce, first mix mint and cinnamon. Blend with honey, sweet wine, and vinegar. Pour the sauce over the apricots, add olive oil, cover, and stew over very low heat for ½ hour or until done. When cooked, thicken liquid with flour. Sprinkle cinnamon or nutmeg over the apricot hors d'oeuvres, and serve.

V-2   GUSTUM DE HOLERIBUS   *Vegetable Relish*   Cook bulbs in stock, olive oil, and wine. When they are cooked, slice suckling pig and chicken livers, chicken legs, and meats from small birds. Cook these with the bulbs. When they have cooked, grind pepper and lovage. Pour stock and wine [over these seasonings]. Add raisin wine to sweeten. Blend with liquid [from the onions and meats]. Recall the onions. [Add the sauce.] Bring [the vegetable relish] to the boil and instantly thicken with cornstarch.

V-3   GUSTUM DE CUCURBITIS FARSILIBUS   *Stuffed Gourd Antepast* From the sides of the gourds carefully cut oblong strips. [Through these openings] hollow out the gourds and then put them in cold water. To make the stuffing for the gourd antepast, first grind pepper, lovage, and oregano. Pour stock [over these seasonings and then] blend with chopped cooked brains. [Into this mixture] dissolve raw eggs. Combine all the ingredients smoothly and add stock. Half cook the hollowed gourds. Stuff them with the relish described above. Replace the oblong strips, bind up the gourds [with the twigs and braise]. Boil them, remove [from the heat], and then fry. The wine sauce is made this way: mix pepper, lovage, and moisten with wine and stock. Add raisin wine and a little olive oil. Pour into a pan and boil. While boiling, thicken with cornstarch. Pour wine sauce over the fried gourds, sprinkle with pepper and serve.

V-4   GUSTUM DE PRAECOQUIIS   *Apricot Antepast*   Take the very small, first-grown, hard-skinned apricots and wash them. Pit them and immerse [the fruit] in cold water. Then arrange them in a stewing dish. [In a mortar] grind pepper and dried mint. Moisten with stock and add honey, raisin wine, wine, and vinegar. Pour this sauce over the prepared apricots in the stewing dish. Add a little oil and cook over a slow fire. After it has boiled, thicken with starch. Sprinkle with pepper and serve.

BOOK IV OF APICIUS,
ALL KINDS OF DISHES,
IS ENDED

Legumes

POTTAGES

℧ Pottages were made of a variety of pulse, or legumes, and grains and were considered by Pliny to be the foods eaten by the earliest Romans. Pottages antedated the discovery of bread-making in Rome, giving rise to the term "pultiphagus" (pottage eater) meaning "a Roman."

It is evident that Romans lived for a long time not on bread but on pottage, since even now foods are called "pulmentaria" [pottages]. *And Ennius, the most ancient Roman poet, recounts as he is describing a famine in Rome caused by a siege, how fathers snatched morsels of pottage out of the hands of their crying children. Consequently the oldest sacred rites and birthdays are celebrated with sacrificial pottage.*

Pliny, 18.19.

I-I   PULTES IULIANAE SIC COQUUNTUR *Pottage Julian* Pour purified spelt into a saucepan. [Add water and] bring to the boil. While boiling, add olive oil. When [the mixture] thickens, stir until the surface is smooth. Now mix two cooked brains with a half pound of meat, ground as for forcemeats. Put this into a pan. [In a mortar] mix pepper, lovage, fennel seed, stock, and a little wine. Add this sauce to the brains and forcemeat, and cook. Afterwards, stir the mixture into the pottage. From this preparation the spelt is made savory. Add it by the ladleful and stir carefully until the pottage has the appearance of a paste.

I-2   PULTES CUM IURE OENOCOCTI *Pottage in Wine Sauce* Season the pottage with wine sauce, season cooked fine wheat flour or spelt in this sauce, and serve with tender pieces of pork made savory by the wine sauce.

I-3   PULTES TRACTOGALATAE *Pottage of Pastry and Milk* Put a pint of milk and a little water in a clean saucepan and heat over a slow fire. Take three circles of dry bread, crumble them, and add them to the milk. To avoid scorching, mix and stir with water. When it has cooked fully on the stove, add honey. A similar pottage can be made with must and milk, salt, and a little olive oil.

PULTES *Pottage* Pour [a quantity of] purified spelt into a saucepan. [Add water and] bring to a boil. When hot, add olive oil. When the mixture thickens, blend [in a mixing bowl] two cooked brains and a half pound of meat ground as for forcemeats. Mix with the brains and put them in a saucepan. [In a mortar] grind pepper, lovage, and fennel seed. Add stock and a little unmixed wine, and pour over the brains and meats. Afterwards, stir the mixture into the pottage. Little by little, make the spelt savory with this preparation. Stir carefully until [the pottage] has the appearance of a paste.[1]

I-4

LENTILS

I find the authorities on the subject consider that the eating of lentils promotes an even temper.

Pliny, 18.31.

LENTICULA EX SPHONDYLIS[2] *Lentils and Parsnips* [Boil the lentils and put them in] a fresh pan. In a mortar, put pepper, cumin, coriander seed, mint, rue, and pennyroyal. Grind. Pour vinegar over [these seasonings]. Add honey, stock, and boiled wine. Mix with vinegar. Pour this sauce into the pan. Add mashed, boiled parsnips, and cook. When well cooked, thicken [with starch] and serve in a mushroom dish with fresh olive oil.

II-1

LENTICULAM DE CASTANEIS *Lentils with Chestnuts* [Boil the lentils.] Take a clean saucepan and put carefully washed chestnuts into it. Add water and a little soda, and cook. When cooked, put pepper, cumin, coriander seed, mint, rue, laser root, and pennyroyal into a mortar. Bruise [these seasonings together]. Pour vinegar over them, and also honey and stock. Blend with [more] vinegar. Pour the sauce over the cooked chestnuts. [Add the lentils.] Add olive oil. Bring to the boil. Stir and taste. If anything is lacking, add it now. When you have poured [the lentils and chestnuts] into a mushroom dish, add fresh olive oil.

II-2

ALITER LENTICULAM *Lentils* Cook [the lentils in water]. When the froth has been skimmed, add leeks and green coriander. [In a mortar]

II-3

Calf's Brains with Fennel Pottage

I-I

2 T. wholewheat pastry flour
1 c. water
2 T. olive oil or butter
¼ lb. cooked calf's brains, chopped
½ lb. ground beef
½ t. ground pepper
½ t. celery seed (or lovage)
pinch of fennel seed
1 c. beef stock
¼ c. white wine

For the pottage, put flour into a pan with water. Bring to a boil, stirring frequently. Add olive oil or butter, stir till smooth, and keep warm. Now mix chopped calf's brains with ground meat and shape into dumplings. Put the meats into a fresh pan and cook in a mixture of pepper, celery seed (or lovage), fennel seed, stock, and wine. When the meats are cooked and seasoned in this sauce, add them spoonful by spoonful to the pottage, and serve.

Lentils and Chestnuts in Coriander Wine Sauce

II-2

1 c. lentils
2½ c. beef or vegetable stock
1 c. shelled chestnuts
½ t. ground pepper
¼ t. cumin
½ t. coriander
1 t. mint
pinch of rosemary (or rue), fennel, and pennyroyal, if available
1 t. wine vinegar
1 T. honey
1 c. vegetable or beef stock
2 T. olive oil or butter

Cook lentils in stock till tender. Drain, reserve stock, and set lentils aside. Take a fresh pan and put chestnuts into it. Cover with water, simmer till cooked, drain, and slice.

Meanwhile, in a mortar, grind pepper, cumin, coriander, mint, and a pinch of rosemary (or rue), fennel, and pennyroyal. Moisten with vinegar and blend with honey. Put the cooked lentils and sliced chestnuts in a pan together with the sauce. Add 1 cup stock and olive oil or butter. Bring to a boil and simmer for a few minutes. Taste, and add honey or vinegar if you wish. Serve the cooked lentils and chestnuts with a little olive oil or melted butter.

Lentils and Leeks

1 c. lentils
2½ c. water
2 heads of leeks, sliced
½ t. coriander
pinch each of fennel,
rosemary (or rue), and
pennyroyal if available
1 t. mint
1 t. wine vineger
1 T. honey
¼ c. vegetable stock
¼ c. boiled white wine
2 T. olive oil or butter
flour
ground pepper

Cook lentils in water, and partially drain, retaining II-3 about a ½ cup of liquid in the pot. Add sliced heads of leeks.

In a mortar, grind coriander seeds, fennel, rosemary (or rue), pennyroyal, and mint. Moisten spices with vinegar. Blend with honey, vegetable stock, and boiled wine. Pour this sauce over the cooked lentils. Bring to a boil, stirring from time to time, and simmer till leeks are tender. Taste, and add honey or vinegar if necessary. Thicken with flour if you wish. Moisten with a few drops of olive oil or butter, sprinkle with pepper, and serve.

Peas with Leeks in Basil Wine Sauce

1 lb. fresh, shelled peas
½ c. water
2 heads of leeks, chopped
½ t. coriander
¼ t. cumin
½ t. ground pepper
½ t. celery seed (or lovage)
pinch each of caraway and
aniseed
¼ t. basil
½ c. chicken or veal stock
¼ c. white wine

Steam peas in a little water, boil, and reserve liquid III-1 in pan when they are done. To this add finely chopped leeks. In a mortar, grind coriander, cumin, pepper, celery seed (or lovage), a pinch of caraway, aniseed, and basil. Blend with stock and white wine. Add this sauce to the peas and leeks, and cook gently over low heat in a covered pan for 25 minutes, stirring from time to time.

grind coriander seed, pennyroyal, laser root, mint, and rue. Moisten with vinegar and add honey, stock, vinegar, and boiled wine. [Pour this sauce into the pan over the lentils and cook.] Add olive oil and stir. If anything is lacking, add it now. Thicken with starch, add some fresh olive oil, sprinkle with pepper, and serve.

PEAS

III-1

[UNTITLED] [*Peas*] Cook the peas and skim them. Then put leeks, coriander, and cumin [into the pan]. [In a mortar] grind pepper, lovage, caraway, aniseed, and fresh basil. Moisten these seasonings with stock and wine. [Add this sauce to the boiled peas and] cook, stirring [from time to time]. [Taste,] add whatever may be lacking, and serve.

III-2

PISAM FARSILEM *Pressed Peas* Boil the peas. Add olive oil to them. Now take a belly [of pork]. [Cut it into squares]. Put this into a pan with stock, the heads of leeks, and green coriander. Simmer. Make small forcemeat squares and cook them in stock with thrushes, meats, or other small birds or chicken slices, and brains previously parboiled in broth. Roast Lucanian sausages and boil a leg of pork, cook leeks in water, and roast half a pint of nuts. [In a mortar] grind pepper, lovage, oregano, and ginger. Pour over these seasonings gravy from the [pan in which the] belly of pork [was cooked] and stir. Then take a pan that has straight edges, one which can be turned over, and cover [the bottom] with caul. Pour olive oil over this, and then sprinkle nuts [on top]. Now put the peas over these, so that the bottom of the pan is covered. Over this, arrange the [boiled] pork, the leeks, and the sliced Lucanian sausage. Once again put peas on top, and cover these alternately with layers of the prepared meats. Continue until the vessel is full. Last of all put a layer of peas atop so that all the ingredients are contained inside. Cook in the oven or over a slow fire, so that the dish cooks firmly through and through. Then in a mortar, put hard-boiled eggs, having first removed the yolks, white pepper, nuts, honey, white wine, and a little stock. Mix these together and put them in a saucepan until they boil. Turn over the pressed peas onto a platter and pour the sauce on top. This is called white sauce.

Baked Peas with Meats and White Sauce

2½ c. fresh, shelled peas
olive oil or butter
1 lb. ham or pork belly, diced
½ c. stock
2 heads of leeks, chopped
1 t. coriander
½ c. poultry forcemeats (see p. 19)
½ c. cooked chicken breast, sliced
¼ lb. calf's brains
2 c. chicken stock
½ lb. Lucanian sausage (see p. 28)
1 c. pine nuts or chopped almonds

First sauce:
1 t. ground pepper
1 T. celery seed (or lovage)
1–1½ t. oregano
½ t. ginger
casings

Second Sauce:
2 hard-boiled egg whites
dash of white pepper
¼ c. finely chopped almonds
1 T. honey
1 c. white wine
2½ c. chicken or veal stock

III-2

Take peas, cook them, drain, and then moisten with a little olive oil or butter. Set aside. Now dice ham or pork. Put the pork in a pan and cover with ½ cup stock, heads of leeks, and coriander. Simmer for 30 minutes on top of stove. Set aside. Now take the forcemeats, the chicken breast, and calf's brains. Put all in a pan, cover with stock, and cook till done. Set aside. Cook Lucanian sausages and set aside. Roast pine nuts or chopped almonds in the oven for a few minutes.

To make the first sauce, in a mortar, grind pepper, celery seed (or lovage), oregano, and ginger. Moisten with ¼ cup liquid from the pork pan. Heat to a boil, and set aside.

Now take a deep, straight-sided (to make it easier to turn upside-down) oiled casserole dish, and line it with casings. Grease this with a little olive oil, then sprinkle the bottom of the dish with the nuts, seasoned with a little of the sauce. Cover with a layer of peas. Make another layer with the diced pork or ham, the leeks, and the sliced sausage. Sprinkle with sauce and add a layer of peas. Cover with the forcemeats and finish with a final layer of peas and sauce. Cook, uncovered, for 40 minutes in a 325°F oven (or cook over low heat).

Meanwhile, make the second sauce with finely minced egg whites, white pepper, almonds, honey, white wine, and stock. Blend and bring to a boil. Simmer for 25 minutes to reduce.

Carefully turn the cooked peas casserole onto a platter. Take off the casings and pour the "white sauce" over the pressed peas. Serve.

III-3

PISUM INDICUM *Peas Indigo* Boil the peas. Skim them. Then chop leeks and coriander. Add [the leeks and coriander] to the pan and simmer. Take little cuttlefish and cook them together with their own ink. [While the cuttlefish are cooking] add olive oil, fish stock, wine, and a bouquet of chives and coriander. When cooked, grind pepper, lovage, oregano, a little caraway, and juices from the pan of peas. Blend with wine and raisin wine. Slice the cuttlefish into very small pieces and add them to the peas. Pour the sauce over all. Sprinkle with pepper [and serve].

⁊ *Peas Indigo.* By this title Apicius did not mean peas from India, but peas which will look as though they have been treated with Indian dye (Indigo) from being cooked with cuttlefish ink.

III-4

[UNTITLED] [*Peas*] Cook the peas, toss, and put them in cold water. When they have cooled, toss them again. Now, chop onion and egg white finely. Season with olive oil, and add a little salt and vinegar. [Drain the peas and transfer to a serving dish]. Pour the yolk of soft-boiled egg into a mushroom dish. Pour the fresh olive oil [and vinegar sauce] over [the dish] and serve.

Peas Indigo with Squid in Wine

2 c. fresh, shelled peas
2 heads of leeks, chopped
½ t. coriander
1 c. squid or small cuttlefish (Sepiola rondoletti)
1 T. olive oil
½ c. fish stock
¼ c. white wine
1 T. chives, finely chopped

Cook the peas, drain, leaving ½ cup liquid, and reserve the rest for sauce. Then add leeks and coriander. Simmer 15 minutes. Meanwhile cover cleaned
cuttlefish or squid with water, and cook in their ink
till tender. While they are cooking add the olive oil,
fish stock, white wine, chives, and coriander.

III-3

Sauce:
1 t. coriander
½ t. ground pepper
½ t. celery seed (or lovage)
¼ t. oregano
pinch of caraway
½ c. peas stock
¼ c. white wine
¼ c. sweet raisin wine or
muscatel
ground pepper

To make a sauce, grind the coriander, pepper, celery
seed (or lovage), oregano, and caraway. Add to the
stock reserved from the peas. Combine with white
and sweet wines. Bring the sauce to a boil, simmer
to reduce, and keep hot.

Now drain the cooked cuttlefish, chop very finely,
and add them to the peas in their liquid. Cook together for a few minutes, drain, and serve in the hot
sauce with a sprinkling of pepper.

Chilled Peas Vinaigrette

2 c. shelled, fresh peas
1 medium onion, finely
chopped
2 hard-boiled egg whites
3 T. olive oil
1 T. cider vinegar
pinch of salt
(1 soft-boiled egg yolk)

Steam peas, drain, and immerse in cold water.
When the peas are cold, drain, and toss to remove
liquid.

Into a mixing bowl, chop onion very finely. Add
chopped egg whites, fresh olive oil, vinegar, and salt.
Pour the chilled peas into a serving dish. (If desired,
add the yolk of a soft-boiled egg to the peas.) Season
with the vinaigrette sauce, and serve.

III-4

III-5 PISAM VITELLIANAM SIVE FABA *Vitellian Peas or Beans* Cook the peas [or beans] and stir until the texture is smooth. Now grind pepper, lovage, and ginger. Over these seasonings put the yolks of hard-boiled eggs, three ounces of honey, stock, wine, and vinegar. Put all of these with the ground seasonings into a pan. Heat this sauce with olive oil until it boils. Then season the peas with it, stirring if it is lumpy so that the texture of the dish is smooth. Add some honey and serve.

¶Aulus Vitellius was Roman Emperor for nine depressing months until December, 69 A.D., when he was murdered by the supporters of his successor, Vespasian. He was distinguished only by his extreme cruelty and gluttony.

The most infamous of Vitellius' banquets was the dinner given by his brother to commemorate the Emperor's arrival in Rome from the provinces. They say that 2,000 of the most costly fish and 7,000 birds were served on that occasion. But Vitellius himself surpassed this with the dedication of a dish he described as "The Shield of Minerva the Guardian of the City" because of its colossal size: In this dish, he united the livers of wrasse, pheasants' and peacocks' brains, flamingoes' tongues, and the roes of moray eels. . . . Because he was a man whose gluttony was not only unlimited but also untimely and sordid, he could never control himself even when offering a sacrifice to the gods from robbing the very altars of their pieces of flesh and wheat cakes, almost out of the fires themselves, and then from gulping them down on the spot.

Suetonius, "Vitellius," 13.

III-6 ALITER PISA SIVE FABA *Peas or Beans* When [the peas or beans have been boiled and] skimmed, grind honey, stock, boiled wine, cumin, rue, celery seed, olive oil, and wine. Stir. Serve with ground pepper and forcemeat dumplings.

Pureed Vitellian Ginger Peas or Beans

2 c. fresh, shelled peas or green beans
1 t. ground pepper
1 t. celery seed (or lovage)
½ t. ginger
3 hard-boiled egg yolks
1 T. honey
½ c. vegetable stock
¼ c. white wine
1 T. white wine vinegar
2 T. olive oil

III-5

Steam peas or green beans till tender and puree them.

In a mortar, grind pepper, celery seed (or lovage), and ginger. To this, add the crumbled egg yolks, honey, stock, white wine, and vinegar. Mix and put this sauce in a pan. Bring to a boil, add a little olive oil, and stir. Combine the pea puree with the sauce, stir till smooth, and serve.

Peas or Beans with Meat Dumplings

2 c. shelled, fresh peas or green beans
cooked beef or pork dumplings

III-6

First, cook the vegetables and reserve stock.

Prepare dumplings using the recipe for *Seasoned Fowl Forcemeat Dumplings* (see p. 22), replacing the fowl meats with an equal amount of pork or beef.

Sauce:
½ t. cumin
pinch of rosemary (or rue)
½ t. celery seed
2 t. honey
½ c. vegetable stock
¼ c. boiled white wine
2 t. olive oil
¼ c. white wine
ground pepper

For the sauce, grind together in a mortar, cumin, rosemary (or rue), and celery seed. Mix with the honey, stock, boiled wine, olive oil, and wine. Bring this sauce to a boil, then stir into the dish of peas or beans. Add cooked beef or pork dumplings. Serve with a sprinkling of pepper.

III-7   ALITER PISAM SIVE FABA *Peas or Beans* Prepare the boiled skimmed peas or beans with Parthian laser, stock, and boiled wine. Pour a little olive oil on top and serve.

⟨ Parthian laser was imported from Parthis (Iran) in the first century A.D. It seems that it was mixed and ground together with pine nuts, which would absorb the flavor. The pine nuts were used as the seasoning, while the laser remained in the storage cask.

III-8   PISAM ADULTERAM VERSATILEM [*Flattered*] *Peas Upside-down* Cook the peas. Into a pan, put brains, or small birds, or thrushes boned by the breast. Add Lucanian sausage, livers, and chicken giblets, stock, and olive oil. Cook the brains [and meats] with a bunch of heads of leeks, and chopped green coriander. Mix pepper and lovage and stock . . .

⟨ Apicius describes the peas as "adulteram versatilem." The adulterer, in classical Latin, was one who unlawfully made love to another's wife through the arts of flattery. In this case, the peas are "flattered" by the accompaniment of expensive meats.

III-9   PISAM SIVE FABAM VITELLIANAM *Peas or Beans Vitellian* Cook the peas or beans. When they have been skimmed, put in leeks, coriander, and mallow flowers. While these are simmering, grind pepper, lovage, oregano, and fennel seed [in a mortar]. Moisten with stock and wine, and put [the sauce] into the pan [with the peas or beans]. Add olive oil and bring to the boil. Stir. Before serving, pour fresh olive oil on top.

> *For dinner the tails of lizard fish*
> *Or beans barely dressed in olive oil*
> *But to your friends you send hares,*
> *Mushrooms, boars, mullets, and oysters —*
> *Papylus, you have neither an appetite nor a mind!*
>
> Martial, 7.77.

Peas or Beans in Parthian Fennel Sauce

2 c. shelled, fresh peas or green beans

Steam the peas or beans till tender, and reserve III-7 stock.

Sauce:
½ t. fennel
½ c. vegetable stock
¼ c. boiled white wine
olive oil

Make a sauce with the fennel, stock, and boiled white wine. Bring to a boil, then simmer for 25 minutes to reduce. Combine the peas with the sauce. Sprinkle with olive oil and serve.

Peas with Sausage and Calf's Brains

½ lb. sliced calf's brains (or deboned chicken breast)
¼ lb. Lucanian sausage, sliced (see p. 28)
½ c. chicken livers and giblets
½ c. chicken or veal stock
2 t. olive oil
2 heads of leek, sliced
1 t. coriander
2 c. shelled, fresh peas

In a casserole, put sliced brains or chicken slices. Add III-8 sliced sausage, chicken livers and giblets, stock, olive oil, leeks, and ground coriander. Braise, covered, for one hour in a 325°F oven. Meanwhile, steam the peas, and reserve stock.

Sauce:
1 t. ground pepper
1 t. celery seed (or lovage)
½ c. vegetable stock
¼ c. white wine
2 t. olive oil

For the sauce, first grind together pepper and celery seed (or lovage). Blend with stock, white wine, and olive oil, heat and bring to a boil, then simmer 15 minutes to reduce. Turn the cooked peas onto a serving dish. Cover with the braised meats, and season with the sauce.

LEGUMES IN THE POD³

IV-1   CUM FABA *Beans* Cook the beans. [In a mortar] grind pepper, lovage, cumin, and green coriander. Moisten with stock. Blend wine and stock with these seasonings. Put in the pan and add olive oil. Simmer over a slow fire and serve.

IV-2   CONCHICLAM APICIANAM *Legumes in the Pod Apicius* Cook peas in the pod in a clean vessel of Cumaean clay. Add to these, sliced Lucanian sausage, forcemeat dumplings made from pork, other [sliced] meats, and [sliced] leg of pork. Grind pepper, lovage, oregano, aniseed, dried onion, and green coriander. Moisten with stock. Blend with wine and stock. Pour this sauce into the clay vessel [with the peas and meats]. Add olive oil. Puncture throughout so that the oil may be absorbed [by the pods]. Cook over a slow fire until done, and serve.

IV-3   CONCHICLAM DE PISA SIMPLICI *A Dish of Plain Peas* Cook and skim the peas. Then put a bunch of leeks and coriander [into the pan]. While [these are] cooking, grind pepper, lovage, and oregano [in a mortar]. Add a bouquet garni [of green herbs] and mix. Blend with stock. [Pour the sauce over the peas.] Add olive oil. Cook over a slow fire and serve.

IV-4   CONCHICLA COMMODIANA *Legumes Commodus*⁴ Cook and skim the peas. [In a mortar] grind pepper, lovage, aniseed, and dried onion. Pour a little liquid from the pan [over these seasonings], and blend with wine and stock. Mix [this sauce with the vegetables] in the pan until it is absorbed. Next, crack four eggs. Add this many eggs for each pint of peas [prepared above]. Stir them well and put all into a clay pot. Cook over the fire and serve when firm.

     ⸿ Lucius Aulius Aurelius Commodus was Emperor from 180 to 192 A.D. and succeeded his father, the philosopher, Marcus Aurelius.

IV-5   ALITER CONCHICLAM SIC FACIES *Legumes* Chop a chicken into small pieces and cook it in stock, olive oil, and wine. To this, add chopped onion, finely ground coriander, and brains with the membranes removed. When [the chicken is] cooked, lift it from the pot and

Peas or Beans Vitellian with Leeks and Fennel

2 c. shelled, fresh peas or
green beans
water
2 leeks, thinly sliced
1 t. coriander
5 grape or small cabbage
leaves

Steam peas or beans for 15 minutes, and reserve III-9
stock. Now add leeks, coriander, and grape or cabbage leaves. Simmer gently for 10 minutes more.

Sauce:
½ t. ground pepper
1 t. celery seed (or lovage)
1 t. oregano
pinch of fennel seeds
½ c. vegetable stock
¼ c. white wine
olive oil or butter

Meanwhile, in a mortar, grind pepper, celery seed
(or lovage), oregano, and a pinch of fennel seeds.
Combine with stock and wine. Bring to a boil, then
simmer slowly for 20 minutes to reduce. Pour the
sauce over the vegetables, stirring from time to time.
Sprinkle with fresh olive oil or melted butter, and
serve.

Beans in the Pod in Coriander Sauce

1 lb. fresh, unshelled beans

Steam beans for 10 minutes. Drain. IV-1

Sauce:
¼ t. ground pepper
½ t. celery seed (or lovage)
¼ t. cumin
1 t. coriander
1 c. chicken or veal stock
½ c. white wine
1 T. olive oil or butter

In a mortar, grind together pepper, celery seed (or
lovage), cumin, and coriander. Blend with stock and
white wine. Pour this sauce over the beans, and add
olive oil or butter. Simmer together gently, stirring,
until the beans are fully cooked and the flavors
mingled.

Beans Apicius with Sausage and Dumplings

IV-2

1 lb. fresh, unshelled beans
½ c. Lucanian sausage, sliced
½ c. cooked pork forcemeat dumplings
½ c. cooked chicken breast, sliced
½ c. cooked pork shoulder, diced
1 t. ground pepper
1 t. celery seed (or lovage)
1 t. oregano
pinch of aniseed
1 t. coriander
2 t. finely chopped onion
½ c. white wine
1 c. meat stock
2 t. olive oil or butter

Put beans into a clay (or other) cooking pot. Prepar dumplings using the recipe for *Seasoned Fowl Forc meat Dumplings* (see p. 22), replacing the fowl mea with an equal amount of pork. Add the sliced sau sage (see p. 28), pork dumplings, chicken breast, an pork shoulder. Then, in a mortar, grind pepper, ce ery seed (or lovage), oregano, aniseed, and coriar der. Blend with onion, and white wine. Pour th mixture over the beans and meats in the pot, an add stock and olive oil or butter. Stir togethe cover, and simmer gently until beans are tender.

Beans and Leeks in a Simple Sauce

IV-3

1 lb. fresh unshelled beans
1 t. coriander
3 leeks, sliced
1½ c. water

In a pan, combine beans with leeks and coriande Add water, and bring to a boil, then simmer ove low heat for 30 minutes. After 15 minutes, continu to cook in the following sauce.

Sauce:
½ t. ground pepper
1 t. celery seed (or lovage)
1 t. oregano
¼ t. thyme
rosemary (or rue)
½ c. chicken or veal stock
1 T. olive oil or butter
ground pepper

For the sauce, in a mortar, grind together peppe celery seed (or lovage), oregano, thyme, and ros mary (or rue). Blend with the stock. Fifteen minut before they are cooked, pour the sauce over the ve etables. Add olive oil or butter. Continue to simm over low heat until the vegetables are done, stirrir from time to time. Serve, with a sprinkling of peppe

Commodus' Beans with Aniseed and Eggs

1 lb. fresh, unshelled beans
½ c. water

Put beans in a pan with water, cook lightly, drain, and reserve liquid.

IV-4

Sauce:
1 t. ground pepper
½ t. celery seed (or lovage)
pinch of ground aniseed
2 t. chopped onion
½ c. chicken or veal stock
½ c. white wine
3 raw egg yolks

For the sauce, in a mortar, grind pepper, celery seed (or lovage), and aniseed. Moisten with a tablespoon of liquid from the beans. Combine with onions, stock, white wine, and well beaten egg yolks. Pour over the drained beans. Transfer everything to a casserole, and cook gently in a 325°F oven until the dish is firm. Serve.

Beans and Chicken Quiche with Cumin

1 chicken
½ c. chicken stock
½ c. white wine
2 t. olive oil
small onions, finely chopped
1 t. coriander
(½ lb. calf's brains)
1 lb. fresh, unshelled green beans
1 t. cumin
pepper, to taste
1 t. coriander
3 raw eggs
1 c. stock
pine nuts or chopped almonds

Cut chicken into pieces. Cook for 30 to 40 minutes in a sauce made with the stock, white wine, and olive oil, together with one chopped onion, coriander (and parboiled calf's brains, if you wish). When done, drain, reserve stock, and bone the chicken pieces.

IV-5

Cook the beans in water, without any seasonings, drain, and reserve liquid. Sprinkle one chopped onion, and coriander over the beans. Take a casserole, butter it, and arrange the beans in alternate layers with the chicken pieces (and chopped brains).

Next, in a mortar, grind pepper and cumin. Mix with stock from the pan of meat. Add well beaten eggs and combine with liquid from the cooked beans. Pour over the casserole. Decorate with pine nuts or chopped almonds. Cook gently in a 350° F oven for 30 minutes, and serve when firm.

remove the bones. [Next, boil peas without seasoning.] Take onion and coriander and chop finely and scatter over the unseasoned cooked peas. In a casserole, arrange variously the peas, the chicken, and the brains. [For the sauce, first] grind pepper and cumin. Then moisten [these seasonings] with gravy [from the pan of chicken and brains]. Into the mortar, crack two eggs and beat. Finally, pour [into the mortar] liquid from the boiled peas. Stir. Add to the casserole. Decorate with pine nuts and cook over a slow fire. Serve [when firm].

IV-6   ALITER CONCHICLA CONCHICLATUS PULLUS VEL PORCEL-LUS *Chicken or Suckling Pig with Legumes in the Pod* Remove the breast bone of the chicken. Straighten the thigh bones of the bird and join them together. [Bind them with twigs and then] prepare the legumes in the pod stuffing. Fill the chicken or pig by turns with washed peas, brains, Lucanian sausage, et cetera. [For the sauce] grind pepper, lovage, oregano, and ginger. Pour stock [over this, and] blend with raisin wine and wine. Cook. Add a little of this sauce to the stuffing materials as you cram them in layers inside the chicken. Cover the cavity with skin, and place the stuffed chicken into a covered pan. Put in the oven and cook very slowly. Serve.

Chicken or Suckling Pig Stuffed with Green Beans

4 lb. roasting chicken
1½ c. fresh, unshelled
green beans
½ c. calf's brains (or lamb
forcemeats, see p. 21)
½ c. Lucanian sausage (see
p. 28), pork sausage, or
blood sausage

Sauce:
1 t. pepper or 1 T. roughly
ground peppercorns
¼ t. celery seed (or lovage)
½ t. oregano
½ t. ginger
½ c. chicken or beef stock
1 T. sweet raisin wine or
muscatel
¼ c. white wine
casing
flour
white pepper

IV-6

Prepare the sauce by grinding pepper, celery seeds (or lovage), ginger, and oregano in a mortar. Mix these with the stock, sweet wine, and white wine. Bring to a boil, then simmer the sauce for 15 minutes.

Next, stuff the chicken with layers of beans, alternating with chopped brains and sliced sausage. Pour a little of the sauce into each of the layers. Skewer and tie the bird with string, and put in a roasting pan. Roast for 30 minutes in a 400°F oven, then lower temperature to 300°F and cook for 1 to 1½ hours.

Serve with a gravy made from the pan drippings thickened with flour, using additional chicken stock as needed, and sprinkle with white pepper.

Green Beans in Coriander Sauce

2 c. green beans
1 c. bean stock
1½ t. coriander
1 T. butter
½ t. cumin
1 T. chives, chopped

VI-1

Steam green beans for 10 minutes or until tender. Make a sauce with stock from the steaming pan, coriander, and cumin. Bring to a boil, then simmer over low heat for 25 minutes to reduce. Add to the beans and reheat. Serve with butter and a garnish of chives.

This dish is a good complement to many of the fowls and roasts of Books VI and VIII, and enlivens the fish dishes of Book X.

SPELT AND BARLEY [SOUPS]

V-1   ALICAM VEL SUCUM TISANAE SIC FACIES *Spelt or Barley Soup* Soak the grain or barley in water the day before, then hull it. Put it [in a saucepan] on the fire. When it has boiled, add sufficient olive oil, a bouquet garni of aniseed, dried onion, savory, and a pig's knuckle to give flavor to the soup. Add ground green coriander and salt. When all has cooked thoroughly, remove the bouquet garni and transfer [the grain] into another cooking vessel, such that it will not be scorched in the bottom of the pan. Stir till smooth and strain over the pig's knuckle. Then grind pepper, lovage, a little dried pennyroyal, cumin, and ground silphium. Pour honey, vinegar, boiled wine, and stock [over these seasonings], and then pour the whole mixture into the saucepan over the pig's knuckle. Cook over a slow fire.[5]

V-2   ALITER TISANAM *Another Barley Soup* [Into a pot] pour chick-peas, lentils, and peas. Grind the barley and then boil it with these vegetables. When is has boiled well, add olive oil as required. Into the soup, chop leeks, coriander, aniseed, fennel, beets, mallows, and soft cabbage. Put these finely chopped vegetables into a saucepan. Boil the cabbage and grind fennel seed, oregano, silphium, and lovage. Moisten these seasonings with stock and pour them along with boiled cabbage into the soup over the vegetables and barley. Stir. Garnish with finely chopped cabbage [leaves].[6]

GREEN BEANS AND BAIAN BEANS

❡Baiae was a popular resort (near Naples), famous for its warm baths, scenery, and the excellence of its oysters. From Apicius' title, it appears that the beans grown in the district of Baiae were also highly esteemed by Romans of the first century A.D.

VI-1   [UNTITLED] [*Green Beans*] Green beans are served cooked with stock, olive oil, green coriander, cumin, and chopped chives.

VI-2   ALITER [*Green Beans*] Fry the green beans and serve with stock.

Green Beans in Mustard Sauce

2 c. green beans

Steam the green beans in a little water till tender, and partially drain.

VI-3

Sauce:
½ t. mustard seed
pinch of rosemary (or rue)
¼ t. cumin; 2 t. honey
¼ c. pine nuts or almonds 1
t. wine vinegar
¾ c. beef stock

To prepare the mustard sauce, grind together mustard seed, rosemary (or rue), and cumin. Add to honey, finely chopped nuts, vinegar, and stock. Heat the sauce, then pour it into the pan of cooked green beans. Stir and simmer for a few minutes. Serve with butter and a sprinkling of pepper.

Beans with Celery and Leeks

2 c. choice green beans

Steam green beans until tender, drain, and reserve liquid.

VI-4

Sauce:
1 t. ground rosemary
1 c. celery, chopped
2 heads of leeks, chopped
1 t. wine vinegar
2 t. olive oil or butter
½ c. bean or vegetable stock
¼ c. boiled white wine

Meanwhile, mix rosemary (or a pinch of rue), celery, and chopped leeks, vinegar, olive oil or butter, stock, and boiled wine. Bring to a boil, then simmer gently for 25 minutes to reduce. Pour over cooked green beans, and serve.

Kidney Beans or Chick-peas in Fennel Sauce

½ c. kidney beans or
chick-peas
⅛ c. vegetable stock
⅛ c. white wine
¼ t. ground pepper
salt
1 T. fennel
2–3 hard-boiled eggs

Prepare beans ahead of time as in preceding recipe, then make the following sauce.

VIII-2

Combine stock with wine, pepper, salt to taste, and fennel, and bring to a boil. Simmer for 5 minutes over low heat, then combine with cooked beans, reheat, and serve. Drain and serve with sliced hard-boiled eggs.

Alternatively, pre-cook, drain, chill, and season in a cold sauce made with stock, white wine, pepper, salt, and fennel. Decorate with hard-boiled eggs.

611-3

VI-3   ALITER [*Green Beans*] Prepare the green beans with ground mustard, honey, small nuts, rue, cumin, and vinegar. Serve.

VI-4   [UNTITLED] [*Baian Beans*] Finely slice boiled Baian beans. Serve with rue, green celery, leeks, vinegar, olive oil, stock, and a little boiled wine or raisin wine.

FENUGREEK

VII   [UNTITLED] [*Fenugreek*] [Prepare] fenugreek in stock, olive oil, and wine.

❡The seeds of fenugreek (*Trigonella foenumgraecum*) were, it seems, from their place in Apicius' catalogue of pottages and legumes, cooked and eaten as a dish in their own right. Nowadays, fenugreek is regarded more as an herb and is used as a seasoning for curries. Cato described it as fodder for cattle.

KIDNEY BEANS AND CHICK-PEAS

VIII-1   [UNTITLED] [*Kidney Beans and Chick-peas*] Serve fresh kidney beans and chick-peas with salt, cumin, olive oil, and a little wine.

VIII-2   ALITER FASEOLUS SIVE CICER *Kidney Beans or Chick-peas* You will enjoy them fried in wine sauce and pepper. [Alternatively] boil them and serve in a dish with eggs, fresh fennel, pepper, stock, and a little boiled wine, in place of saltfish. Serve them this way or more simply, just as they are [that is, uncooked].

How many eloquent writers feed the moths and bookworms
When cooks alone can buy their polished lines?

Martial, 6.61.

**BOOK V OF APICIUS,
LEGUMES,
IS ENDED**

Of Birds

OF OSTRICH

❡Ostrich meats were popular amongst people of Apicius' class, not so much for their succulence as for their scarcity.

I-I   IN STRUTHIONE ELIXO   *Of Boiled Ostrich*   [Mix] pepper, mint, roasted cumin, celery seed, dates, honey, vinegar, raisin wine, stock, and a little olive oil. Blend these ingredients in a saucepan and boil. Then thicken the sauce with starch. Arrange the boiled ostrich parts on a platter and pour the sauce over them. Sprinkle pepper on top. If, however, you wish to cook [the ostrich] in the spices themselves, add spelt.

I-2   ALITER IN STRUTHIONE ELIXO   *[Sauce] for Boiled Ostrich*   Use pepper, lovage, thyme or savory, honey, mustard, vinegar, stock, and olive oil.

OF CRANE, DUCK, PARTRIDGE, TURTLEDOVE, WOOD PIGEON, DOVE, AND DIFFERENT BIRDS

II-I   GRUEM VEL ANATEM   *Crane or Duck*   Wash and dress the bird, and put it in a pot. Add water, salt, and aniseed. When the bird is half cooked and the flesh firm, take it out [of the vessel] and put it into another saucepan with olive oil and stock and a bouquet of oregano and coriander. When [the bird is] nearly cooked, add a little boiled wine for coloring. [For the sauce] blend pepper, lovage, cumin, coriander, laser root, rue, boiled wine, and honey. Add gravy [from the bird and some] vinegar. Stir. Pour the sauce into a saucepan, heat, and thicken with starch. Put [the bird] onto a platter and pour the sauce on top.

II-2   IN GRUE IN ANATE VEL IN PULLO   *Of Crane, Duck, or Chicken*   [For the sauce, blend] pepper, dried onion, lovage, cumin, celery seed, pitted Damascus plums [damsons], honey wine, vinegar, stock, boiled wine [and olive oil]. Cook. When cooking crane, its head should not touch the boiling water, but should remain without. After the bird is cooked, wrap it in a hot linen cloth and pull out the head. Then the

Roast Duck in Spiced Gravy

3 lb. duck
3 c. water
1 t. salt
¼ t. aniseed
water
2 T. butter or olive oil
1 c. duck stock
1 t. oregano
1 T. coriander
½ c. boiled wine

To prepare the duck, simmer it for 30 minutes in water seasoned with salt and aniseed. Remove the bird from the pot, reserving the stock, put it in a roasting pan, and season with a mixture of butter or olive oil, stock, oregano, and coriander. (At this point, an "Apician" stuffing may be added, made of sausage, damsons or dates, almonds, and spices.) Roast in a 375°F oven for 1½ hours, basting from time to time. For the last 30 minutes add the boiled red wine to the pan.

II-I

Sauce:
½ t. ground pepper
1 t. celery seed (or lovage)
½ t. cumin
¼ t. coriander
pinch of fennel
½ t. rosemary (or a pinch of rue)
½ c. boiled wine
dash of wine vinegar
c. gravy from roasting pan
flour

To make the sauce, grind pepper, celery seed (or lovage), cumin, coriander, fennel, and rosemary (or rue) in a mortar. Add to boiled wine (see p. 306), vinegar, and gravy from the roasting pan. Bring the sauce to a boil, simmer to blend flavors, and thicken with flour. Serve the duck on a platter with the sauce.

tendons shall follow after, leaving only the meat and bones behind . . . for the tendons of the crane are difficult to chew.

⁋ By the first century A.D., both the Damascus plum and the Egyptian had been transplanted to the Italian peninsula, and it was no longer necessary to import them across the Mediterranean, preserved in honey and boiled wine.

II-3   GRUEM VEL ANATEM EX RAPIS *Crane or Duck with Turnips* Wash and prepare the bird and then boil it in water, salt, and aniseed until [the crane or duck is] half cooked. Now boil the turnips vigorously so they lose their smell. Remove the bird from the pot and wash it a second time. Then put [the bird] into a roasting pan with olive oil and stock and a bouquet garni of chives and coriander. Take the rinsed turnips and chop them finely, and sprinkle the parts over the meat. Before the bird is fully roasted, add some boiled wine to give color [to the meal]. Make the sauce thus: [blend] pepper, cumin, coriander and laser root, and add vinegar and gravy from the roasting pan. Empty the contents of the mortar over the bird [and the diced turnips], and cook [together]. Thicken [the extra gravy] with starch and add this to the turnips. Sprinkle with pepper and serve.

II-4   ALITER IN GRUEM VEL ANATEM ELIXAM *[Sauce] for Boiled Crane or Duck* Mix pepper, lovage, cumin, dried coriander, mint, oregano, nuts, dates, stock, olive oil, honey, mustard, and wine.

II-5   ALITER GRUEM VEL ANATEM *Crane or Duck* Roast the bird, and pour this sauce over it: grind pepper, lovage, oregano, stock, honey, and a little vinegar and olive oil. Cook this sauce well and add starch. While the sauce is bubbling, add rings of boiled, sliced gourds or Egyptian beans. If you have them on hand, cook chicken feet and livers [and put them with the roast crane or duck]. [Arrange the bird] on a platter and sprinkle with finely ground pepper before serving.

II-6   ALITER IN GRUE VEL ANATE ELIXA *[Sauce] for Boiled Crane or Duck* [Blend] pepper, lovage, celery seed, colewort, coriander, mint, dates, honey, vinegar, stock, boiled wine, and mustard. Make this same sauce to cook with roast [crane or duck].

Plum Sauce for Roast Duck and Chicken

½ t. ground pepper
2 t. chopped onion
1 T. lovage (or celery seed)
1 t. cumin
½ t. celery seed
½ c. damsons (or plums)
¼ c. mead or 1 T. honey
2 c. chicken stock
dash of wine vinegar
½ c. boiled wine
1 T. olive oil or butter

II-2

In a mortar, grind together pepper, onion, lovage (or celery seed), cumin, and celery seed. Add chopped damsons. Blend with mead or honey, stock, vinegar, boiled wine, and olive oil or butter. Bring to a boil and simmer for 30 minutes over very low heat. Serve with the roasted duck or chicken.

Roast Duck in a Blanket of Turnips

3 lb. duck
1 t. salt
¼ t. aniseed
3 turnips, cooked
1 T. olive oil or butter
1 c. turnip stock
1 T. chives, chopped
1 T. coriander

⅓ c. sweet red wine or port
1 c. bread crumbs
½ c. thinly sliced head of leek
1 t. coriander

Sauce:
¼ t. each pepper & cumin
½ t. coriander
pinch of fennel
1 t. wine vinegar
1 c. pan gravy

II-3

Simmer the duck in water seasoned with salt and aniseed for 30 minutes. Meanwhile, cook the turnips in water, drain them, and save the liquid from the pot. Put the bird in a roasting pan and season with a mixture of butter or olive oil, turnip stock, chives, and coriander.

For a stuffing to complement the bird, mix bread crumbs with leek and coriander. Mash the cooked turnips to a pulp and spread in a blanket over the duck. Roast, uncovered, in a 375°F oven for 1½ hours. One hour before serving, add sweet wine or port with which to baste the roast. Finish in the following sauce.

To make the sauce, in a mortar, grind together pepper, cumin, coriander, and fennel. Add to vinegar and gravy from the roasting pan. Pour this sauce over the bird and the turnips, and cook together for the last 15 minutes. Thicken the gravy with flour, and serve with a sprinkling of pepper.

Nut Sauce for Braised Duck

II-4

½ t. ground pepper
1 t. celery seed (or lovage)
½ t. cumin
1 t. coriander
1 t. mint
½ t. oregano
⅛ c. pine nuts or almonds
⅛ c. dates
2 c. duck or chicken stock
1 T. olive oil or butter
1 T. honey
½ t. mustard seed
½ c. red wine

In a mortar, grind together pepper, celery seed (or lovage), cumin, coriander, mint, and oregano. Add finely chopped nuts and chopped dates. Combine with stock, olive oil or butter, honey, mustard seed and wine. Bring to a boil, then simmer for 25 minutes to reduce. Pour over the braised duck and serve.

Zucchini Sauce for Roast Duck

II-5

½ t. ground pepper
½ t. celery seed (or lovage)
½ t. oregano
2 c. chicken stock
1 c. pan gravy
1 T. honey
dash of wine vinegar
2 t. olive oil
flour
1 medium zucchini, ½ acorn
or butternut squash, or
2 c. broad beans
1 c. chicken livers
ground pepper

This sauce is to be poured over the duck 20 minutes before the bird is done.

First, in a mortar, grind pepper, celery seed (or lovage), and oregano. Combine with stock and gravy from the roasting pan. Add honey, vinegar, and olive oil or butter. Bring this sauce to a boil and thicken with flour. Add parboiled, sliced zucchini, squash, or lightly cooked broad beans. Pour over the duck and finish cooking. (Add lightly sautéed chopped chicken livers, if you wish.) Serve the bird in the sauce, and sprinkle with finely ground pepper.

Date Sauce for Braised Duck

½ t. ground pepper
1 t. lovage (or celery seed)
1 t. celery seed
pinch of mustard seed (or rocket seed)
1 t. coriander
sprig of mint
¼ c. dates, finely chopped
1 T. honey
1 t. wine vinegar
1 c. chicken stock
½ c. boiled red wine
pinch of mustard seed

II-6

In a mortar, grind together pepper, lovage (or celery seed), celery seed, mustard (or rocket seed), coriander, and mint. Add to chopped dates. Combine with honey, vinegar, stock, boiled wine, and mustard seeds. Bring to a boil, simmer to blend flavors, and pour over the roasting duck 20 minutes before it is done.

Alternatively, braise the bird in the sauce from the beginning, correcting seasonings 20 minutes before the duck is done.

Raisin Sauce for Partridge

½ t. ground pepper
1 t. celery seed (or lovage)
½ t. celery seed
sprig of mint
1 t. ground peppercorns (or myrtle berries)
¼ c. dark raisins
1 T. honey
½ c. red wine
1 c. chicken stock

III-1

In a mortar, grind together pepper, celery seed (or lovage), celery seed, mint, and peppercorns (or myrtle berries). Add to raisins. Mix with honey, red wine, and stock. Bring to a boil and simmer for 20 minutes before serving.

Alternatively, the bird may be braised in this sauce.

Rosemary Sauce for Partridge and Game Birds

½ t. ground pepper
½ t. celery seed (or lovage)
sprig of mint
1 t. rosemary (or rue seed)
1 c. chicken stock
½ c. white wine
1 T. olive oil or butter

III-3

In a mortar, grind together pepper, celery seed (or lovage), mint, and rosemary (or rue) seed. Add stock, white wine, and olive oil or butter. Braise the bird in this mixture until done.

Or roast the bird and serve it in the rosemary sauce.

OF BOILED PARTRIDGE,
HAZEL HEN, AND TURTLEDOVE

III-1   [UNTITLED] [*Sauce for Partridge*] [Combine] pepper, lovage, celery seed, mint, myrtle berries or raisins, honey, wine, vinegar, stock, and olive oil. Serve chilled.

III-2   [UNTITLED] [*Partridge*] Boil the partridge in its feathers, and then pluck the bird while it is still wet. It is possible to cook a newly slaughtered bird in the sauce [described above], so that the flesh does not harden. If the partridge was killed [three or more] days previously, it should be boiled [first and the sauce added afterwards].

III-3   IN PERDICE ET ATTAGENA ET IN TURTURE [*Sauce*] *for Partridge, Hazel Hen, and Turtledove* [Mix] pepper, lovage, mint, and rue seed. Add stock, unmixed wine, and olive oil. Heat.

> *Ringdoves delay then quench the loins:*
> *He who'd lust shouldn't eat this bird.*
>
> Martial, 13.67.

OF WOOD PIGEONS AND DOVES

IV-1   IN ASSIS [*Sauce*] *for Roasted* [*Wood Pigeons and Doves*] [Use a sauce made from these ingredients:] pepper, lovage, coriander, caraway, dried onion, mint, egg yolks, dates, honey, vinegar, stock, olive oil, and wine.

IV-2   ALITER ELIXIS [*Sauce*] *for Boiled* [*Wood Pigeons and Doves*] [In a mortar, bruise] pepper, caraway, celery seed, and parsley. Add country sauce, dates, honey, vinegar, wine, olive oil, and mustard.

IV-3   ALITER [*Sauce for Wood Pigeons and Doves*] Use pepper, lovage, parsley, celery seed, rue, nuts, dates, honey, vinegar, stock, mustard, and a little olive oil.

IV-4   ALITER [*Sauce for Wood Pigeons and Doves*] [Grind] pepper, lovage, and fresh laser. Add [a little] stock and wine. [Simmer.] Pour over the dove or wood pigeon. Sprinkle with pepper and serve.

Sweet Onion Sauce for Roasted Pigeons and Doves

½ t. ground pepper
½ t. celery seed (or lovage)
½ t. coriander
pinch of caraway
sprig of mint
2 t. chopped onion
¼ c. dates, finely chopped
1 t. honey
dash of wine vinegar
1 c. chicken stock
2 t. olive oil or butter
½ c. white wine
2 raw egg yolks

In a mortar, grind together pepper, celery seed (or lovage), coriander, caraway, and mint. Add to onion and chopped dates. Blend with honey, vinegar, stock (including pan drippings), olive oil or butter, and wine. Heat, then thicken with well beaten egg yolks. Pour over the roasting birds, and cook together for the last 20 minutes.

Or pour the sauce over the cooked birds and serve.

IV-I

Parsley-Mint Sauce for Braised Pigeons and Doves

½ t. ground pepper
pinch of caraway
½ t. celery seed
2 t. parsley
¼ c. Country Mint Sauce
(see p. 15)
¼ c. dates
1 t. honey
dash of wine vinegar
½ c. white wine
2 t. olive oil or butter
pinch of mustard seed
1 c. chicken stock with
pan drippings

Cook the birds as you would duck (see p. 125), and braise in this sauce until done. Or roast the parboiled birds and serve them in the sauce.

In a mortar, grind pepper, caraway, and celery seed. Add to parsley, Country Mint Sauce, and chopped dates. Combine with honey, vinegar, wine, olive oil or butter, mustard seed, and stock. Bring to a boil, then gently simmer for 25 minutes to reduce before serving.

IV-2

Sweet Basting Sauce for Pigeons and Doves

IV-3

½ t. ground pepper
1 t. lovage (or celery seed)
2 T. parsley
½ t. celery seed
½ t. rosemary (or rue)
¼ c. dates, finely chopped
1 t. honey
dash of wine vinegar
½ t. mustard seed
2 t. olive oil or butter
1 c. chicken stock with
pan drippings

In a 325°F oven, half cook the birds for 45 minutes in a roasting pan with olive oil or butter, then finish in the sauce, basting occasionally.

In a mortar, grind together pepper, lovage (or celery seed), parsley, celery seed, and rosemary (or rue). Add finely chopped dates. Combine with honey, vinegar, mustard seed, olive oil or butter, and stock. Bring to a boil, then add to the roasting pan.

Simple Basting Sauce for Roast Pigeons & Doves

IV-4

½ t. ground pepper
¼ t. celery seed (or lovage)
½ t. ginger
¾ c. chicken stock
½ c. white wine

In a mortar, grind pepper, celery seed (or lovage), and ginger. Add to stock and wine and stir together. For the last 45 minutes, pour over the roasting birds and cook together, uncovered, in a 325°F oven, basting from time to time.

Spiced Sweet Wine Sauce for Birds and Fowl

V-1

½ t. ground pepper
½ t. cumin
1 t. savory
1 t. celery seed (or lovage)
1 t. mint
¼ c. raisins, damsons, or plums
3 t. honey
½ c. red wine (or myrtle wine)
1 t. wine vinegar
1 c. chicken stock
1 t. olive oil or butter
1 celery stalk

In a mortar, grind pepper, cumin, savory, celery seed (or lovage), and mint. Add to raisins or finely chopped plums. Blend with honey, red wine, vinegar, stock, and olive oil or butter. Bring to a boil, simmer gently for 25 minutes to reduce, stirring with a stalk of celery.

Saffron Nut Sauce for Birds and Fowl

½ t. ground pepper
1 t. parsley
1 t. celery seed (or lovage)
½ t. mint
pinch of saffron
½ c. white wine
¼ c. hazelnuts or almonds, grated
1 T. honey
1 t. wine vinegar
1 c. chicken stock
1 t. olive oil or butter
1 celery stalk
sprig of fresh mint

In a mortar, grind together pepper, parsley, celery seed (or lovage), mint, and a pinch of saffron. Combine with wine. Add roasted grated hazelnuts or almonds, honey, wine, vinegar, and stock. Put olive oil or butter in a pan, heat and add the sauce. Bring to a boil and simmer for 25 minutes over low heat to reduce. Stir with celery and a sprig of mint.

Score the skin of a nearly roasted bird and pour this sauce over it. Cook together for a few minutes in the oven and serve.

v-2

Cumin Nut Sauce for Braised Game Birds

½ t. ground pepper
½ t. lovage (or celery seed)
½ t. cumin
½ t. celery seed
⅓ c. hazelnuts or almonds, grated
1 T. honey
2 c. chicken stock
1 t. wine vinegar
2 t. olive oil or butter

In a mortar, grind together pepper, lovage (or celery seed), cumin, and celery seed. Add grated hazelnuts or almonds, honey, stock, vinegar, and olive oil or butter. Bring to a boil, then simmer for 25 minutes to reduce.

v-3

SAUCES FOR VARIOUS BIRDS

v-1   [UNTITLED]   [*Sauce for Various Birds*]   [Combine] pepper, roasted cumin, lovage, mint, raisins or pitted damsons, and a little honey. Blend with myrtle wine, vinegar, stock, and olive oil. Heat and stir with a bouquet of celery and savory.

v-2   ALITER IUS IN AVIBUS   *Another Sauce for Birds*   Mix pepper, parsley, lovage, dried mint, and saffron. Pour wine [over these ingredients]. Add hazelnuts or roasted almonds, a little honey, wine, vinegar, and stock. Put this sauce into a warming pan and then add oil. Simmer and stir with a sprig of green celery and Italian catmint. Score [the skin of the bird] and then pour [the sauce over the flesh].

v-3   IUS CANDIDUM IN AVEM ELIXAM   *White Sauce for Boiled Bird* Combine pepper, lovage, cumin, celery seed, roasted hazelnuts or almonds or other shelled nuts, a little honey, stock, vinegar, and olive oil.

v-4   IUS VIRIDE IN AVIBUS   *Green Sauce for Birds*   [Combine] pepper, caraway, Indian spikenard, cumin, bay leaf, green herbs of any kind, dates, honey, vinegar, a little wine, stock, and olive oil.

v-5   IUS CANDIDUM IN ANSERE ELIXO   *White Sauce for Boiled Goose* [Mix] pepper, caraway, cumin, celery seed, thyme, onion, laser root, roasted nuts, honey, vinegar, stock, and olive oil.

v-6   AD AVES HIRCOSAS OMNI GENERE   *How to Prepare Hircinous* [*High*] *Birds of All Kinds*   [Blend] pepper, lovage, thyme, dried mint, hazelnuts, dates, honey, vinegar, wine, stock, olive oil, boiled wine, and mustard. You can make [the bird] more savory and more nourishing, and you can preserve [the richness of] the fat, if you put it into the oven wrapped in a coating of flour and olive oil.

     ⊄ This recipe is useful for birds which have been hung too long (in the case of pheasant, for example, more than 10 days or until mortification has begun), or birds which feed in marshes and streams, and thus have a disagreeably "fishy" smell. The invention of the refrigerator has reduced the quanitity of seasonings with which meats and fowl are prepared, but to my mind, something of the individuality of each animal has also been lost in the process.

Green Herb Sauce for Game Birds

½ t. ground pepper
pinch of caraway
¼ t. cumin
pinch of spikenard, if
available
pinch of bay leaf
fresh herbs to taste (thyme,
oregano, lovage, or
celery leaf)
¼ c. dates, finely chopped
1 t. wine vinegar
¼ c. white wine
¾ c. chicken stock
2 t. olive oil or butter

In a mortar, grind together pepper, caraway, cumin, v-4
spikenard, and bay leaf. Add the green herbs tied in
a cheesecloth, finely chopped dates, vinegar, wine,
stock, and olive oil or butter. Bring to a boil, then
simmer gently for 20 minutes to reduce. Remove
herbs and serve.

Sweet and Sour Sauce for Roast Goose

10 lb. goose

Sauce:
1 t. ground pepper
¼ t. caraway
1 t. cumin
1 t. celery seed
½ t. thyme
½ t. ginger
¼ c. hazelnuts or almonds
1 T. honey
1 T. wine vinegar
1 c. chicken stock
2 t. olive oil or butter

To release the fat, parboil the goose in a pan half v-5
covered with water. Then roast the goose slowly in
a 350° F oven for 3 to 3½ hours. One hour before it
is done, add this sweet and sour sauce, and baste
with it from time to time.

In a mortar, grind together pepper, caraway, cumin, celery seed, thyme, and ginger. Add to grated
or very finely chopped hazelnuts or almonds. Blend
with honey, vinegar, stock, and olive oil or butter.
Bring to a boil, then simmer over low heat for 20
minutes to reduce.

V-7   ALITER AVEM [*Bird*] Into the belly of the bird, put fresh chopped olives. Sew up the bird and boil. Remove the cooked olives [and serve separately].

OF FLAMINGO

My scarlet wings give me my name, but gourmands
  Relish my tongue.
What if my tongue should speak?

Martial, 13.71.

VI-1   [UNTITLED] [*Flamingo*] Free the flamingo of its feathers. Wash, dress, and put it in a pan. Add water, salt, aniseed, and a little vinegar. When the bird is half cooked, bind a bouquet of chives and coriander and cook [with the flamingo]. Before the bird is fully cooked, pour boiled wine over it for coloring. [To make the sauce] put into a mortar, pepper, cumin, coriander, laser root, mint, and rue. Bruise [these seasonings together], pour vinegar [over them], and add some dates and gravy from the pan. Empty the contents of the mortar into the same pan [with the flamingo]. Thicken the sauce with starch and pour it over the bird. Serve. The same method is used for parrot.

VI-2   ALITER [*Sauce for Flamingo*] Roast the flamingo. [In a mortar] mix pepper, lovage, celery seed, fried sesame seed, parsley, mint, dried onion, and dates. Add honey, wine, stock, vinegar, olive oil, and boiled wine. Blend [and heat. Pour over the flamingo and serve.]

> ❡Pliny disgustedly said it was Apicius who taught that flamingo tongues had an exquisite taste. It was made famous by the dreadful emperor Caligula (37–41 A.D.), who enjoyed the flamingo tongue ragout, supposedly invented by Apicius (10.68).

VI-3   AVES OMNES NE LIQUESCANT *So That the Flesh of All Kinds of Birds May Not Spoil* It is better to boil them in their feathers. Previously, however, they should be drawn by the throat or by the rump.

Seasonings for Cooking "High" Poultry

1 t. salt
½ t. aniseed
1 t. ground pepper
½ t. celery seed (or lovage)
1 t. thyme
1 t. mint
¼ c. hazelnuts or almonds
¼ c. chopped dates
1 T. honey
1 T. wine vinegar
½ c. white wine
2 c. chicken stock
2 t. olive oil or butter

v-6

First put the no longer fresh bird in a pot, with water seasoned with salt and aniseed. Cook for 30 minutes. Now transfer the prepared bird to a roasting pan and add a blended mixture of these strong seasonings: pepper, celery seed (or lovage), thyme, mint, finely chopped nuts and dates, honey, vinegar, wine, stock, and olive oil or butter. Heat this mixture to a boil, then add to the roasting pan. Baste from time to time until done.

Because of the flamingo's rarity, no modern version of the recipe is included here. However, in Roman times, the serving of such rare birds was a culinary status symbol.

Sesame Seed Sauce for Roast Goose

½ t. ground pepper
1 t. celery seed (or lovage)
1 t. toasted sesame seeds
1 t. parsley
1 t. mint
1 t. dried onion
1 t. honey
½ c. white wine
1 c. chicken stock
1 t. wine vinegar
2 t. olive oil or butter

vi-2

In a mortar, grind together pepper, celery seed (or lovage), sesame seeds, parsley, mint, and dried onion. Blend with honey, white wine, stock, vinegar, and olive oil or butter. Bring to a boil and simmer gently for 25 minutes to reduce. Or cook together with the roast bird for the last 25 minutes.

OF GOOSE

VII   ANSEREM ELIXUM CALIDUM EX IURE FRIGIDO APICIANO *Boiled Goose Served Hot with Cold Apician Sauce* [In a mortar] mix pepper, lovage, coriander seed, mint, and rue. Pour a little stock and olive oil [over the seasonings]. Blend. Dry the boiled goose while it is piping hot in a clean linen cloth. Pour the cold sauce [over the bird] and serve.

OF CHICKEN

VIII-1   IN PULLO ELIXO IUS CRUDUM *Uncooked Sauce for Boiled Chicken* Throw into a mortar, aniseed, dried mint, and laser root. Moisten [these seasonings] with vinegar. Add dates, pour in stock, a little mustard and olive oil, and boiled wine. Blend, and then serve [with boiled chicken].

VIII-2   PULLUM ANETHATUM *Aniseed Chicken* [Prepare the same aniseed sauce as above, and] blend with a little honey and stock. Take the cooked chicken out of the pan and dry it with a clean linen cloth. Score [the skin of the bird] and pour the [aniseed] sauce into the clefts until it is completely absorbed. Then roast the chicken, basting it with a feather in its own juices. Sprinkle with pepper and serve.

VIII-3   PULLUM PARTHICUM *Parthian Chicken* Open the chicken by the rear, dress it on a square dish. [In a mortar] bruise pepper, lovage, and a little caraway. Moisten with stock. Blend with wine. Set the chicken in a vessel made of Cumaean clay. Over the bird, pour the sauce. Dissolve fresh laser in warm water, and put this liquid [in the clay pot] with the chicken. Cook and sprinkle with pepper before serving.

❡The Parthians traditionally ruled the lands between the Euphrates in the West and the Indus in the East, and thus enjoyed the position of middlemen on the trade routes between Rome and the Oriental empires of India and China.

In this recipe, the word "Parthian" refers to an elaborate

Hot Braised Goose Served with Cold Sauce Apicius

1 medium braised goose

After cooking, take the goose out of the pot and blot it dry. VII

Sauce:
½ t. ground pepper
¼ t. celery seed (or lovage)
½ t. coriander
pinch of rosemary (or rue)
1 c. defatted goose or chicken stock
2 t. olive oil

For the sauce, in a mortar, grind pepper, celery seed (or lovage), coriander, mint, and rosemary. Mix with stock and olive oil. Then bring to a boil and simmer gently for 10 minutes. Chill. Serve with the hot goose.

Pungent Ginger Dressing for Braised Chicken

¼ t. aniseed
1 t. mint
½ t. ginger
1 T. wine vinegar
1 date, finely chopped
¼ c. chicken stock
¼ t. mustard seed
3 T. olive oil
½ c. boiled white wine
(see p. 306)

To make this cold dressing for serving with braised chicken, first grind aniseed, mint, and ginger. Combine with vinegar, chopped date, chicken stock, mustard seed, olive oil, and boiled white wine. VIII-1

(This sauce can also be used with green salads.)

Aniseed Chicken

VIII-2

4 lb. chicken

Take the whole chicken and braise in water for approximately 20 minutes. Drain, reserve stock, and wipe dry.

Sauce:
¼ t. aniseed
1 t. mint
½ t. ginger
1 t. wine vinegar
3 dates, finely chopped
1 c. chicken stock
¼ t. mustard seed
2 t. olive oil
½ c. boiled white wine (see p. 306)
1 t. honey
ground pepper

For the sauce, combine aniseed, mint, ginger, vinegar, dates, stock, mustard, olive oil, boiled white wine, and honey. Heat to the boiling point and simmer gently for 20 minutes.

Now score the chicken's skin and pour aniseed sauce over it. Roast in a 300°F oven for 2 hours, basting frequently with the liquid from the roasting pan. Sprinkle with mild pepper before serving.

Caraway-Ginger Chicken in a Clay Pot

VIII-3

4 lb. chicken
Sauce:
1 t. pepper
½ t. celery seed (or lovage)
¼ t. caraway
½ c. chicken stock
¼ c. white wine
½ t. ginger
½ c. hot water

To make the sauce, combine pepper, celery seed (or lovage), caraway, stock, white wine, and ginger with hot water. Pour this sauce over the chicken, and cook in a covered clay pot till the bird is tender.

Almond Sauce for Guinea Hen or Chicken

3 lb. guinea hen or chicken
1 t. ginger
1 t. ground pepper

Sprinkle ginger and pepper over the dressed guinea   VIII-5
hen or chicken. Roast in a 350–400°F oven for 1
hour or till done.

Sauce:
¼ t. ground pepper
½ t. cumin
½ t. coriander
pinch of fennel
pinch of rosemary (or rue)
¼ c. dates, finely chopped
¼ c. almonds or filberts,
grated
1 t. wine vinegar
1 c. chicken stock
1 t. olive oil or butter
ground pepper

For the sauce, grind pepper, cumin, coriander, fennel, and rosemary (or rue) in a mortar. Add to finely
chopped dates, and grated almonds or filberts. Blend
with vinegar, stock, and olive oil or butter. Bring
the sauce to a boil and pour over the roast bird.
Sprinkle with a little pepper, and serve.

Chicken with Ginger or Fennel

4 lb. chicken
½ t. ground pepper
½ t. celery seed (or lovage)
1 t. ginger or ½ t. fennel
1 c. chicken stock
½ c. white wine
ground mild pepper

Prepare the bird and put it in a clay pot (or covered   VIII-6
casserole). In a mortar, grind together pepper, celery seed (or lovage), and ginger or fennel. Combine
with stock and white wine. Cook chicken in a 375°F
oven in this sauce for 1½ hours, basting occasionally. Serve with a sprinkling of mild pepper.

Ginger Marinade for Roast Chicken Pieces

1 t. ginger
1 t. ground pepper
¼ c. olive oil
1 T. parsley
chicken stock

Blend ground ginger, pepper, olive oil, stock to   VIII-7
cover meat and parsley. Leave chicken parts in the
marinade overnight, then bake, covered, at 400°F
in a clay pot (or casserole) until done.

method of dressing the chicken. Pliny, for one, was not impressed by such foreign influences in Roman kitchens:

Then came the artists of the kitchens, and chickens were dressed to exhibit their haunches, or were split along their backs, and by spreading out from a single foot were made to cover whole serving dishes. And so the Parthians consigned their own culinary fashions to our Roman cooks. But in all this ostentation, no one dish pleases everyone, and here a haunch is praised, and elsewhere a breast.

Pliny, 10.71.

VIII-4   PULLUM OXYZOMUM *Chicken Seasoned with Sour Sauce* Take one-eighth of a pint of olive oil, a small but sufficient amount of... slightly less of stock, and the same of vinegar. Add six scruples of pepper, one of parsley, and a bouquet of chives. [Simmer, season the chicken with the sour sauce, and serve.]

VIII-5   PULLUM NUMIDICUM *Numidian Guinea Hen* Dress the guinea hen, boil it, take it out, then [sprinkle] with laser and pepper, and roast. Grind pepper, cumin, coriander seed, laser root, rue, dates, and nuts. Moisten with vinegar, and add honey, stock, and olive oil. Blend. When this sauce has boiled, thicken with starch and pour over the chicken. Sprinkle with pepper and serve.

VIII-6   PULLUM LASERATUM *Chicken with Laser Spice* Open the chicken by the rear. Wash and dress the bird and put it in a clay pot. [In a mortar] grind pepper, lovage, and fresh laser. Moisten these seasonings with stock. Add wine and stock, and blend. Pour the sauce over the chicken [and cook in the clay pot]. When ready, sprinkle with pepper and serve.

VIII-7   PULLUM PAROPTUM *Lightly Roasted Chicken* Use a little laser, six scruples of pepper, one-eighth of a pint of olive oil, one-eighth of a pint of stock, and a little parsley.

VIII-8   PULLUM ELIXUM EX IURE SUO *Chicken in Its Own Broth* [In a mortar] grind pepper, cumin, a little thyme, fennel seed, mint, rue, and laser root. Moisten with vinegar. Add dates and pound. Blend with honey, vinegar, stock, and olive oil. [Take the boiled] chicken, cool it, and dry it [with a cloth]. Pour [sauce] over and serve.

Chicken in Thyme Sauce

4 lb. cooked chicken
½ t. ground pepper
1 t. thyme
½ t. cumin
pinch of fennel
1 t. mint
pinch of rosemary (or rue)
1 t. wine vinegar
¼ c. dates, finely chopped
1 t. honey
2 c. chicken stock
2 t. olive oil or butter

To make the sauce, in a mortar, grind pepper, VIII-8
thyme, cumin, fennel, mint, and rosemary (or
rue). Blend with vinegar, chopped dates, honey,
stock, and olive oil. Bring to a boil, then simmer the
cooked chicken for 30 minutes in this sauce before
serving, basting occasionally.

Chicken with Squash in Hot Thyme Sauce

Add 1 t. ground mustard to the thyme sauce de- VIII-9
scribed in the preceding recipe. Serve chicken and
sauce together with cooked squash, vegetable marrow, zucchini, or pumpkin.

VIII-9   PULLUM ELIXUM CUM CUCURBITIS ELIXIS   *Boiled Chicken with Boiled Gourds*   Make the sauce described above, add mustard, pour over [the boiled chicken and gourds] and serve.

VIII-10   PULLUM ELIXUM CUM COLOCASIIS ELIXIS   *Boiled Chicken and Boiled Egyptian Beans [Kidney Beans]*   Make the sauce described above. Pour [over the chicken and beans] and serve. This [sauce] can be made for boiled [chicken] and . . .

VIII-11   [UNTITLED]   [*Chicken*]   . . . Use Colymbadian olives. Do not stuff the chicken too vigorously, but leave a little space, lest it burst asunder while it is cooking. The chicken should be lowered, in a basket, into the pot and raised from time to time during boiling, and lowered lest it burst asunder.

> ⟨ Colymbadian olives were named for their method of prepara-
> tion. The finest large olives from Ancona (a seaport on the Adri-
> atic), were placed in pots containing olive oil that had been sea-
> soned with herbs. They were called "floating" or "swimming"
> olives after the Greek word "kolumbos" (swimming bath). As
> they lay in the amphora, the olives absorbed the flavors of the
> herbs suspended in oil. These were the finest and most expen-
> sive. More commonly, olives were prepared and seasoned in
> brine. Fennel was added to the water before the salt. Colym-
> badian olives or the brine-soaked Halmadian olives were custo-
> marily served at the beginning of the meal, but if the dinner was
> an elaborate one, they could also appear at the conclusion.

VIII-12   PULLUS VARDANUS   *Chicken Vardanus*   Cook the chicken in a sauce made of these ingredients: stock, olive oil, wine, and a bouquet of chives, coriander, and savory. After cooking, grind pepper [in a mortar] with one-sixth of a pint of nuts. Pour over liquid from the chicken pan and throw away the bouquet. Add to this mixture a cup of milk, and blend. Pour the sauce over the chicken and heat until it boils. Beat egg whites [and use them] to thicken the sauce. Arrange the chicken on a platter, and pour the sauce described above over it. This is called white sauce.

Chicken Vardanus with Chives and Hazelnuts

2 lbs. chicken parts
2 T. olive oil

Take chicken parts and brown them in olive oil.

VIII-12

First sauce:
1 c. chicken stock
2 t. olive oil or butter
½ c. white wine
1 T. fresh chives, chopped
1½ t. coriander
1½ t. savory or sage

For the first sauce, mix stock, olive oil, white wine, chives, coriander, and savory or sage, according to taste. Cover, and cook the browned chicken parts in this sauce until done.

Second sauce:
ground pepper, to taste
¼ c. hazelnuts or almonds, finely chopped
½ c. pan juices
1 c. milk
flour

Now, in a mortar, grind pepper, mix with finely chopped nuts, and add to sauce from the chicken pan. Blend with the milk, pour over the cooked chicken, and bring to a boil. Thicken the sauce with flour. Add water to achieve desired consistency, and serve over the chicken pieces.

Browned Chicken Frontinian

3 lb. chicken, cut into parts
2 T. olive oil or butter

Brush chicken with olive oil or butter. Roast for 30 minutes in a 375°F oven to brown the meat. When done, finish in the following sauce.

VIII-13

Sauce:
pinch of aniseed
½ t. savory
½ t. coriander
2 T. olive oil
1 c. chicken stock
1 T. chives
(½ c. white wine)
ground pepper

To make the sauce, grind aniseed, savory, and coriander in a mortar. Combine with olive oil, stock, and chives. Put in a cooking pot with the browned chicken parts, and cook till done, basting from time to time with the sauce mixed with the chicken juices. (If you wish, add white wine to the mixture.) Serve the chicken in the sauce with a sprinkling of pepper.

Chicken and Parsley Dumplings in Wine Sauce

VIII-14

2 lbs. chicken breasts
2 T. olive oil
1 medium onion, chopped
½ c. white wine
½ t. coriander
½ c. chicken stock
1 c. milk
salt
2 T. honey
1 T. water

Dumplings:
1 t. parsley
½ c. all purpose flour
1 raw egg
milk

Sauce:
¼ t. pepper
½ t. celery seed (or lovage)
1 t. oregano
1 t. honey
½ c. boiled wine (see
p. 306)
1 c. chicken stock

Sauté onion until soft, in olive oil. Now add the chicken breasts and continue cooking till they are brown. Add the white wine, coriander, and stock. Simmer for 40 minutes and set aside, putting the gravy into a fresh saucepan. To this, add milk, salt to taste, honey, and water, and keep warm over low heat.

Meanwhile, make 10 very small dumplings. First mix parsley with flour. Then put an egg in a measuring cup and add milk to fill ⅓ of the cup. Mix, then stir into the parsley and flour. Now heat the gravy-milk liquid until it boils, and add the dumpling mix by individual spoonfuls. Cover and simmer for 5 minutes, then uncover and simmer five more minutes.

For the sauce, grind together pepper, celery seed (or lovage), and oregano. Mix with honey, boiled wine, and stock. Bring to a boil, then simmer for 25 minutes to reduce. Pour the sauce over the reheated chicken and dumplings, and serve.

Almond Ginger Stuffing for Chicken

4 lb. chicken
½ t. ground pepper
¼ t. celery seed (or lovage)
2 t. ginger
½ lb. ground beef
½ c. boiled wheat berries
1 c. cooked calf's
brains, chopped
3 raw egg yolks
½ c. chicken or beef stock
1 t. olive oil
whole peppercorns
½ c. almonds

To make this stuffing for a roast chicken (or suckling pig), combine ground pepper, celery seed (or lovage), and ginger, with ground beef, boiled wheat, and chopped calf's brains. Bind with well beaten egg yolks. Add stock to moisten, olive oil, a few roughly ground peppercorns, and the almonds (whole or chopped, as you wish).

VIII-15

Stuffed Roast Chicken in White Sauce

4 lb. chicken

Stuff the chicken with the *Almond Ginger Stuffing* in the preceding recipe and roast it in the oven.

VIII-16

Sauce:
2 T. butter
2 T. white pastry flour
1 c. milk
1 T. parsley
ground pepper

To make the sauce, first melt butter over low heat in a saucepan. Combine with flour, gradually add milk, and simmer till thickened, stirring constantly. Stir in parsley and pour over the cooked fowl. Serve at once, with a sprinkling of pepper.

VIII-13   PULLUM FRONTONIANUM *Chicken Frontinian* Roast the chicken a little to brown it, and then season it with stock, olive oil, a bouquet of aniseed, chives, savory, and green coriander. When the bird is done, remove it [from the pan] and arrange it on a platter that you have soaked with boiled wine. Sprinkle with pepper, and serve.

VIII-14   PULLUS TRACTOGALATUS *Chicken Prepared in Pastry and Milk* Cook the chicken in stock, olive oil, wine, onions, and a bouquet of coriander. After cooking, take the bird out of this sauce [and set aside]. In a fresh saucepan, put milk and a little salt, honey, and a very little water [that is, a third part]. Heat gently over a slow fire. Take crumbled pastry and add it, little by little, to the liquid. Stir continuously to avoid scorching. Put the chicken, whole or separated into parts [in the pastry-and-milk]. Serve on a platter, over which this sauce is to be poured. [Grind] pepper, lovage, and oregano. Add honey, a little boiled wine, and chicken gravy. Blend, boil the sauce in a pan, thicken with starch, and serve.

VIII-15   PULLUS FARSILIS *Stuffed Chicken* Draw the chicken by the neck, as for chicken in gravy. Grind pepper, lovage, and ginger. [Pound with] chopped meat, boiled spelt, and brains stewed in gravy. Break eggs [into this] and combine so that the stuffing has a consistent texture. Add stock, a little olive oil, peppercorns, and an abundance of nuts. Blend. Now take this stuffing and fill up the insides of a chicken or suckling pig, taking care to leave a little room free. In a similar manner you can prepare the stuffing for a boned capon.

VIII-16   PULLUS LEUCOZOMUS *Chicken with White Sauce* Draw the bird and dress it according to the recipe above. Open it at the breast bone. Now mix water with a copious quantity of Spanish oil. Stir and thicken with starch until the liquid has been consumed. [Cook the bird in the white sauce.] When [the bird is] done, take it out with whatever leeks [sic] remain. Sprinkle with pepper and serve.

BOOK VI, OF BIRDS,
IS ENDED

Gourmet Recipes

STERILE SOW'S WOMB, SKIN, CRACKLING, SPARE RIBS, AND TROTTERS

I-1 VULVAE STERILES *Sterile Sows' Wombs* Take Cyrenaic or Parthian laser and a combination of vinegar and stock. Serve.

I-2 IN VULVA STERILI *[Sauce] for Sterile Sow's Womb* [Combine] pepper, celery seed, dried mint, laser root, honey, vinegar, and stock.

I-3 VULVAE STERILES *Sterile Sow's Womb* Serve with pepper, stock, and Parthian laser.

I-4 VULVAE STERILES *Sterile Sow's Womb* Serve with pepper, stock, and a little spiced wine.

I-5 CALLUM LIBELLI COTICULAE UNGELLAE *Skin, Crackling, Spare Ribs, and Trotters* Serve with pepper, stock, and laser.

I-6 VULVAM UT TOSTAM FACIAS *Grilled Sterile Sow's Womb* First roll the womb in bran and then steep in brine.[1] Cook.

SOW'S BELLY[2]

II-1 [UNTITLED] *[Sow's Belly]* Boil the belly and then bind it with reeds. Sprinkle with salt and put in the oven or on a gridiron. Roast it a little. Mix pepper, lovage, stock, wine, and raisin wine. Thicken [the sauce] with starch and pour over the sow's belly.

II-2 SUMEN PLENUM *Stuffed Sow's Belly* Grind pepper, caraway, and salted sea urchin. [Fill the belly,] sew it together, and cook. [This dish] should be eaten with fish-pickle and mustard.

LIVER OF ANIMALS FATTENED ON FIGS

III-1 IN FICATO OENOGARUM *Wine Sauce for Liver of Animals Fattened on Figs* Use pepper, thyme, lovage, stock, a little wine, and olive oil.

III-2 ALITER *[Liver of Animals Fattened on Figs]* Score with a reed and steep in stock. [Grind] pepper, lovage, and two laurel berries. Then roll the liver in caul and grill. Serve.

Tripe with Fennel Cream Sauce

1 lb. sliced tripe
6 small onions
water

Sauce:
2 T. butter
2 T. flour
1 c. milk
1 c. beef stock
1 t. wine vinegar
pinch of ground fennel
⅛ t. ground pepper
pinch of salt

Simmer the tripe with the halved onions and water   I-I
for 4 hours in a covered pan. Drain, then finish
cooking over low heat for 1 hour, with the onions,
in the following cream sauce.

For the sauce, first melt the butter over low heat.
Slowly add flour, then the milk. Mix with the stock,
vinegar, fennel, pepper, and salt. Pour over the tripe
and onions, and finish cooking till the tripe is done.

Tripe with Honey Ginger Sauce

1 lb. sliced tripe

Sauce:
⅛ t. ground pepper
¼ t. ginger
1 t. celery seed
1 t. honey
1 t. wine vinegar
2 c. beef stock
1 t. mint
pinch of salt

Simmer the tripe for 4 hours in water, in a covered   I-2
pan, and drain. Then finish cooking for 1 hour in the
following sauce.

For the sauce, in a mortar, grind together pepper,
ginger, and celery seed. Add to honey, vinegar, and
beef stock. Pour over the tripe and cook gently
together. Twenty minutes before serving, add mint.
Salt to taste, and serve.

Tripe with Cinnamon-Nutmeg Sauce

I-4

1 lb. sliced beef tripe

Simmer the tripe in a covered pan for 4 hours, then drain and finish cooking for 1 hour in the following spiced wine sauce.

Sauce:
½ c. beef stock
½ c. white wine
⅛ t. cinnamon
pinch of nutmeg
⅛ t. ground pepper

For the sauce, combine beef stock with white wine, and spice the mixture with cinnamon and nutmeg. Pour over the tripe and cook gently together till the tripe is done. Sprinkle with pepper and serve.

Seasonings for Spare Ribs, Cheeks, and Crackling

I-5

ground pepper
reduced pork stock
ginger

Simmer meat for 2 hours in water seasoned to taste with pepper, reduced pork stock, and ginger.
    Alternatively, cook meat in water, and finish for 20 minutes in seasoned stock.
    Serve in wine sauce. (See p. 306.)

Pork Liver in Celery Wine Sauce

III-1

1 lb. pork liver
olive oil

Slice and sauté the liver in olive oil, and serve in a reduced wine sauce.

Sauce:
½ t. pepper
½ t. thyme
1 t. celery seed (or lovage)
¾ c. pork or chicken stock
¼ c. red wine
1 t. olive oil

To make the sauce, in a mortar, grind together pepper, thyme, and celery seed (or lovage). Combine with stock, red wine, and olive oil. Bring the sauce to a boil, simmer to reduce for 20 minutes, and pour over the liver slices.

Broiled Pork Liver with Bacon Slices

1 lb. pork liver

Marinade:
1 c. pork or chicken stock
½ t. ground pepper
1 t. celery seed (or lovage)
6 cloves (or laurel berries)
3–4 bacon slices
wine sauce

Pound the liver and steep for 2 hours in a marinade   III-2
of stock seasoned with pepper, celery seed (or lovage), and a few crushed cloves (or laurel berries).
Wrap the marinated liver in bacon slices, and broil
in oven.

Serve with reduced wine sauce from preceding
recipe.

Marinated Pork Hors D'oeuvres

1 lb. choice pork or beef

Marinade:
1 t. ground pepper
1 t. celery seed (or lovage)
pinch of aniseed
1 t. cumin
½ t. ginger
5 cloves or laurel berries
pork or beef stock

Cut meat into 1 inch cubes. In a mortar, grind pep-   IV-1
per, celery seed (or lovage), aniseed, cumin, ginger,
and a few cloves (or laurel berries). Blend with sufficient stock to cover meat. Put the meat into a dish
and steep in the marinade overnight. Then drain
and roast 1 hour in a 325°F oven.

Sauce:
½ t. ground pepper
½ t. celery seed (or lovage)
1 c. pork or beef stock
sweet raisin wine or muscatel
flour

For the sauce, grind together pepper and celery seed
(or lovage). Add to stock, and sweeten with wine to
taste. Bring to a boil and thicken with flour. Drench
the hors d'oeuvres with this sauce and serve.

MEAT HORS D'OEUVRES

IV-1

OFELLAS OSTIENSES *Ostian* Hors D'oeuvres* On the skin, mark out [bite-sized] pieces of choice meat, but leave the skin intact. Grind pepper, lovage, anise, cumin, silphium, and one laurel berry. Pour stock [over these seasonings and] blend. Pour [the mixture] into an angular vessel over the hors d'oeuvres. Steep. When the meat has reposed for two or three days in the marinade, bind it with twigs in the shape of a [Roman] ten, and put it in the oven. After cooking, separate the pieces of meat which you have marked out from each other. Grind pepper and lovage. Pour stock over these seasonings and add a little raisin wine for sweetness. Cook and then thicken the gravy with starch. Drench the hors d'oeuvres [with this sauce] and serve.

IV-2

OFELLAS APICIANAS *Hors D'oeuvres Apicius* Remove the bones from pieces of meat. Roll into the shape of a wheel, binding them with twigs. Put in the oven. When it is browned, remove [from the oven] and, to expel moisture, dry the meat on a gridiron over a slow fire, taking care the meat does not scorch. [For the sauce, first] grind pepper, lovage, cyperus, and cumin. Blend with stock and raisin wine. Stir. Put the morsels of meat and the sauce into a saucepan. After cooking, remove the hors d'oeuvres from the pan and dry them. Serve them without sauce. Sprinkle with pepper and serve. If the meat should be fatty, remove the skin before the pieces are bound with twigs. In this way, also, it is possible to make these hors d'oeuvres from the belly of the animal.

IV-3

OFELLAE APROGINEO MORE *Hors D'oeuvres in the Manner of Wild Boar* Steep [the pieces of meat] in [a marinade of] oil and stock. Seasoning is put into this when it is cooked. While it is on the fire, the [following] sauce is added and boiled again: ground pepper, green herbs, honey, and stock. Add starch when the sauce is boiling. Or, the morsels of meat may be simply boiled without [the marinade of] stock and olive oil, but sprinkled with pepper. Add the sauce described above and cook.

---

* Ostia was (and is) a seaport on the mouth of the Tiber River.

Spiced Pork Hors D'oeuvres Apicius

lb. choice pork (fillet, loin)

Sauce:
½ t. ground pepper
½ t. celery seed (or lovage)
pinch of ginger
¼ t. cumin
¾ c. pork or chicken stock
¼ c. raisin wine
ground pepper

Cut meat in strips, roll, and secure with toothpicks   IV-2
(or twigs). Brown the pieces in a 300°F oven, and
wipe away melted fat.

For the sauce, in a mortar, grind pepper, celery
seed (or lovage), ginger, and cumin. Blend with
stock and raisin wine. Slowly cook the meat in this
sauce. When done, remove the hors d'oeuvres from
the sauce and allow them to dry. Sprinkle each with
a little pepper and serve.

Pork Hors D'oeuvres with Green Herb Sauce

1 lb. choice pork

Marinade:
2 t. olive oil
1 c. pork or chicken stock
1 t. thyme
2 t. celery seed (or lovage)
1 t. oregano
1 t. rosemary

Sauce:
¼ t. ground pepper
1 t. fresh mint, chopped
½ t. fresh thyme
½ t. fresh oregano
pinch of fresh rosemary
(or rue)
1 t. honey
1 c. pork or chicken stock
flour

Cut the meat into 2 inch cubes. Steep the pieces for   IV-3
8 hours in a marinade of olive oil and stock seasoned
with thyme, celery seed (or lovage), oregano, and
rosemary (or rue). Put the morsels in a braising pan
and cook gently in the marinade for one hour.

Meanwhile prepare a sauce. Combine ground
pepper, fresh herbs (chopped mint, thyme, oregano,
rosemary or rue), honey, and stock. Bring the sauce
to a boil, then thicken with flour. Serve the hors
d'oeuvres in the sauce.

Alternatively, marinate the pieces of meat, then
remove them from the marinade and cook with a
sprinkling of pepper. Then finish cooking in the
green herb sauce described above.

IV-4 ALITER OFELLAS *Another Hors D'oeuvre* Fry [the pieces of meat] carefully until they are almost cooked. Now take one-twelfth of a pint of the best stock and a twelfth of a pint each of water, vinegar, and olive oil. Blend. Put this, mixed with the meat pieces, into an earthenware dish. Fry and serve.

IV-5 ALITER OFELLAS *Another Hors D'oeuvre* [Cook the pieces of meat] in a frying pan with a generous quantity of wine sauce. Sprinkle with pepper and serve.

IV-6 ALITER OFELLAS *Another Hors D'oeuvre* Steep pieces of meat in water, having sprinkled them before with salt and cumin. Then fry them carefully.

ROASTS[3]

V-1 ASSATURAM *Roast Meat* Roasted plain in the oven and sprinkled with plenty of salt, serve with honey.

V-2 ALITER ASSATURAS *Roast Meats* [Grind] six scruples of parsley and six each of laser and of ginger. Add five laurel berries, green herbs, six scruples each of laser root, of oregano, and of cyperus. [Mix with] a little costmary, three scruples of pellitory, six scruples of celery seed, twelve scruples of pepper, and stock and olive oil to suffice.

V-3 ALITER ASSATURAS *Roast Meats* Take dried, crushed seeded myrtle berry and mix with cumin, pepper, honey, stock, boiled wine, and olive oil. [Cook] and thicken with starch. First boil the meat and then roast it a little, with salt. Pour [the sauce] over [the roast meat]. Sprinkle with pepper and serve.

V-4 ALITER ASSATURAS *Roast Meats* [Pound] six scruples each of pepper, of lovage, of parsley, of celery seed, of aniseed, of laser root, and of hazelwort. Add a little pellitory and six scruples each of cyperus, of caraway, of cumin, and of ginger. [Blend with] half a pint of stock and one-eighth of a pint of oil.

V-5 ASSATURAS IN COLLARE *Of Roast Neck* Boil and pour [a sauce made from] pepper, green herbs, honey, and stock into a shallow pan [and add the boiled neck]. Then roast in the oven until done. However, you may wish to roast the boiled neck without condiments, pouring the sauce, hot, over the dry roast when it is cooked.

Savory Pork or Beef Hors D'oeuvres

1 lb. choice pork or beef
olive oil
1½ T. pork or beef stock
1½ T. water
1½ T. mild wine vinegar
1½ T. olive oil

Cut the meat into thin 2-inch squares. Then sauté   IV-4
the morsels in olive oil until they are nearly done.

Next combine stock, water, vinegar, and olive oil.
Pour into a cooking pot, and add the meats. Finish
cooking over low heat, and serve.

Tart Sauce for Roast Meats

1 t. parsley
1 t. fennel
½ t. ginger
5 crushed laurel berries or
peppercorns
½ t. basil
½ t. thyme
1 t. oregano
pinch of mint (or costmary)
½ t. chamomile (or pellitory)
1 t. celery seed
½ t. ground pepper
2 t. olive oil
1½ c. beef stock

In a mortar, grind parsley, fennel, ginger, laurel ber-   V-2
ries or peppercorns, basil, thyme, oregano, mint,
chamomile, celery seed, and ground pepper. Combine with olive oil and mix with stock. Bring to a
boil, simmer for 15 minutes, then remove from heat
and chill. Serve a little of the sauce with slices of cold
roast beef.

Alternatively, add the mixture to the roasting
pan, baste the meat, and serve the reduced sauce
with the finished roast.

Roast Meats with Myrtle Wine Sauce

v-3

3 lb. pot or rump roast
water

Sauce:
3-4 myrtle berries, cloves or
juniper berries
½ t. cumin
½ t. ground pepper
1 T. honey
1 c. beef stock
¼ c. boiled red wine (see
p. 306)
1 T. olive oil
(flour)
ground pepper

Simmer the pot roast or rump roast in a covered pan
with water for about 2 hours. Remove from the pot
and reserve stock.

In a mortar, grind together cloves, myrtle or juniper
berries, cumin, and pepper. Combine with honey,
stock, boiled red wine, and olive oil. Bring to a boil,
then roast meat for 1 hour, basting with the sauce, in
a 325°F oven. Thicken sauce with flour, if you wish.
Sprinkle roast with pepper and serve with the sauce.

Roast Mutton with Thyme Sauce

v-5

3-4 lb. neck of mutton
2 c. water

Sauce:
½ t. ground pepper
2 t. thyme
1 t. oregano
1 T. honey
2 c. mutton stock

Simmer the neck of mutton with water in a covered
pan for a ½ hour and reserve liquid. Transfer meat
to a roasting pan.

To make the sauce, grind together pepper, thyme,
and oregano. Combine with honey and stock. Pour
over the mutton and roast in a 350°F oven for
hours or until done, basting with the sauce.

Alternatively, roast meat without the sauce, simmer sauce 25 minutes to reduce, and serve with
finished roast.

Rosemary-Ginger Sauce for Braised Meats

½ t. ground pepper
½ t. celery seed (or lovage)
½ t. oregano
½ t. rosemary (or rue)
pinch of ginger
1 T. chopped onion
¼ c. boiled wine
2 t. honey
½ t. cider or white vinegar
1 t. olive oil or butter
1 c. beef, pork, or
other meat stock
(flour)

In a mortar, grind pepper, celery seed (or lovage), oregano, rosemary (or rue), and ginger. Add chopped onion. Mix with boiled wine, honey, vinegar, olive oil, and stock. Heat, simmer to reduce for 25 minutes, and serve with cooked, drained meats. Or, the sauce can be thickened into a gravy with flour.

VI-I

OF BOILED MEATS AND CHOICE CUTS

VI-1   IUS IN ELIXAM OMNEM *Sauce for All Boiled Meats* [Mix] pepper, lovage, oregano, rue, silphium, dried onion, wine, boiled wine, honey, vinegar, and a little olive oil. Dry [the boiled meats] and then wrap in a linen cloth [and press out the remaining moisture]. Pour the sauce over the boiled meats.

VI-2   IUS IN ELIXAM *Sauce for Boiled Meats* [Mix] pepper, parsley, stock, vinegar, dates, shallots, and a little olive oil. Pour over [the meat] when the sauce is hot.

VI-3   IUS IN ELIXAM *Sauce for Boiled Meats* Combine pepper, dried rue, fennel seed, onion, dates, stock, and olive oil.

VI-4   IUS CANDIDUM IN ELIXAM *White Sauce for Boiled Meats* [Combine] pepper, stock, wine, rue, onion, nuts, spiced wine. Add a little soaked bread to thicken the sauce and olive oil. Cook and pour the sauce [over boiled meats].

VI-5   ALITER IUS CANDIDUM IN ELIXAM *Another White Sauce for Boiled Meats* [Combine] pepper, caraway, lovage, thyme, oregano, shallots, dates, honey, vinegar, stock, and olive oil.

VI-6   IN COPADIIS IUS ALBUM *White Sauce for Choice Cuts* [Mix] pepper, cumin, lovage, rue seed, and damsons. Pour wine [over these ingredients]. Blend with honeyed wine and vinegar. [Stir] a little thyme and oregano [into the sauce].

VI-7   ALITER IUS CANDIDUM IN COPADIIS *Another White Sauce for Choice Cuts* [Mix] pepper, thyme, cumin, celery seed, fennel, mint, myrtle berry and raisins. Blend with honey wine. Stir the sauce with a sprig of savory.

VI-8   IUS IN COPADIIS *Sauce for Choice Cuts* [Combine] pepper, lovage, caraway, mint, spikenard, bay leaf, the yolk of an egg, honey, honey wine, vinegar, stock, and olive oil. Stir with a bouquet garni of savory and chives. Thicken with starch.

VI-9   IUS ALBUM IN COPADIIS *White Sauce for Choice Cuts* [Mix] pepper, lovage, cumin, celery seed, thyme, soaked nut kernels, soaked and cleaned nuts, honey, vinegar, stock, and olive oil.

Onion Date Sauce for Braised Meats

½ t. coarsely ground pepper
2 T. chopped fresh parsley
1 c. beef, pork, or other meat stock
1 t. cider or white vinegar
2 T. chopped dates
1 T. shallots or onions
1 t. olive oil or butter

Mix pepper, parsley, stock, vinegar, finely chopped dates and shallots, and olive oil or butter.

A ½ hour before meat is done, heat, then pour into the braising pan over the drained meats. Finish cooking the meats in the sauce, basting occasionally.

VI-2

Onion Fennel Sauce for Braised Meats

½ t. coarsely ground pepper
½ t. rosemary (or rue)
pinch of fennel
1 T. chopped onion
2 T. chopped dates
1 c. beef, pork, or other meat stock
2 t. olive oil or butter

In a mortar, grind pepper, rosemary (or rue), and fennel. Add finely chopped onion and dates. Combine with stock and olive oil or butter.

A ½ hour before meat is done, drain the meat, then finish cooking and basting the drained meats in the sauce. Serve.

VI-3

Almond Wine Sauce for Braised Meats

½ t. ground pepper
1 c. beef, pork, or other meat stock
¼ c. white wine
pinch of rosemary (or rue)
1 T. onion, finely chopped
¼ c. almonds or pine nuts, finely chopped
1 c. spiced white wine (see Spiced Wine Apicius, p. 3)
2 t. olive oil or butter
(flour)

Mix pepper, stock, white wine, rosemary (or rue), finely chopped onion and nuts, spiced wine, and olive oil or butter. Bring to a boil, then simmer for 25 minutes to reduce. Thicken with flour, if you wish. Serve the sauce with the cooked meats.

Or omit flour and finish cooking the lightly cooked (drained) meats in the sauce.

VI-4

Caraway-Oregano Sauce for Braised Meats

VI-5

½ t. coarsely ground pepper
pinch of caraway or
aniseed
1 t. celery seed (or lovage)
½ t. thyme
½ t. oregano
2 T. chopped shallots or
onions
2 T. chopped dates
1 t. honey
1 t. cider or white vinegar
2 c. beef, pork, or
other meat stock
2 t. olive oil or butter

In a mortar, grind pepper, caraway or aniseed celery seed (or lovage), thyme, and oregano. Add to finely chopped shallots and dates. Blend with honey, vinegar, stock, and olive oil or butter.

A ½ hour before meat is done, drain the meat heat sauce and pour into the braising pan over the drained meats. Continue cooking to reduce sauce and serve with meat.

Damson Sauce for Braised Meats

VI-6

½ t. coarsely ground pepper
½ t. cumin
1 t. celery seed (or lovage)
1 t. rosemary (or rue)
½ t. thyme
½ t. oregano
¼ c. damsons or plums
¼ c. white wine
¼ c. mead or 1 T. honey
1 t. cider vinegar or white
wine vinegar
1 c. beef, pork, or
other meat stock

In a mortar, grind together pepper, cumin, celery seed (or lovage), rosemary (or rue), thyme, and oregano. Add sliced plums. Blend with white wine mead or honey, vinegar, and stock.

A ½ hour before meat is done, drain meat, heat sauce and pour it into the braising pan. Finish cooking meat in the sauce.

Raisin Thyme Sauce for Braised Meats

¼ t. coarsly ground pepper
½ t. thyme
¼ t. cumin
1 t. celery seed
pinch of fennel
sprig of fresh mint
4–5 peppercorns (or juniper or myrtle berries)
¼ c. raisins
¼ c. mead or 1 T. honey
1 c. beef, pork, or other meat stock
savory, to taste

In a mortar, first grind together pepper, thyme, cumin, celery seed, fennel, and fresh mint. Add to peppercorns (or myrtle berries) and raisins. Combine with mead or honey and stock. Heat and stir in savory, to taste.

A ½ hour before meat is done, drain meat and pour sauce into pan with it. Finish cooking the meat in the sauce.

vi-7

Wine Egg Sauce for Braised Meats

½ t. coarsely ground pepper
1 t. celery seed (or lovage)
pinch of caraway
sprig of mint
1 t. bay leaf
1 t. spikenard (or bay leaves)
1 raw egg yolk
1 t. honey
¼ c. mead or sweet white wine
1 t. white wine vinegar or cider vinegar
2 t. beef, pork, or other meat stock
2 t. olive oil or butter
small bouquet garni of savory and chives
flour

Grind together pepper, celery seeds (or lovage), caraway, mint, bay leaf, and spikenard, if available. Blend with well beaten egg yolk, honey, mead or sweet wine, vinegar, stock, and olive oil or butter. Add savory and chives tied in cheesecloth.

A ½ hour before meat is done, drain meat and add sauce to it. Finish cooking in the sauce. Remove bouquet garni of savory and chives, and serve sauce with meat.

vi-8

Pepper Nut Sauce for Braised Meats

VI-9

½ t. coarsely ground pepper
1 t. lovage (or celery seed)
¼ t. cumin
½ t. celery seed
½ t. thyme
¼ c. almonds, walnuts, pine,
or pistachio nuts
1 t. honey
1 t. white wine vinegar or
cider vinegar
1 c. beef, pork, or
other meat stock
2 t. olive oil or butter

In a mortar, grind together pepper, lovage (or celery seed), cumin, celery seed, and thyme. Add to finely chopped nuts. Blend with honey, vinegar, stock, and olive oil or butter.

A ½ hour before meat is done, drain the meat, add the sauce, and cook till done. Serve the meat with the sauce.

Mustard Wine Sauce for Braised Meats

VI-10

¼ t. ground pepper
½ t. celery seed
pinch of caraway
¼ t. savory
pinch of saffron
1 T. shallots or onion,
chopped
3 T. almonds, chopped
2 T. dates, chopped
1 c. beef, pork, or
other meat stock
2 t. olive oil or butter
pinch of ground mustard
½ c. white wine

In a mortar, grind together pepper, celery seed, caraway, savory, and saffron. Add finely chopped shallots or onions, almonds, and dates. Blend with stock, olive oil, and a little mustard. Heat and add wine.

A ½ hour before meat is done, drain the meat and pour sauce over it. Finish cooking meat in the sauce and serve together.

Almond Parsley Sauce for Braised Meats

½ t. coarsely ground pepper
½ t. ground pepper
½ t. celery seed (or lovage)
2 T. parsley
1 T. shallots or onions
¼ c. almonds, finely chopped
2 T. dates, chopped
1 t. honey
1 t. white wine vinegar or
cider vinegar
1 c. beef, pork, or
other meat stock
¼ c. white wine
2 t. olive oil or butter

In a mortar, grind together pepper, celery seed (or   VI-11
lovage), and parsley. Add chopped shallots or onions, almonds, and dates. Blend with honey, vinegar,
stock, wine, and olive oil or butter.

A ½ hour before meat is done, drain the meat,
and pour sauce over it. Finish cooking the meat in
the sauce and serve together.

Peppercorn Leek Sauce for Braised Meats

2 hard-boiled eggs, chopped
¼ t. pepper
1 t. cumin
1 T. parsley, chopped
¼ c. thinly sliced leeks
6 coarsely ground pepper-
corns (or myrtle berries)
1 T. honey
1 t. white wine vinegar or
cider vinegar
1½ c. beef, pork, or
other meat stock
2 t. olive oil or butter

Mix finely chopped hard-boiled eggs with pepper,   VI-12
cumin, and chopped parsley. Add leeks, and coarsely ground peppercorns (or myrtle berries). Combine
with honey, vinegar, stock, and olive oil or butter.

A ½ hour before meat is done, drain the meat,
and pour sauce over it. Finish cooking the meat in
the sauce and serve together.

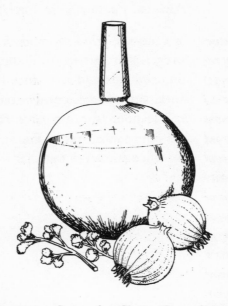

VI-10   IUS IN COPADIIS *Sauce for Choice Cuts* [Mix] pepper, celery seed, caraway, savory, saffron, shallots, roasted almonds, dates, stock, olive oil, and a little mustard. Add boiled wine to color [the sauce].

VI-11   IUS IN COPADIIS *Sauce for Choice Cuts* [Mix] pepper, lovage, parsley, shallots, roasted almonds, dates, honey, vinegar, stock, boiled wine, and olive oil.

VI-12   IUS IN COPADIIS *Sauce for Choice Cuts* [Mix] chopped hard-boiled eggs, pepper, cumin, parsley, cooked leek, myrtle berries, a goodly quantity of honey, vinegar, stock, and olive oil.

VI-13   IUS IN ELIXAM ANETHATUM CRUDUM *Aniseed Marinade for Pork Delicacies* [Grind] pepper, aniseed, dried mint, and laser root. Pour vinegar [over these seasonings]. Add dates, honey, stock, and a little mustard. Blend with boiled new wine and with olive oil. Use this [marinade] also with neck of pork.

VI-14   IUS IN ELIXAM ALLECATUM *Fish-pickle Sauce for Boiled Meats* [Mix] pepper, lovage, caraway, celery seed, thyme, shallots, dates, and strained fish-pickle. Blend these ingredients with honey and wine. Sprinkle chopped green celery over [the sauce]. Add oil and serve [with boiled meats].

Aniseed Marinade for Braised Pork Tidbits

pork cubes
Marinade:
½ t. coarsely ground pepper
½ t. ground aniseed
sprig of mint
½ t. ginger
2 t. white wine vinegar or
cider vinegar
¼ c. dates, finely chopped
2 t. honey
2 c. pork stock
1 t. ground mustard
½ c. boiled white wine (see
p. 306)
2 t. olive oil

In a mortar, grind together pepper, aniseed, mint, VI-13 and ginger. Moisten with vinegar. Add to finely chopped dates, honey, stock, and a little mustard. Stir in boiled wine and olive oil. Pour over the meat and leave in the marinade for at least six hours before cooking and serving.

This marinade is also good for braising sweetbreads.

(By reducing the aniseed to ¼ t., the wine to ¼ c., and stock to 1 c., an excellent sauce can be made with these marinade ingredients.)

Fish-pickle Sauce for Braised Choice Meats

½ t. coarsely ground pepper
½ t. lovage (or celery seed)
pinch of caraway
½ t. celery seed
½ t. thyme
2 T. shallots or 1 T. onion,
chopped
2 T. dates, chopped
1 T. fish pickle (see p. 305)
1 t. honey
½ c. white wine
1 c. pork or beef stock
2 t. olive oil
chopped celery stalks
ground pepper

First, grind together pepper, lovage (or celery seed), VI-14 caraway, celery seed, and thyme. Add to chopped shallots, dates, and fish-pickle. Blend with honey, wine, stock, and olive oil. Heat and add to drained, nearly cooked meats. Finish cooking meats in sauce until the liquid has been reduced by half.

Serve meats in the sauce, each portion garnished with finely chopped celery and sprinkled with freshly ground pepper.

PAUNCH

VII-I

[UNTITLED] [*Paunch*] Take the paunch of a pig and empty it scrupulously, first washing it with a solution of vinegar and salt, and then with water. Then fill the stomach with these ingredients: pounded and ground pork mixed with three brains with the membranes removed, raw eggs, nuts, and peppercorns. Blend this stuffing with a sauce made of these ingredients: ground pepper, lovage, silphium, anise, ginger, and a little rue, the best stock [to moisten], and a little olive oil. Fill the belly with the stuffing, taking care to leave a little empty space lest the stomach burst asunder during cooking. Bind up the two openings with twigs and put it into a pot of boiling water. Lift it out of the pot and pierce [the belly] with a needle, so that it may not burst. When [the stomach is] half cooked, lift it out of the boiling water and hang in woodsmoke to give it color. Then put it into the boiling water a second time and make sure it cooks thoroughly. Add stock, wine, and a little oil. Open it with a small knife and season with stock and lovage.

❡ In modern times, the stomach of the pig is not highly regarded. Two thousand years ago it was considered to be a great delicacy along with the womb, glandules, testicles, and cheeks. Then as now, all parts of the pig were scrupulously cleaned before use.

VII-2

VENTREM UT TOSTUM FACIAS *Grilled Paunch* First roll the stomach in bran, then steep in brine. Cook.

TESTICLES AND KIDNEYS

VIII

LUMBULI ASSI ITA FIUNT *Small Roast Testicles* Cut them open and stretch the two sides apart. [Liberally] sprinkle [the exposed testicles] with ground pepper, nuts, coriander chopped minutely, and ground fennel seed. Close the testicles and sew them together. Enfold with caul, and then brown [the testicles] in olive oil and stock. Next, roast in the oven or on a small gridiron.

HAM

[UNTITLED] [*Ham*] Boil the ham with a generous quantity of dried figs and with three laurel leaves. Then take off the skin and inscribe the ham with checker-shaped cuts. Fill these with honey. Make a paste of wheat flour and olive oil, and completely cover the ham like a skin. When the crust has baked, remove the ham from the oven and serve as is.

IX-1

PERNAE COCTURAM *Preparation of a Ham* Simply boil [the ham] in water with dried figs, as is the custom. Serve with bread pieces and boiled wine or spiced wine. Even better, serve with cakes made of new wine and wheat flour.

IX-2

PETASONEM EX MUSTEIS *Pestle or Shoulder of Pork with Cakes Made from New Wine and Wheat Flour* Boil the shoulder of pork [in water] with two pounds of barley and twenty-five dried figs. When it has boiled thoroughly, take off the skin and scorch the fat on a red hot brazier. Then cover [the seared flesh] with honey. But, it is better to smear the pork with honey and put it in the oven to cook until it colors. In a saucepan, heat and blend raisin wine, pepper, a bouquet of rue, and unmixed wine. Pour half [of the pepper sauce] over the shoulder of pork. Pour the other half over pieces of cake made of new wine and flour. When the biscuit has supped up all that it can, pour any sauce that remains over the meat. [Add the saturated biscuit to the roasting pan. Finish cooking and serve.]

IX-3

LARIDI COCTURA *Preparation of Bacon* Cover with water and cook with a lot of dill. Sprinkle with a few drops of oil and a little salt.

IX-4

You thought me cruel and greedy, Rusticus,
When I whipped the cook who burned our dinner.
If I unjustly beat him for a trifling offense,
Tell me, what worse crime can my cook commit?

Martial, 8.23.

Roast Kidneys for One

VIII

1 pair veal, lamb, or
pork kidneys
¼ t. ground pepper
¼ c. roasted almonds, finely
chopped
½ t. coriander
pinch of fennel
2 T. olive oil
2 t. meat stock
fish-pickle (see p. 305)
bacon

Remove the fat from the kidneys and discard. Cut kidneys lengthwise without separating them, into two parts. Spread them, and season with pepper, almonds, coriander, fennel, olive oil, and stock, or fish-pickle, if on hand. Close the kidneys and secure with toothpicks. Wrap in rashers of bacon, and roast in a 350° oven for about 35 minutes.

Baked Ham

IX-I

4–5 lb. ham
1 c. figs
3 laurel or bay leaves
½ c. liquid honey

Pastry:
2½ c. flour
½ t. baking powder
½ t. salt
1 c. shortening
1 raw egg
water
½ t. cider vinegar or
lemon juice

Place the ham in a pan and half cover with cold water. Bring to a boil and simmer for 1 hour, then drain and discard the water. Add figs, laurel or bay leaves, and fresh water. Simmer for a further 45 minutes. Take ham from the pot, cool it, and remove the skin. Score ham deeply, and drench the incisions with liquid honey.

Make the pastry as directed below, roll it out and pull it around the ham. Smooth the ends for a more pleasing appearance.

Bake in a 350°F oven for 15 minutes or until pastry browns.

For the pastry, mix flour, baking powder, and salt. Cut the shortening into the mixture. In a bowl, beat the egg and add sufficient water to it to make ¾ cup of liquid. Add vinegar or lemon juice. Blend wet and dry ingredients with a fork, then cool the dough in the refrigerator for 1 hour before using it with the ham.

"Must" Cake for Roast Pork

Must cake:
2 c. white flour
3 t. baking powder
½ c. shortening
½ c. honey
2 raw eggs
1 c. cottage cheese
¼ t. aniseed
¼ t. cumin
bay leaves
¼ c. white grape juice or must

Sift together flour, baking powder, aniseed, and cumin. Combine shortening, eggs, and honey. Combine dry ingredients with cottage cheese and then with other wet ingredients. Lastly, stir in the grape juice. Pour the batter into a greased and floured loaf pan. Decorate with bay leaves and bake in a 350°F oven for 40 minutes or until done.

IX-3

Pepper sauce:
½ c. sweet raisin wine or muscatel
½ c. grape juice or new wine
pinch of rosemary, rue, or sage
½ t. ground pepper

To make pepper sauce, combine, raisin wine or muscatel, grape juice, a pinch of rosemary, rue or sage, and pepper. Bring to a boil, and simmer to blend flavors.

Serve a roast shoulder or leg of pork in the pepper sauce, with slices of sauce-saturated must cake.

IX-4

Bacon with Dill

8 thick rashers of Canadian bacon
½ c. water
½ t. dill

In a frying pan, barely cover bacon with water seasoned with dill. Fry the bacon, but do not allow it to become crisp. If desired, serve with a sprinkling of olive oil and salt to taste.

LIVER AND LUNGS

X-1   IECINERA HAEDINA VEL AGNINA SIC COQUES *Liver of Kid or Lamb* Make honey-water, and into it mix eggs and some milk. Make incisions in the liver and let them absorb [the liquid]. Then cook in wine sauce. Sprinkle with pepper and serve.

X-2   ALITER IN PULMONIBUS *Lungs* Wash the lungs in milk and allow them to absorb as much of it as possible. [In a mortar] break two eggs, and add a few grains of salt and a spoonful of honey. Blend these ingredients and pour [the preparation] into the lungs. Boil the lungs and then cut them up. Now mix pepper, stock, raisin wine, and unmixed wine [into a sauce]. Fry the lungs and pour the wine sauce over them.

> *How parsley thrives and gourds grow large*
> *How endive loves to drink from streams.*
>
> Virgil, "Georgics," 4.120–21.

Marinated Liver of Kid or Lamb

1 lb. lamb, pork, calf, or
goat liver
½ c. milk
1 raw egg
¼ c. water
2 T. honey
2 T. olive oil
½ c. boiled red wine (see
p. 306)
ground pepper

If necessary, remove membrane from liver, and   x-1
with a knife make a few superficial incisions. Prepare a sweet marinade with milk, well beaten egg,
and water mixed with honey. Immerse the scored
liver in the marinade and steep for 6 hours.

Into a hot frying pan, pour olive oil. Add the
prepared liver slices, and turn to brown both sides.
Add the wine and simmer for 3 minutes on each
side. Serve with a sprinkling of pepper.

Lungs Apicius

1 pair lamb's lungs
2 c. beef or chicken stock
2 raw eggs
1 t. honey
salt
olive oil or butter

Casserole sauce:
½ t. ground pepper
¾ c. beef or chicken stock
1 t. thyme
1 t. celery seed (or lovage)
1 t. oregano
1 medium onion, chopped
¼ c. red wine or grape juice

Wash the lungs and cut in strips, removing the   x-2
larger arteries. Place in a pot with stock, bring to
a boil, and simmer for 2 hours. Drain, and season
with well beaten eggs, honey, and salt to taste. Next,
sauté lightly in olive oil or butter. Remove from the
pan and place in a casserole with the following
sauce.

To make the sauce, grind together thyme, celery
seed (or lovage), and oregano. Combine with onion,
stock, and wine or juice. Cook covered in a 300°F
oven for 2 hours, and serve.

Prepared in this way, the lungs taste much like
kidneys.

HOMEMADE SWEETS AND HONEYED CHEESES

❡The paucity of recipes for Roman pastries and desserts in Apicius' *Cookery* does not accurately reflect their significance in the cookery of the ancient world. The recipes for these, along with culinary medicine and wine making, are in my opinion in the books missing from *The Roman Cookery of Apicius* as it has come down to us. Their existence can be inferred from a multitude of scattered sources in Greek and Roman history and literature.

XI-1   DULCIA DOMESTICA *Homemade Sweets* Take palms or dates, with the stones removed, and stuff them with nuts or nut kernels and ground pepper. Salt the dates on top and bottom and fry in cooked honey, and serve.

❡In the preparation of sweets, Apicius used the word "pepper" loosely. In the first century A.D., cinnamon and nutmeg were thought by the Romans to have common points of origin with pepper. They were, in those days, prohibitively expensive.

XI-2   ALITER DULCIA *Sweets* Strip off pieces of the best African must cake and immerse them in milk. When they have drunk [up all the milk they can, form them into small cakes]. Bake them in the oven, but not for long lest they become too dry. [After baking] remove [from the oven and] pour honey over the cakes while they are still hot. Puncture them so that they may drink [up the honey]. Sprinkle with pepper and serve.

> *Arise: even now boys are buying their morning*
>   *pastries*
> *And the roosters of the dawn are everywhere alive*
>   *with calls.*
>
>   Martial, 14.223.

Dates Alexandrine

20 (whole) dates
20 blanched almonds
1 t. cinnamon
butter
salt
liquid honey

Remove pits from dates. Roll almonds in cinnamon XI-1 and stuff one in each date. Place dates on a greased pan. Sprinkle salt over the dates, then coat each one with honey. Glaze in a 450°F oven for 10 minutes, then serve.

Sweet "Roman Toast"

white bread
milk
olive oil or butter
liquid honey

Remove the crusts from the bread, and slice it. Dip XI-3 in milk and sauté in olive oil or butter. Sprinkle honey on top and serve.

This recipe omits the egg customarily added with "French" toast, but is delicious nonetheless.

"Peppered" or Cinnamon Sweet Cakes

1¼ c. pastry flour
1 t. baking powder
½ t. ground rosemary (or rue)
⅓ c. almonds, chopped
1 t. cinnamon
¼ c. sweet raisin wine or muscatel
¼ c. grape juice or new wine
2 T. honey or brown sugar
milk
filberts (or hazelnuts)

Mix flour with baking powder. Blend with rose- XI-4 mary (or rue), almonds, and cinnamon. In a measuring cup combine sweet wine with grape juice (or new wine) and honey. Add milk to make 1 cup of liquid. Mix with the dry ingredients and bake in a 9-inch round pan, in a 375°F oven for 30 minutes. Garnish with roasted chopped nuts and serve.

For a rich variation, lightly spread liquid honey over the warm cake, and decorate with chopped nuts. Then prick the surface here and there with a fork and drizzle 2–3 T. of wine into the cake.

> *A thousand sweets my hands have shaped*
> *For them alone the careful bees have toiled.*

> Martial, 14.222.

xi-3   ALITER DULCIA *Sweets* Strip the crusts from wheaten loaves and break the loaves into large pieces. Soak them in milk and fry in olive oil. Pour honey over them and serve.

xi-4   DULCIA PIPERATA *Peppered Sweets* ... put [pepper,] honey, wine, raisin wine, and rue. To this, add nut kernels and nuts and boiled spelt. [Bake and] add chopped roasted filberts, and serve.

xi-5   ALITER DULCIA *Sweets* Mix pepper, [chopped] nuts, honey, rue, and raisin wine. Cook in milk and pastry. Thicken with a little egg and bake. Pour honey on top, sprinkle [with filberts], and serve.

xi-6   ALITER DULCIA *Sweets* Take the finest wheat flour and cook it in boiling water until a stiff paste results. Spread this upon a platter [to cool]. When cold, cut it into the shape of sweetcakes and fry these in the best olive oil. Remove [them from the pan]. Pour honey over them, sprinkle with pepper and serve. The result is even better if [the wheat flour is cooked] not in water, but in milk.

xi-7   TYROPATINAM *Custard* Take sufficient milk for the size of the cake pan. Mix the milk with honey just as if you were making milk-food. Then put in five eggs to a pint of the honey-milk mixture, or three eggs to half a pint. Dissolve the eggs into the milk so that the resulting mixture is smooth. Strain into a clay vessel and cook over a slow fire. When the custard is firm, sprinkle with pepper and serve.

xi-8   OVA SPONGIA EX LACTE *Egg Sponge in Milk* Take four eggs, one half pint of milk, and an ounce of olive oil. [Beat and] dissolve so that the mixture is smooth. Into a shallow pan, pour a little oil and heat [until it bubbles]. Then add the ingredients which you have mixed. When the egg sponge is cooked on the bottom, turn it onto a round dish. Pour honey [on top], sprinkle with pepper, and serve.

❡In fact, this is Apicius' recipe for a simple omelette.

Rich Sweet Cakes

2 t. cinnamon
½ c. almonds, chopped
½ t. ground rosemary (or rue)
2 c. pastry flour
2 t. baking powder
¼ c. sweet raisin wine or muscatel
1 egg
4 T. honey or brown sugar
¼ c. milk
filberts or pecans

In a mixing bowl, put cinnamon, chopped almonds, and rosemary (or rue). Add flour, baking powder, and mix. Next, combine sweet wine, well beaten egg, honey, and milk. Blend and stir into the dry ingredients. Bake in a 375°F oven in a greased 9 inch round pan for 30 minutes. Pour a little honey on top of the finished cake, garnish with nuts, and serve.

XI-5

Roman Custard

2 c. milk
¼ c. honey or sugar
3 egg yolks
¼ t. nutmeg or cinnamon

To make the custard, first pour the milk into a bowl. Mix with honey and then scald in a saucepan. Remove from heat and add well beaten egg yolks. Add nutmeg or cinnamon and stir well. Pour into individual molds or into a baking dish. Bake uncovered at 325°F for 1 hour, or until set. Sprinkle with cinnamon or nutmeg, and serve.

XI-7

Honey Omelette

4 eggs
½ c. milk
4 T. butter or oil
2 T. liquid honey
cinnamon or nutmeg

Take the eggs, milk, and butter and combine. With butter, grease a shallow pan or skillet and then heat. When the melted butter begins to bubble, pour in the eggs and cook the omelette. Do not fold. Serve with honey poured on top and a sprinkling of cinnamon or nutmeg.

XI-8

For a Roman mushroom omelette, add ¼ cup of choice mushrooms prepared with coriander and wine (as in *Sautéed Mushrooms*, ms. 179).

XI-9   MELCAS   *Cheese Sweetened with Honey*   [Serve] with pepper and fish-pickle, or [with a seasoning of] salt, olive oil, and coriander.

The smoke of any hearth can age a cheese,
But those made in the street of the Velabriaus*
Have drunk the fire.

Martial, 13.126.

He who eats baked or boiled cheese will need no other poison.

Anthimus, 81.

BULBS

⁊ The Latin word used by Apicius is "bulbos," which I have translated here as onion, the edible bulb most commonly eaten in modern times. Two thousand years ago, however, the peoples of the Mediterranean were accustomed to using many other kinds of bulbs in cookery and in medicine, of which the squill was, in Pliny's words (19.30), "verum nobilissima" (truly the most renowned).

XII-1   [UNTITLED]   [*Onions*]   Serve with olive oil, fish-pickle, vinegar, and a little sprinkling of cumin.

XII-2   ALITER   [*Onions*]   Pound the onions and boil in water. Then fry in olive oil. Make the sauce [from these ingredients:] thyme, pennyroyal, pepper, oregano, honey, a little vinegar, and if you like, a little fish-pickle. Sprinkle with pepper and serve.

XII-3   ALITER   [*Onions*]   Take boiled onions, press them and put them into a dish. Then add thyme, oregano, honey, vinegar, boiled wine, dates, stock, and a little olive oil. [Blend.] Sprinkle with pepper and serve.[4]

XII-4   ALITER   [*Onions*]   Serve fried onions in wine sauce.

*The Velabrum was a street in the Rome of Apicius famous for its cheesemongers.

Fish-pickle Cheese Hors D'oeuvres

c. mild white farmer's cheese
2 T. honey
2 T. mild fish-pickle (see p. 305)
½ t. ground pepper

Coarsely grate the cheese, then combine with honey, XI-9 fish-pickle, and coarsely ground pepper.

Alternatively, combine the grated cheese with ⅛ t. salt, 3 t. olive oil, 1 t. coriander, and 2 T. honey.

Both versions should be chilled before serving them as appetizers. They are very good with thin, crisp breads or toast.

Onion Relish

3–4 onions, chopped
2 T. olive oil
¼ c. mild fish-pickle (see p. 305)
1 T. white wine vinegar or cider vinegar
¼ t. cumin

Mix the chopped onions with the olive oil, fish- XII-1 pickle, vinegar, and cumin. Serve as a relish.

Hot Onion Sauce

4 onions, chopped
2 T. olive oil or butter
Sauce:
½ t. thyme
¼ t. mint (or pennyroyal)
½ t. ground pepper
1 t. oregano
1 t. honey
2 t. white wine vinegar or cider vinegar
½ c. onion stock
1 T. fish-pickle (see p. 305)

Strew the onions in a frying pan. Combine all the XII-2 other ingredients and pour them over the onions. Heat and simmer for 5 minutes, or till onions are cooked.

This is a hot sauce and a fitting complement to beef, lamb, goat, etc.

ASH MUSHROOMS AND MUSHROOMS BOLETINE⁵

❡The high esteem in which the edible mushrooms of the genus *Boletus* were held by Apicius' contemporaries can be appreciated from the following epigram:

> *To send presents of silver and gold*
> *Or cloaks and togas*
> *Is easy;*
> *But giving some boleti . . .*
> *That's hard.*

Martial, 13.48.

XIII-1   FUNGI FARNEI *Ash Mushrooms* Boil [them in water]. Dry and then serve hot with fish-pickle mixed with pepper.

XIII-2   IN FUNGIS FARNEIS [*Sauce*] *for Ash Mushrooms* [Mix] pepper, boiled wine, vinegar, and olive oil.

> *Among those foods which are eaten thoughtlessly, I would justly place mushrooms. Although their flavor is excellent, mushrooms have fallen into disgrace by a shocking instance of murder: they were the means by which the Emperor Tiberius Claudius was poisoned by his wife Agrippina; and by doing this she gave to the world and to herself another poison, one worse than all the others: her own son, Nero.*

Pliny, 22.92.

XIII-3   ALITER FUNGI FARNEI *Ash Mushrooms* Boiled and served in salt, olive oil, wine, and chopped coriander.

XIII-4   BOLETOS FUNGOS *Mushrooms Boletine* [Prepare] in boiled wine with a bouquet of green coriander. When done, remove the coriander and serve.

XIII-5   BOLETOS ALITER *Mushrooms Boletine* Take the caps of these mushrooms and serve them with a sprinkling of fish-pickle or salt.

XIII-6   BOLETOS ALITER *Mushrooms Boletine* Take the stalks of the mushrooms and chop them. Pour into a fresh dish. Then add pepper, lovage, and a little honey. Blend with stock and a little olive oil.

Wine Sauce for Mushrooms

mushrooms
olive oil or butter
red wine
red wine vinegar
ground pepper

Slice mushrooms and sauté in olive oil or butter. Combine red wine and vinegar (1 t. vinegar to ½ c. wine), add to mushrooms, and finish cooking them. Serve with a sprinkling of pepper.

XIII-2

Sautéed Mushrooms

mushrooms
olive oil
red wine
pinch of salt
coriander

Sauté mushrooms in olive oil. Cook gently till done in red wine seasoned with a pinch of salt and ground coriander to taste.

XIII-3

Mushrooms with Coriander

mushrooms
¼ t. coriander to ½ c. boiled
wine (see p. 306)

Use a small saucepan and pour in just enough boiled wine to cover the mushrooms. For each half cup of wine use ¼ t. coriander. Cook mushrooms gently in the wine and coriander.

To be utterly authentic, the coriander should be freshly picked and tied into a bouquet, allowing the mushrooms to absorb the seasoning of the coriander. Discard the bouquet before serving.

XIII-4

Mushrooms with a Rich Sauce

¼ lb. choice mushrooms

Sauce:
¼ t. ground pepper
½ t. celery seed (or lovage)
1 t. honey
2 T. mushroom liquid or
stock
2 T. olive oil or butter

Select choice mushrooms and slice them parallel to the stems. Cook them for three minutes in the following sauce.

For the sauce, grind together pepper and celery seed (or lovage). Combine with honey, mushroom liquid, and olive oil or butter. Bring to a boil, lower heat, and finish cooking with the mushrooms.

Alternatively, the mushrooms can be served raw with the hot sauce poured on top.

XIII-6

TRUFFLES

℄ The truffle was esteemed by gourmets as highly in the ancient world as it is today.

XIV-I   [UNTITLED] [*Truffles*]   Peel the truffles, boil, sprinkle with salt, and transfix with twigs. Grill lightly and put in a pan in olive oil, stock, boiled wine, wine, pepper, and honey. After cooking, thicken [the sauce] with starch. Arrange the truffles [in a dish] and serve [in the sauce].

XIV-2   ALITER TUBERA   *Truffles*   Boil them, sprinkle with salt, infix with twigs, and grill lightly. In a saucepan, put stock, fresh olive oil, boiled wine, a little wine, roughly ground peppercorns, and a little honey. Boil and thicken [the sauce] with starch, and then puncture the truffles in order that they may drink up the sauce. Take out the twigs. Remove when the truffles have absorbed as much of the sauce as they can. Serve. If you wish, roll the same truffles in pork sausage skin, roast, and serve in this way.

XIV-3   ALITER TUBERA   *Truffles*   Simmer in wine sauce, pepper, lovage, coriander, rue, stock, honey, wine, and a little oil.

XIV-4   ALITER TUBERA   *Truffles*   Simmer [the truffles] in pepper, mint, rue, honey, oil, and a little wine. Serve.

> *Our tender crowns burst from nourishing soil*
> *Of earth's fruits second to mushrooms only,*
> *   We the truffles.*

Martial, 13.50.

XIV-5   ALITER TUBERA   *Truffles*   Boil the truffles with leeks and then serve [in a sauce of] salt, pepper, chopped coriander, unmixed wine, and a little olive oil.

XIV-6   ALITER TUBERA   *Truffles*   [Mix] pepper, cumin, silphium, mint, celery, rue, honey, and vinegar or wine, salt or fish-pickle, and a little olive oil.

Roasted Truffles in Wine

truffles
salt
1 c. veal stock
2 t. olive oil
¼ t. ground pepper
1 t. honey
½ c. white wine
flour

Wash, season with salt, and brown truffles in the oven. Then slice and simmer for 5 minutes in a mixture of stock, olive oil, pepper, honey, and wine. Thicken the sauce with flour, and serve.

Alternatively, after browning the truffles, puncture them with a fork, then simmer 5 minutes in the sauce.

XIV-1,
XIV-2

Lovage Sauce for Truffles

fresh truffles
Sauce:
¼ t. ground pepper
½ t. celery seed (or lovage)
¼ rosemary (or pinch of rue)
1 c. veal stock
½ c. white wine
2 t. olive oil
flour

Grind together pepper, celery seed (or lovage), and rosemary (or rue). Combine with stock, wine, and olive oil. Bring the sauce to a boil, then simmer together with sliced or punctured truffles for 5 minutes, and serve.

XIV-3

Rosemary Mint Sauce for Truffles

fresh truffles
Sauce:
¼ t. ground pepper
sprig of mint
pinch of rosemary (or rue)
1 t. honey
1 T. olive oil
½ c. white wine

Combine pepper, fresh mint, rosemary (or rue), with honey, olive oil, and wine. Bring to a boil, then simmer truffles in this sauce for 10 minutes, and serve.

XIV-4

THE EGYPTIAN BEAN

℄ The Egyptian bean (commonly known today as taro root) was regarded as a delicacy by the Romans of Apicius' day, and they ate not only the tubers but also the beans, the stalks, and the stems. The tuber, however, was considered the choice part then as now.

XV

IN COLOCASIO   *[Sauce] for Egyptian Bean*   [Mix] pepper, cumin, rue, honey, stock, and a little olive oil. When it has boiled, thicken [the sauce] with starch.

SNAILS

Fulvius Lippinus began the practice of breeding snails in the district of Tarquinii [now Trachina] a little before the civil war fought by Pompey the Great [50–48 B.C.]. He separated the different kinds of snails so that each had its own vivarium in which to breed: the white snails found in the district of Reate; the Illyrian snails famous for their extraordinary size; the African snails characterized by their fertility; and the African Sun snails known for their excellent quality.

Lippinus also invented a technique of fattening them with must and spelt and other kinds of food so that the fattened snails could satisfy a feast. Indeed, Marcus Varro wrote that this passion for the art of breeding snails reached the stage where a single shell could contain twenty pints.

Pliny, 9.82.

XVI-1

COCHLEAS LACTE PASTAS *Snails Fed with Milk* Take the snails and wipe them off with a sponge. Remove the membranes so that the snails may emerge [from their shells]. For one day, put them in a vessel with milk and salt, and then for a few days afterwards, only with milk. Cleanse them of their dross every hour. When the snails have become too large for their shells, fry them in olive oil. Add a little wine sauce and serve. Similarly, snails can be fattened on meat.

Truffles with Leeks

2 oz. truffles
3 heads of leeks
1 c. water

Chop leeks into 1 inch segments and combine with washed, sliced truffles. Place in a pot with water and bring to a boil, then drain and reserve stock.   XIV-5

Sauce:
¼ t. salt
¼ t. ground pepper
½ t. coriander
½ c. white wine
2 t. olive oil

Meanwhile, combine salt, pepper, coriander, and add stock from the pan. Stir in wine and olive oil. Bring this sauce to a boil, then add leeks and truffles to it, and simmer for 5 to 10 minutes more.

Spiced Celery Sauce for Truffles

a small quantity of fresh truffles

Wash, then slice or puncture truffles with a fork.   XIV-6

Sauce:
¼ t. ground pepper
pinch each of cumin, fennel, and rosemary (or rue)
sprig of mint
½ c. chopped celery
1 t. white wine vinegar or cider vinegar
½ c. white wine
dash of salt or 2 t. fish-pickle (see p. 305)
2 t. olive oil
1 c. vegetable stock

For the sauce, grind together pepper, cumin, fennel, rosemary (or rue), and mint. Add celery, vinegar, wine, salt or fish-pickle, olive oil, and stock. Add to the truffles, bring to a boil, and simmer together for 5 minutes, then serve.

Sautéed Snails in Fennel Sauce

XVI-2

12–15 snails
1 c. veal stock
pinch of fennel
¼ t. ground pepper
1 T. olive oil

Remove the snails from their shells. Lightly sauté in olive oil seasoned with salt. Then cover with the following sauce and simmer till snails are done.

For the sauce, mix stock, fennel, pepper, and olive oil, and combine with snails.

Snails Poached with Cumin

XVI-3

12–15 snails
1 c. veal stock, or ½ c. white wine and ½ c. veal stock
¼ t. ground pepper
¼ t. cumin

Remove the snails from their shells and place in a cookpot. Add stock and seasonings. Bring to a boil and simmer together till done.

Eggs Poached in Wine Sauce

XVII-1

4 chicken or duck eggs
2 T. chopped onion
1 c. red wine
¼ c. oregano
½ t. celery seed (or lovage)
salt, to taste
ground pepper, to taste

Grind together oregano, celery seed (or lovage), and pepper. Combine with onion, wine, and salt, and pour into a pan. Bring to a boil, then simmer. Carefully add eggs and poach according to taste.

Roman Scrambled Eggs

1 T. butter
4 eggs
3 T. chicken stock
3 T. white wine
⅛ t. fennel
ground pepper, to taste

Melt butter in a pan. Combine eggs with chicken XVII-2 stock, wine, fennel, and pepper. Then pour into pan and scramble the mixture till done.

Sauce for Soft-boiled, Poached, or Scrambled Eggs

½ t. ground pepper
½ t. celery seed (or lovage)
1 T. finely chopped almonds
¼ c. mild fish-pickle (see
p. 305)
1 t. honey
½ c. chicken stock

Grind together pepper, celery seed, and almonds. XVII-3 Combine with fish-pickle, honey, and stock. Bring to a boil and serve with cooked eggs.

XVI-2   COCHLEAS *Snails* Grill them with pure salt and olive oil. Pour [a sauce of] laser, stock, pepper, and olive oil [over the cooked snails].

XVI-3   COCHLEAS ASSAS *Poached Snails.* [As the snails are cooking] pour [a seasoning of] stock, pepper, and cumin over them continually.

XVI-4   ALITER COCHLEAS *Snails* Immerse live snails in milk and wheat flour. When they have fattened, cook.

EGGS

℟ Eggs were customarily served at the "gustatio," or hors d'oeuvre courses at the beginning of a Roman dinner.

XVII-1   OVA FRIXA *Fried Eggs* [Fry them in] wine sauce.

When a tide of white flows around saffron yolks,
    Season the eggs with the liquor of Spanish mackerel.
                                    Martial, 13.40.

XVII-2   OVA ELIXA *Boiled Eggs* [Serve in a dressing of] stock, olive oil, and unmixed wine, or [season with] stock [mixed with] pepper and laser.

When the young Julia Augusta was pregnant with Tiberius
Caesar by Nero, she very much wanted to give birth to a boy and
so she made use of a method of divination used by young women.
She kept an egg warm in her bosom, and when she had to set it
aside she consigned it to a nurse so that the warmth would not be
interrupted . . . and nor was this method of divination false.
                                    Pliny, 10.76.

XVII-3   IN OVIS HAPALIS *Of Soft-boiled Eggs* [Garnish with] pepper, lovage, soaked nut kernels, pine nuts, honey, vinegar, and stock.

BOOK VII OF APICIUS,
THE GOURMET,
— IS ENDED —

Quadrupeds

OF WILD BOAR

❡ Apicius prepared wild boar in a way similar to suckling pig and pork except that the wild boar meat was marinated for one day in water, salt, and cumin. Although wild boars live to considerable age, only the young animals (up to a year) were cooked and served whole.

1-1   APER ITA CONDITUR *Wild Boar* Clean the meat with a sponge. Sprinkle it with salt and ground cumin and let it remain this way [overnight]. On the next day, roast it in the oven. When cooked, [serve in a sauce of] ground pepper, gravy from the boar, honey, stock, boiled wine, and raisin wine.

1-2   ALITER IN APRO *Wild Boar* Boil in sea water with a sprig of laurel until the meat is soft. Remove the skin. Serve with salt, mustard, and vinegar.

1-3   ALITER IN APRO *Wild Boar* Grind pepper, lovage, oregano, seeded myrtle berries, coriander, and onions. Pour honey, wine, stock, and a little olive oil [over these ingredients, and blend]. Simmer and thicken [the sauce] with starch. Roast the wild boar in the oven and then pour the sauce [over it]. This recipe will serve for all kinds of wild game.

1-4   IN APRUM ASSUM IURA FERVENTIA FACIES SIC *Roast Wild Boar in Hot Sauce* [Mix] pepper and fried cumin, celery seed, mint, thyme, savory, saffron, roasted small nuts or roasted almonds, honey, wine, one-eighth of a pint of stock, and a little olive oil. [Pour this sauce, boiling hot, over the roast and serve.]

1-5   ALITER IN APRUM ASSUM IURA FERVENTIA *Another Hot Sauce for Roast Wild Boar* [Mix] pepper, lovage, celery seed, mint, thyme, roasted nuts, wine, vinegar, stock, and a little olive oil. When the juices from the meat are bubbling in the roasting pan, pour in the ball of ground seasonings from the mortar, adding a bouquet garni of dried onion and rue. Stir. If you wish to make [this sauce] richer, thicken it with egg whites, stirring gradually. Serve [the meat] with a sprinkle of ground pepper.

Roast Pork or Boar with Cumin in Wine

4–6 lb. boar or pork roast

Marinade:
1 t. salt
water
1 t. myrtle berries, or juniper berries, or cloves
2 t. peppercorns
2 t. cumin

Sauce:
2 t. honey
½ c. chicken or pork stock
¼ c. red wine
½ t. ground pepper
roasting pan juices

Wipe the roast dry. Immerse for 24 hours in a marinade of salt, water, myrtle berries, peppercorns, and cumin. Roast uncovered in a 350°F oven for 30 minutes per pound.

To make the sauce, combine pepper, honey, stock, and pan juices. Bring to a boil and simmer for 30 minutes. Serve with the slices of meat.

Alternatively, braise the meat slowly in stock seasoned to taste with pepper. One hour before it is done, drain the pan, pour the sauce over the roast and finish cooking, spooning the sauce over the meat from time to time.

If you like, sprinkle additional cumin over the roast as it cooks.

1-1

Coriander Sauce for Pork, Beef, and Venison

4–6 lbs. roast meat

Sauce:
½ t. ground pepper
2 t. celery seed (or lovage)
1 t. oregano
3–4 dried myrtle berries, or juniper berries, or cloves
1 t. green coriander
2 T. chopped onion
1 t. honey
1 c. pork or beef stock
½ c. red wine
1 T. olive oil or butter

In a mortar, grind together pepper, celery seed (or lovage), oregano, dried myrtle berries, and coriander. Add chopped onion, to taste. Blend with honey, stock, red wine, and olive oil or butter. Bring to a boil and simmer for 30 minutes. Then pour over the roast meat slices.

Alternatively, finish cooking the roast in the sauce for ½ hour.

1-3

I-6   IUS IN APRUM ELIXUM *Sauce for Boiled Wild Boar* [Combine] pepper, lovage, cumin, silphium, oregano, nuts, dates, honey, mustard, vinegar, stock, and olive oil.

I-7   IUS FRIGIDUM IN APRUM ELIXUM *Cold Sauce for Boiled Wild Boar* [Combine] pepper, caraway, lovage, fried coriander seed, aniseed, celery seed, thyme, oregano, shallots, honey, vinegar, mustard, stock, and olive oil.

I-8   ALITER IUS FRIGIDUM IN APRUM ELIXUM *Another Cold Sauce for Boiled Wild Boar* [Combine] pepper, lovage, cumin, aniseed, thyme, oregano, a little silphium, more of colewort seed, wine, a few green herbs, onions, Pontic hazelnuts or roasted almonds, dates, honey, vinegar, a little unmixed wine, boiled wine for color, stock, and olive oil.

I-9   ALITER IN APRO *For Wild Boar* Combine pepper, lovage, oregano, celery seed, laser root, cumin, fennel seed, rue, stock, wine, and raisin wine. Bring [this sauce] to the boil. When it has boiled, thicken with starch. Coat the inside and outside of the boar with sauce and serve.

I-10   PERNA APRUNA ITA IMPLETUR TERENTINA *Filled Gammon of Wild Boar Terentine* With a knife, cut the joint carefully so as to separate the skin from the flesh and so that the meat can be completely covered by sauce poured from a little horn. Now grind pepper, laurel berry, and rue. If you wish, add laser. Add the best stock, boiled wine, and [a few] drops of fresh olive oil. When it is stuffed, sew the opening through which it was stuffed back into place and put the meat into a pan. Boil in sea water with tender shoots of laurel and anise.

> *My cook wants a mountain of peppercorns*
> *And then he'll waste my best Falernian wine*
> *To make his precious fish-pickle recipe*
> *And now that enormous boar he's bought*
> *Won't even fit the stove: by the father of the gods*
> *I swear he's trying to bankrupt me.*

Martial, 7.27.

Cumin Sauce for Roast Pork

4–6 lb. roast pork

Sauce:

1 t. coarsely ground
pepper (or more)

1 t. cumin

1 t. celery seed

½ t. chopped fresh mint

½ t. savory

pinch of saffron

¼ c. ground roasted pine
nuts or almonds

1 c. pork or beef stock

2 t. olive oil or butter

In a mortar, grind peppercorns and cumin. Add celery seed, chopped fresh mint, savory, saffron, and roasted pine nuts or almonds. Blend with stock and olive oil or butter. Bring the sauce to a boil, simmer for five minutes, pour over the roast, and serve.

1-4

Hot Sauce for Roast Pork

4–6 lb. roast pork

Sauce:

½ t. coarsely ground pepper

1 t. lovage (or celery seed)

1 t. celery seed

1 t. chopped fresh mint

1 t. thyme

¼ c. grated or finely
chopped almonds

½ c. red wine

1 t. wine vinegar or
cider vinegar

1 c. pork or beef stock

2 t. olive oil or butter

2 T. chopped onion

½ t. rosemary (or rue)

(2 egg whites)

In a mortar, grind pepper, lovage, celery seed, chopped mint, thyme, and nuts. Blend with wine, vinegar, stock, and olive oil or butter. Add this sauce to the juices in the roasting pan, then add the chopped onion, and stir. Bring to a boil and simmer for 25 minutes, then serve with the roast meat.

For a richer texture, gradually add two egg whites to the sauce and stir gently. Serve with a sprinkling of pepper.

1-5

Sweet Sauce for Roast Pork

1-6

4–6 lb. roast pork
Sauce:
½ t. coarsely ground pepper
1–2 t. lovage (or celery seed)
½ t. cumin
⅛ t. fennel
1 t. oregano
⅛ c. pine nuts, almonds, or pistachio nuts
⅛ c. chopped dates (or sultanas)
2 t. honey
¼ t. mustard seed
1 t. wine or cider vinegar
1 c. pork or beef stock
2 t. olive oil or butter

In a mortar, grind pepper, lovage (or celery seed), cumin, fennel, and oregano. Combine with finely chopped nuts, dates, honey, mustard seed, vinegar, stock, and olive oil or butter. Bring to a boil and simmer for 25 minutes, then serve with the cooked meat.

Alternatively, braise the meat in it for the last 25 minutes.

Cold Sauce for Roast Pork or Ham

1-7

4–6 lb. roast pork or ham
Sauce:
½ t. ground pepper
pinch of caraway
1 t. lovage (or celery seed)
1 t. coriander
pinch of aniseed
1 t. celery seed
½ t. thyme
¼ t. oregano
1 T. shallots or onions, chopped
1 t. honey
1 t. wine or cider vinegar
⅛ t. mustard seed
1 c. pork, chicken, or beef stock
2 t. olive oil or butter

In a mortar, grind pepper, caraway, lovage, coriander, aniseed, celery seed, thyme, and oregano. Add to shallots or onions. Blend with honey, vinegar, mustard seed, stock, and olive oil or butter. Bring to a boil, then simmer for 25 minutes. Chill, and serve with slices of meat. Or serve hot, if you wish.

Cold Wine Sauce for Roast Pork or Ham

4–6 lb. roast pork or ham

Sauce:
½ t. ground pepper
1 t. celery seed (or lovage)
½ t. cumin
½ t. thyme
½ t. oregano
pinch of fennel
⅛ t. mustard (or colewort seed)
½ c. red wine
½ t. rosemary, and of rue, if available
2 T. chopped onion
⅛ c. roasted hazelnuts or almonds, finely chopped
⅛ c. dates, finely chopped
1 t. honey
1 t. wine vinegar or cider vinegar
1 T. boiled red wine (see p. 306)
1 c. pork or beef stock
2 t. olive oil or butter

In a mortar, grind pepper, celery seed (or lovage), cumin, thyme, oregano, fennel, and mustard (or colewort) seed. Combine with wine, rosemary (and rue), onion, chopped nuts and dates. Blend with honey, vinegar, boiled wine, stock, and olive oil or butter. Bring to a boil, then simmer for 25 minutes. Chill, and serve with roast pork or ham. Or serve hot, if you wish.

1-8

Sweet Wine Sauce for Roast Pork

1-9   4–6 *lb. roast pork*

Sauce:
½ *t. ground pepper*
1 *t. lovage (or celery seed)*
1 *t. oregano*
1 *t. celery seed*
½ *t. cumin*
pinch of fennel seed
½ *t. rosemary (or rue)*
1 *c. pork or beef stock*
¼ *c. red wine*
¼ *c. sweet raisin wine or muscatel*
flour

In a mortar, grind pepper, lovage, oregano, celery seed, cumin, fennel seed, and rosemary (or rue). Blend with stock, red wine, and sweet wine. Bring the sauce to a boil, simmer to blend flavors, and thicken with flour. Coat the sides of the roast with the sauce, and serve.

Alternatively, baste the roasting meat in the sauce for the last hour of cooking, then thicken sauce, and serve.

Ham in Terentine Sauce

1-10   4 *lb. ham with bone in*

Sauce:
½ *t. coarsely ground pepper*
4–5 *t. cloves (or juniper or laurel berries)*
½ *t. rosemary (or rue)*
pinch of fennel
¼ *c. pork or beef stock*
¼ *c. red wine*
1 *t. olive oil or butter*

Simmer ham for 1 hour in water, changing to fresh water after 30 minutes. Drain, cool meat, and separate skin from the flesh, leaving it attached at the small end. Score the ham, then season it with the reduced sauce below. Tie skin back in place with string, and bake in a 350°F oven for 2½ hours.

To make the sauce, grind together pepper, cloves or juniper berries, and rosemary (or rue). Add a pinch of fennel. Combine with stock, red wine, and olive oil or butter. Bring to a boil, simmer to reduce, and use as described above.

OF VENISON

This animal does not suffer from illnesses of fever, and even is itself a preventative for this dread disease. We understand that lately certain noble ladies have become accustomed to tasting venison every day in the morning, and in their old age have been free from fevers. But they consider this cure to be valid only if the deer is slain by a single wound.

Pliny, 8.50.

IUS IN CERVUM *Sauce for Venison* Grind pepper, lovage, caraway, oregano, celery seed, laser root, and fennel seed, and pound [them in a mortar]. Now pour stock, wine, raisin wine, and a little olive oil. Bring [the sauce] to the boil. When it has boiled, thicken with starch. Coat the inside and outside of the cooked venison [with this sauce] and serve.   II-I

This recipe may be used in the preparation of all antlered deer and other kinds of woodland game.

ALITER [*Venison*] Boil the meat and then roast it a little. [For the sauce] mix pepper, lovage, caraway, celery seed, and pour honey, vinegar, stock, and olive oil. Heat [slowly] and then thicken with starch. Pour over the venison [and serve].   II-2

IUS IN CERVO *Sauce for Venison* [Combine] pepper, lovage, shallots, oregano, nuts, dates, honey, stock, mustard, vinegar, and olive oil. [Simmer and pour over the meat.]   II-3

CERVINAE CONDITURA *Sauce for Venison* [Combine] pepper, cumin, green herbs, parsley, onions, rue, honey, stock, mint, raisin wine, boiled wine, and a little olive oil. Bring [the sauce] to the boil and then thicken with starch.   II-4

IURA FERVENTIA IN CERVO *Hot Sauce for Venison* [Combine] pepper, lovage, parsley, cumin, roasted pine nuts or almonds, honey, vinegar, wine, a little olive oil, and stock. Stir.   II-5

EMBAMMA IN CERVINAM ASSAM *Marinade for Roast Venison* [Combine] pepper, spikenard, bay leaf, celery seed, dried onion, green rue, honey, vinegar, stock, dates, raisins, and olive oil.   II-6

Lean, dry venison can be wrapped in bacon or larded. Steaks are first browned in olive oil or butter, then finished in one of the savory sauces below. Cooked roasts may be served with the sauces.

Oregano Sauce for Venison Steaks or Roast

II-I *4 lbs. roast venison or steaks*
Sauce:
¼ t. ground pepper
1 t. celery seed (or lovage)
pinch of caraway
½ t. oregano
¼ t. ginger
pinch of fennel seed
1 c. venison, beef, or chicken stock
¼ c. red wine
2 t. olive oil or butter
flour

In a mortar, grind pepper, celery seed (or lovage), caraway, oregano, ginger, and fennel seed. Blend with stock, wine, and olive oil or butter. Bring the sauce to a boil, then simmer slowly for 25 minutes to reduce, and serve over the cooked venison. Or thicken with flour and serve.

Alternatively, finish the venison steaks in the sauce for a few minutes before serving.

Simple Sauce for Venison

II-2 *4 lbs. roast venison or steaks*
Sauce:
½ t. ground pepper
1 t. lovage (or celery seed)
pinch of caraway
1 t. celery seed
1 t. honey
1 t. wine vinegar or cider vinegar
1 c. venison, beef, or chicken stock
2 t. olive oil or butter
flour

In a mortar, grind peppercorns, lovage, caraway, and celery seed. Blend with honey, vinegar, venison stock, and olive oil or butter. Bring to a boil, then simmer slowly for 25 minutes, and serve with roast venison or with steaks.

Thicken sauce with flour, if you wish, before serving with meat.

Nut Sauce for Venison

4 lbs. roast venison or steaks
Sauce:
½ t. ground pepper
½ t. cumin
¼ c. onions or shallots, chopped
¼ t. oregano
⅛ c. roasted almonds, chopped
⅛ c. dates, chopped
1 t. honey
c. venison, beef, or chicken stock
¼ c. red wine
¼ t. mustard seed
1 t. wine or cider vinegar
2 t. olive oil or butter

Combine pepper, cumin, chopped onions or shallots, and oregano. Add to finely chopped almonds and dates. Blend with honey, stock, wine, mustard seed, vinegar, and olive oil or butter. Bring to a boil, then simmer for 25 minutes. Serve with the cooked venison.

II-3

Sweet Cumin Sauce for Venison

4 lbs. roast venison or steaks
Sauce:
¼ t. ground pepper
½ t. cumin
¼ t. basil
¼ t. rue (or rosemary)
2 t. parsley
½ t. rosemary
½ t. mint
2 T. chopped onion
1 t. honey
c. venison, beef, or chicken stock
¼ c. sweet raisin wine or muscatel
2 t. olive oil or butter
flour

In a mortar, grind pepper, cumin, rosemary, basil, parsley, rue (or rosemary), and mint. Blend with onion, honey, stock, sweet wine, and olive oil or butter. Bring the sauce to a boil, simmer for 25 minutes over low heat, and thicken with flour before serving with the cooked venison.

II-4

Pine Nut Sauce for Venison

II-5   4 lbs. roast venison or steaks

Sauce:

½ t. ground pepper

1 t. celery seed (or lovage)

2 t. parsley

1 t. cumin

¼ c. pine nuts or
almonds, chopped

1 t. honey

1 t. wine or cider vinegar

½ c. red wine

2 t. olive oil or butter

1 c. venison, beef, or chicken stock

In a mortar, grind pepper, celery seed (or lovage), parsley, and cumin. Add to nuts, then blend with honey, vinegar, wine, olive oil or butter, and stock. Bring to a boil, simmer for 25 minutes, then pour over cooked venison, and serve.

Marinade for Venison Pot Roast

II-6   4 lb. venison pot roast

Marinade:

1 t. ground pepper

1 t. crushed bay leaf

1 t. crushed spikenard (or
bay leaf)

1 t. celery seed

1 medium onion, finely chopped

1 t. rosemary (or rue)

1 T. honey

2 T. sharp vinegar

3 dates, finely chopped

¼ c. raisins

1 T. olive oil

2 c. venison or beef stock

Combine pepper, crushed bay leaf and spikenard, celery seed, chopped onion, rosemary (or rue), honey, vinegar, dates, raisins, olive oil, and stock. Marinate, covered, for 8 hours, basting occasionally.

Cook the pot roast in some of the marinade in a covered pot until done.

Plum Sauce For Roast Venison

4 lbs. roast venison
Sauce:
½ t. ground pepper
1 t. lovage
2 t. parsley
¼ c. pitted plums, or
damsons (or prunes)
½ c. red wine
1 t. honey
1 t. wine vinegar or
cider vinegar
1 c. venison, beef, or
chicken stock
2 t. olive oil
1 T. chives
½ t. savory

In a mortar, grind pepper, celery seed (or lovage), and parsley. Soak plums in wine, and combine with the herbs, honey, vinegar, stock, and olive oil or butter. Stir in the chives and savory. Bring the sauce to a boil, simmer and reduce for 25 minutes. Serve with the roast venison.

II-7

Mixed Spice Sauce for Venison Steaks or Cutlets

2 lbs. venison steaks or cutlets
Sauce:
¼ t. ground pepper
1 t. celery seed (or lovage)
pinch of caraway
½ t. cumin
2 t. parsley
½ t. rosemary (or rue)
1 t. honey
½ t. mustard seed
1 t. red wine vinegar
1 c. venison, beef or
chicken stock
2 t. olive oil

In a mortar, grind pepper, celery seed (or lovage), caraway, cumin, parsley, and rosemary (or rue). Blend with honey, mustard seed, vinegar, stock, and olive oil or butter. Bring to a boil and simmer for 25 minutes to reduce. Pour over the cooked meat and serve.

III-1

II-7   ALITER IN CERVUM ASSUM IURA FERVENTIA   *Another Hot Sauce for Roast Venison*   [Combine] pepper, lovage, parsley, damsons soaked [in water or wine], wine, honey, vinegar, stock, and a little olive oil. Stir [with a bouquet of] chives and savory. [Pour the boiling sauce over the meat and serve.]

OF ROEBUCK*

Sooner will roes mate with Apulian wolves
Than Pholoe sin with her shameful lover.

Horace, 1.33.

III-1   IUS IN CAPREA   *Sauce for Roebuck*   [Combine] pepper, lovage, caraway, cumin, parsley, rue seed, honey, mustard, vinegar, stock, and olive oil.

III-2   IUS IN CAPREA ASSA   *Sauce for Roast Roebuck*   [Combine] pepper, green herbs, rue, onion, honey, stock, raisin wine, and a little olive oil. Bring [the sauce] to the boil and [then thicken with] starch.

III-3   ALITER IUS IN CAPREA   *Another Sauce for Roebuck*   [Combine] pepper, green herbs, parsley, a little oregano, rue, stock, honey, raisin wine, and some olive oil. Thicken with starch.

*A small Eurasian deer (*Capreolus capraea*).

Thick Sauce for Venison Steaks or Cutlets

venison steaks or cutlets

Sauce:
¼ t. ground pepper
¼ t. rosemary
¼ t. basil
pinch of rue, if available
1 small chopped onion
1 t. honey
1 c. venison, beef, or
chicken stock
½ c. sweet raisin wine or
muscatel
2 t. olive oil
flour

Marinate the meat for 8 hours in the *Marinade for*   III-2
Venison Pot Roast. Then cook the meat, pour the
following sauce over it, and serve.

For the sauce, first grind together pepper, rosemary, basil (and rue). Add to onion. Blend with
honey, stock, sweet wine, and olive oil. Bring the
sauce to a boil, simmer for 25 minutes and thicken
with flour before serving over the meat.

Basil-Oregano Sauce for Venison Steaks or Cutlets

venison steaks or cutlets

Sauce:
¼ t. ground pepper
½ t. rosemary
¼ t. basil
2 t. parsley
1 t. oregano
pinch of rue, if available
1 c. venison, beef, or
chicken stock
1 t. honey
½ c. sweet raisin wine or
muscatel
2 t. olive oil
flour

In a mortar, grind pepper with rosemary, basil,   III-3
parsley, oregano (and rue). Blend with stock, honey,
sweet wine, and olive oil. Bring the sauce to a boil,
simmer for 25 minutes to reduce, and thicken with
flour before serving.

OF WILD SHEEP

IV-1 IUS IN OVIFERO FERVENS *Hot Sauce for Wild Sheep* [In a mortar, mix] pepper, lovage, cumin, dried mint, thyme, and laser. Moisten [these seasonings] with wine. [Now blend with] damsons soaked [in water or wine], honey, wine, stock, vinegar, some raisin wine for color, and olive oil. Stir with a bouquet of oregano and dried mint.

IV-2 IUS IN VENATIONIBUS OMNIBUS ELIXIS ET ASSIS *Sauce for All Kinds of Wild Game Whether Boiled or Roasted* Take eight scruples of pepper and six scruples each of rue, lovage, celery seed, juniper [berry], thyme, and dried mint. Add three scruples of pennyroyal. Grind all of these seasonings assiduously until they become a very fine powder. Put this into a small vessel together with a fitting quantity of honey. Serve with fish-pickle-and-vinegar.

IV-3 IUS FRIGIDUM IN OVIFERO *Cold Sauce for Wild Sheep* [Combine] pepper, lovage, thyme, fried cumin, roasted pine nuts, honey, vinegar, stock, and olive oil. Sprinkle with pepper [and serve].

BEEF AND VEAL

V-1 VITELLINA FRICTA *Fried Veal [Steak]* [Combine] pepper, lovage, celery seed, cumin, oregano, dried onion, raisins, honey, vinegar, stock, wine, olive oil, and boiled wine.

V-2 VITULINAM SIVE BUBULAM CUM PORRIS VEL CYDONEIS VEL CEPIS VEL COLOCASIIS *Veal or Beef with Leeks or Quince-apples or Onions or Egyptian Beans* [Prepare with] stock, pepper, laser, and a little olive oil.

V-3 IN VITULINAM ELIXAM *[Sauce] for Boiled Veal* [In a mortar] grind pepper, lovage, caraway, and celery seed. [Over this] pour honey, vinegar, stock, and olive oil. Simmer. Thicken [the sauce] with starch, pour over [boiled] veal [and serve].

V-4 ALITER IN VITULINAM ELIXAM *Another [Sauce] for Boiled Veal* [Combine] pepper, lovage, fennel seed, oregano, nuts, dates, honey, vinegar, [veal] stock, mustard, and olive oil.

Hot Mint Sauce for Roast Mutton

3–4 lbs. roast mutton

Roast the mutton and serve it with this sauce.

IV-1

Sauce:
dash of ground pepper
½ t. celery seed (or lovage)
⅛ t. cumin
3 sprigs fresh mint, (or heaped T. dried mint)
¼ t. oregano
pinch of thyme
pinch of fennel
¼ c. red wine
⅛ c. damsons or plums, finely chopped
2 T. honey
⅓ c. mild vinegar
olive oil

For the sauce, first grind together pepper, celery seed (or lovage), cumin, finely chopped mint, oregano, thyme, and fennel. Moisten with a little red wine. Blend with damsons, honey, vinegar, and a few drops of olive oil. Bring to a boil, and simmer for 25 minutes. Serve with the roast mutton.

Cold Sauce for Roast Mutton

3–4 lbs. roast mutton

Roast the mutton and serve it with this cold sauce.

IV-3

Sauce:
¼ t. ground pepper
1 t. celery seed (or lovage)
½ t. thyme
⅛ t. cumin
¼ c. roasted pine nuts or almonds, finely chopped or grated
2 t. honey
1 t. vinegar
1 c. mutton or beef stock
2 t. olive oil

Grind together pepper, celery seed (or lovage), thyme, and cumin. Add nuts, honey, vinegar, stock, and olive oil. Bring to a boil and simmer for 25 minutes. Use when it has cooled. Or serve hot, if you wish, with the roast meat.

Veal in Sweet and Sour Onion Sauce

V-1

1 lb. ¾" veal steak

Sauce:
¼ t. ground pepper
1 t. lovage (or celery seed)
¼ t. celery seed
¼ t. cumin
½ t. oregano
1 medium onion,
finely chopped
2 T. raisins
1 t. honey
1 t. red wine vinegar
¼ c. red wine
2 t. olive oil
½ c. veal juices or beef stock

Sauté the meat lightly in olive oil. Skim the fat from the frying pan, preserve juices, and finish cooking in the following sauce.

For the sauce, first grind together pepper, lovage (or celery seed), celery seed, cumin, and oregano. Add chopped onion, raisins, honey, vinegar, red wine, olive oil, and veal juices. Blend. Pour the sauce into the pan with the veal, cover, and cook very gently for 1 hour.

Veal with Leeks, Apples, and Broad Beans

V-2

1 lb. veal or stewing beef, cubed
2 T. flour
1 t. ginger
½ t. ground pepper
2 T. olive oil
1 c. beef or vegetable stock
1 onion, chopped
1 c. leeks, chopped
3 medium cooking apples, peeled and chopped
1 c. broad beans
ginger
mild ground pepper

Roll 1-inch cubes of veal in flour, ginger, and pepper. Sear in olive oil. Put the browned meat in a covered baking dish and add stock. Cook in a 300°F oven for 40 minutes, then add onions, leeks, apples, and broad beans. Continue cooking for 40 minutes more or until beans are done.

Before serving, stir the apples into the liquid to make a thick sauce, and sprinkle a little more ginger or mild pepper over the dish.

Caraway Sauce for Baked Veal

1 lb. thick veal cutlets
olive oil or butter
½ t. ground pepper
½ c. beef stock or water

Trim fat from the veal. Brown cutlets in olive oil v-3 or butter, then place in a covered baking dish. Add stock seasoned with pepper, and cook for 1 hour in a 325°F oven, or until done.

Sauce:
½ t. ground pepper
1 t. lovage (or celery seed)
large pinch of caraway
1 t. celery seed
2 T. honey
dash of vinegar
1 c. veal or beef stock
2 t. olive oil or butter
flour

For the sauce, grind together pepper, lovage, (or celery seed) caraway, and celery seed. Blend with honey, vinegar, stock, and olive oil. Heat the sauce, simmer slowly for 25 minutes, and then thicken with flour. Pour the sauce over slices of cooked veal and serve.

Fennel Nut Sauce for Roast Veal or Cutlets

1 lb. roast veal or cutlets

Prepare veal as in preceding recipe. v-4

Sauce:
½ t. pepper
1 t. celery seed (or lovage)
large pinch of fennel
½ t. oregano
¼ c. almonds, chopped
¼ c. dates, chopped, or raisins
2 T. honey
2 c. veal or beef stock
½ t. mustard seed
2 t. butter

In a mortar, grind pepper, celery seed (or lovage), fennel, and oregano. Add to chopped nuts and dates. Blend with honey, stock, mustard seed, and butter. Simmer for 25 minutes, and serve over slices of roast or sautéed meat.

OF KID AND LAMB

VI-1   COPADIA HAEDINA SIVE AGNINA   *Choice Cuts of Kid or Lamb*
Cook them with pepper and stock. [Serve] with [a sauce of] sliced green beans, stock, pepper, laser, fried cumin, pieces of bread, and a little olive oil.

VI-2   ALITER HAEDINAM SIVE AGNINAM EXCALDATAM   *Kid or Lamb Washed in Warm Water*   Put the choice cuts of meat into a pan. Add onions, coriander chopped very finely, ground pepper, lovage, and cumin. Add stock, olive oil, and wine. Cook, transfer to a stewing dish, and thicken [the gravy] with starch. [Serve.]

VI-3   [ALITER HAEDINAM SIVE AGNINAM EXCALDATAM]   [*Kid or Lamb Washed in Warm Water*]   Prepare the lamb's meat with the ground seasonings in the mortar [written above], before cooking. Goat's meat, however, should receive the ground seasonings during cooking.

VI-4   HAEDUM SIVE AGNUM ASSUM   *Roast Kid or Lamb*   First cook in stock and olive oil, [then remove from the pan and] score [the flesh]. Pour [a sauce of] pepper, laser, stock, and a little olive oil [over the incisions]. Roast [the kid or lamb] on a gridiron. [When done] pour [more of] the same sauce over the meat, sprinkle with pepper, and serve.

VI-5   ALITER HAEDUM SIVE AGNUM ASSUM   *Roast Kid or Lamb*
Use half an ounce of pepper, six scruples of wild spikenard, a little ginger, six scruples of parsley, a little laser, half a pint of the best quality stock, and one-eighth of a pint of olive oil.

When lambs are fat and vines are mellow
Then shadows that deeply lie at the foot of mountains
Are soon to follow.

Virgil, "Georgics," 1.341–42.

Choice Cuts of Lamb or Kid in Thick Bean Sauce

-3 lbs. choice cuts of lamb or kid (leg, loin, rack)
1 t. ground pepper
1 c. beef or other meat stock

Season meat with pepper, add stock, and roast in a VI-1 325°F oven for 2 hours or till done.

Sauce:
1 c. sliced green beans
1 c. vegetable or beef stock
dash of ground pepper
1 t. ginger
¼ t. cumin
1 t. butter
½ c. bread bits or crumbs

For the sauce, combine beans, stock, pepper to taste, ginger, and cumin, and simmer for 25 minutes over low heat. Before serving, add bread bits, and pour over slices of the cooked meat.

The bread crumbs serve the same function as would flour, to thicken the sauce. They seemed to be a culinary treat for Apicius.

Lamb or Kid in Coriander Onion Sauce

-3 lbs. choice cuts of lamb or kid (leg, loin, rack)
1 medium onion, chopped
½ t. coriander
¼ t. celery seed (or lovage)
¼ t. cumin

Season the meat with onion, coriander, celery seed VI-2 (or lovage), and cumin. Roast, uncovered, in a 300°F oven for 2 hours. (After 1½ hours, add more spices to taste, if you wish.)

Sauce:
½ t. coriander
¼ t. celery seed (or lovage)
¼ t. cumin
1 medium onion, chopped
2 c. vegetable or beef stock
2 t. butter
½ c. red wine
flour

For the sauce, in a mortar, grind together coriander, celery seed (or lovage), and cumin. Add to onion, and combine with stock, butter, and wine. Bring to a boil and simmer slowly for 25 minutes. Thicken with flour and serve over the slices of meat.

Roast Lamb or Kid in Ginger Sauce

VI-4

3–4 lb. lamb or kid roast
2 T. olive oil or butter

Sauce:
½ t. ground pepper
1 t. ginger
½ c. vegetable or beef stock
1 T. olive oil or butter

Take the roast and moisten it with olive oil or butter. Roast uncovered for 1 hour at 325°F. Then score the roast lightly with a sharp knife, and over the incisions pour the sauce made with pepper, ginger, stock, and olive oil or butter. Continue roasting for 1 hour or till done, then serve with the same sauce.

Parsley Sauce for Roast Lamb or Kid

VI-5

2–3 lb. lamb or kid roast
¼ t. ground pepper
1 small crushed bay leaf
1 t. parsley
½ t. ginger
1 c. vegetable or beef stock
2 t. butter

Of course, this recipe was given by Apicius for a whole animal. To season a 2–3 lb. roast use the adapted quantities of ingredients, combine, and simmer for 20 minutes before serving with the meat.

Lamb or Kid in Cream Sauce

VI-6

3–4 lb. lamb or kid roast

Season meat with salt and pepper. Roast in a 325°F oven for 2 hours or until done.

Sauce:
¼ t. ground pepper
½ t. thyme
½ t. celery seed (or lovage)
2 t. butter
1 T. flour
⅔ c. white wine
⅔ c. cream
1 T. roasting pan liquid

For the sauce, grind together pepper, thyme, celery seed (or lovage). In a saucepan, melt butter and stir in flour to make a paste. Mix with wine, spices, and bring to a boil. Simmer and carefully stir in cream and liquid from roasting pan. Serve with slices of roast meat.

HAEDUS SIVE AGNUS SYRINGIATUS ID EST MAMMOTESTIS   VI-6
Milk-fed Kid or Lamb Hollowed Out Like a Shepherd's Pipe   Bone [the lamb or goat] carefully from the neck, so that it becomes like a bag. Carefully empty the intestines of the animal by blowing through them from the head, so that the ordure will be forced out through the nether part. Wash scrupulously with water. Then fill with a mixture of [stuffing] and stock. [Put them back inside the kid.] Sew up [the animal] at the shoulder and cook in the oven. When [the baby kid or lamb is] done, pour this sauce, boiling, over it: milk, ground pepper, stock, boiled wine reduced one-half and boiled wine reduced one-third, and olive oil. While [the sauce is] yet bubbling, add starch [to thicken it].

Alternatively, [the animal] can be put into a net or basket and bound together carefully and then lowered into a vessel of boiling water seasoned with a little salt. Cook it for a considerable period, until it has boiled well three times, take it out and then boil it once again [but this time] in the sauce written above. The boiling sauce also should be poured over the meat [when it is served].

ALITER HAEDUS SIVE AGNUS SYRINGIATUS   *Kid or Lamb*   VI-7
Hollowed Out Like a Shepherd's Pipe   [Cook with] one pint of milk, four ounces of honey, one ounce of pepper, and a little salt and laser. For the sauce, [mix] one-eighth of a pint each of olive oil, stock and honey, eight ground dates, half a pint of good wine, and a little starch [to thicken].

HAEDUS SIVE AGNUS CRUDUS   [*Seasoning for*] *Raw Kid or*   VI-8
Lamb   Rub [a mixture of] olive oil and pepper [into the skin] and then generously sprinkle pure salt and coriander seed [over it]. Put into the oven, and serve [when] roasted.

> *The well dressed throng applauds:*
> *You weren't eloquent, Pomponius,*
> *But your dinner was.*
>
> Martial, 6.48.

VI-9   HAEDUM SIVE AGNUM TARPEIANUM   *Tarpeian Kid or Lamb*
Before cooking, prepare and sew up. [Make a marinade of] pepper,
rue, savory, onion, a little thyme, and stock. Thoroughly moisten the
kid: steep it [in the sauce to make the meat soft]. Then put [the kid] in a
pan with some olive oil [and roast in the oven]. When [the meat is]
completely cooked, pour this sauce into the [same] pan: grind savory,
onion, rue, dates, stock, wine, boiled wine, and olive oil. [Cook to-
gether] until the sauce has thickened, and then turn [the meat with the
sauce] onto a ring-shaped dish. Sprinkle with pepper and serve.

⁋This dish is probably named in memory of Tarpeia, a Roman
traitoress. Early in Rome's history, Romulus carried off the
women of the neighboring Sabines in order to procure wives for
his followers. In the ensuing war, Sabine warriors besieged the
Capitoline Hill, then an outpost of the fledgling Roman city. A
Roman maiden, Tarpeia, offered to open the citadel in return
for "the things the Sabines wore on their left arms," by which
she meant their golden bracelet. They accepted her offer but
then rewarded her treachery by crushing her to death with the
weight of their shields, which they *also* wore on their left arms
(Florus, *Epitome*, 1.1).

VI-10   HAEDUM SIVE AGNUM PARTHICUM   *Parthian Kid or Lamb*
[Prepare the meat and] put it in the oven. [Now make a sauce by]
grinding pepper, rue, onion, savory, pitted damsons, a little laser, wine,
stock, and olive oil. [Boil the sauce]. [Put the roast] on a platter and
drench it with boiling sauce. [This dish] is served with vinegar.

> *In 300 verses you praise the baths*
> *Of Ponticus the gourmet:*
> *You want to dine, Sabellius, not to bathe.*
>
> Martial, 9.19.

Marinated Lamb or Kid in Savory Sauce

3–4 lb. lamb or kid roast

Marinade:
2 t. ground pepper
1 t. rosemary (or rue)
1½ t. savory
2 onions, finely chopped
1 t. thyme
2 c. vegetable or beef stock

Sauce:
1 t. savory
pinch of rosemary (or rue)
1 onion, finely chopped
¼ c. dates, finely chopped
1 c. meat stock or pan juices
¼ c. red wine
¼ c. boiled red wine
2 t. olive oil

VI-9

Marinate the roast (or whole prepared animal) overnight in a covered pan containing the pepper, rosemary (or rue), savory, chopped onion, thyme, and stock. Baste occasionally.

Roast in a fresh pan in a 325°F oven with a little olive oil.

Meanwhile, prepare the sauce. Grind savory and rosemary (or rue) together. Add to chopped onion and dates. Blend with the stock, red wine, boiled wine (see p. 306) and 2 t. olive oil. Twenty minutes before serving, when roast is nearly done, pour the sauce over it and cook together, letting the sauce thicken. Serve the meat in the sauce.

Plum Sauce for Roast Lamb or Kid

3–4 lb. lamb or kid roast

Sauce:
½ t. ground pepper
pinch of rosemary (or rue)
1 onion, finely chopped
¼ t. savory
6 damsons or plums, pitted
½ t. ginger
½ c. red wine
1 c. vegetable or beef stock
1 T. olive oil
mild wine or cider vinegar

VI-10

First roast the lamb or kid in a 325°F oven for 2 hours or until done.

Meanwhile, make a sauce with the following ingredients. Combine pepper, rosemary (or rue), chopped onion, savory, damsons or plums, ginger, red wine, stock, and olive oil. Bring the sauce to a boil, and simmer for 25 minutes to reduce. Pour over each serving at the table, and sprinkle with a little vinegar.

VI-II   HAEDUM LAUREATUM EX LACTE *Suckling Kid Crowned with Laurel and Milk* Dress the kid, bone it, remove its intestines with curdled milk, and wash. Into a basin or mortar, put pepper, lovage, laser root, two laurel berries, and a little pellitory. Add two or three brains. Grind all together, and then pour stock and flavor with salt. Blend. Over these ingredients, strain two pints of milk and two spoonsful of honey. [Combine.] Now fill up the intestines with this stuffing and arrange them on top of the kid, in a ring. Cover this with sausage skin or papyrus leaf, and bind with twigs. Now put the kid in a [roasting] pan or shallow pan and cook in olive oil and wine. When [the meat is] half cooked, [make a sauce] by grinding pepper, lovage, and juices from the roasting pan. Add a little boiled wine. Grind. Pour [the sauce] over the roast [and put it back in the oven]. When completely done, thicken the sauce with starch, [decorate the kid with laurel] and serve.

OF SUCKLING PIG

VII-1   PORCELLUM FARSILEM DUOBUS GENERIS *Suckling Pig Stuffed in Two Ways* Prepare [the pig]. Clean through its throat and hang from the neck. Before browning, open the skin under the earlaps. Put Terentine stuffing into a cow's bladder. Fix a bird keeper's pipe to the neck of the bladder, through which you squeeze into the ear of the pig as much of the stuffing as possible. After this, cover [the earlaps] with papyrus and fasten securely, and prepare the other stuffing. You make it thus: grind pepper, lovage, oregano, and a little laser root. Pour stock [over this] and add cooked brains, raw eggs, boiled spelt, and pork gravy. [Blend.] If you have them on hand, add small birdmeats. Mix [the stuffing] with nuts, peppercorns, and stock. Fill [the interior of] the suckling pig [with these ingredients], cover the opening with papyrus, and fasten it with clasps. Put [the stuffed suckling pig] into the oven [and roast]. When cooked, remove the papyrus, [arrange on a platter], anoint [with olive oil], and serve.

VII-2   ALITER PORCELLUM *Suckling Pig* [Cook with] salt, cumin, and laser.

Stuffed Roast Suckling Kid with Wine Sauce

8–10 lb. suckling kid

Roast the kid in a 325°F oven for 2 hours.   VI-II

Stuffing:
½ t. ground pepper
½ t. celery seed (or lovage)
½ t. ginger
2 cloves or 1 laurel berry
¼ t. salt
pinch of chamomile
1 lb. cooked, browned calf's brains
2 c. bread crumbs
1 raw egg
2 t. honey
7–8 sausage casings
grease-proof paper or foil

Sauce:
½ c. vegetable or chicken stock
1 T. butter
½ c. red wine

Gravy:
pan juices
¼ t. ground pepper
½ t. celery seed (or lovage)
¼ c. red boiled wine (see p. 306)
pan juices
flour
laurel fronds

To make the stuffing, first grind together pepper, celery seed (or lovage), ginger, and cloves (or laurel berry). Add salt and chamomile. Chop cooked calf's brains, combine with bread crumbs, and well beaten egg sweetened with honey, and combine with seasonings to make forcemeats. Fill casings with this stuffing and tie into a ring.

Next, season the roast with the sauce made from stock, butter, and wine. Place the sausage on top, and return to the oven. After 1 hour remove the sausage, and, if it is a larger animal, continue roasting the kid 1 hour more.

Make the gravy by combining pan juices with pepper, celery seed (or lovage), and wine. Heat to a boil and add flour to thicken. Decorate the finished roast with the sausage ring, and serve slices of meat in the gravy.

For a more authentic version of this recipe, decorate the kid with a plaited crown of laurel before serving.

Pork Roast Stuffed with Nuts and Sausage

VII-1

1 leg of pork

Stuffing:
½ t. ground pepper
1 t. celery seed (or lovage)
½ t. oregano
½ t. ginger
2 T. pork or chicken stock
1 lb. cooked calf's brains
1 raw egg
2 c. bread crumbs
⅓ c. cooked chicken breast,
finely chopped
2 T. pine nuts or almonds,
finely chopped
Myrtle Sausage (see p. 21)
foil

For the stuffing, in a mortar, grind together pepper, celery seed (or lovage), oregano and ginger. Moisten with stock. Add to finely chopped calf's brains, and combine with bread crumbs, well beaten egg, chicken breast, and chopped nuts.

Bone the pork leg and fill with the stuffing. Cover the openings with foil and fasten with string. Roast in a 350°F oven, 35–40 minutes a pound.

Serve the roast pork leg with slices of myrtle sausage.

Roast Pork Apicius

VII-2

3–5 lb. pork roast
5 medium onions
3 t. cumin
salt
1 t. ground ginger
1 t. thyme
1 t. coriander
1 c. pork or chicken stock
1 T. flour
ground pepper

Liberally sprinkle the pork with cumin, and roast in a 350°F oven, 35 minutes per pound. After 1 hour, add salt to taste, ginger, thyme, and coriander. Add whole medium onions to the pan.

When the meat is done, use onions and drippings to make a gravy. Thicken the gravy with flour and serve with slices of pork sprinkled with pepper.

Since suckling pig is often difficult to obtain, some of these recipes substitute roast leg of pork or roast pork loin.

PORCELLUM LIQUAMINATUM *Suckling Pig in Gravy* Remove the organs from the belly of the pig, so that some of the meat is left in it. [In a mortar] grind pepper, lovage, and oregano. Pour stock [over these seasonings and then] add one portion of brains and two eggs. Blend well. Now take the pig and boil it a little to harden the skin. Then stuff [the suckling pig], fasten it with clasps, and lower it in a basket into a pan of briskly boiling water. When done [remove it from the pan and put it on a serving dish]. Undo the clasps to allow the juice to flow out. Sprinkle with pepper and serve.

VII-3

PORCELLUM ELIXUM FARSILEM *Boiled Stuffed Suckling Pig* Remove the belly and then half cook the pig. [In a mortar] mix pepper, lovage, and oregano. Pour stock [over these seasonings and add] a quantity of cooked brains appropriate [to the size of the pig to be stuffed]. Add a similar quantity of eggs, and stir until they are combined. Blend with [more] stock. Now chop sausages that were cooked whole. First wash the suckling pig with stock, stuff it, bind it with clasps, and lower it in a basket into a pan of briskly boiling water. When [the meat is] cooked, wipe it with a sponge and serve without pepper.

VII·

PORCELLUM ASSUM TRACTOMELINUM *Roast Suckling Pig Stuffed with Pastry and Honey* Clean the pig, taking care to remove the organs by [means of] the throat. Dry [the pig]. Now grind one ounce of pepper with honey and wine, and put [this mixture] on [the fire] until it boils. Add to this, pieces of dried pastry. Mix with the seasonings in the roasting pan. Stir with a sprig of green laurel. Let [these ingredients] simmer until the texture thickens, becoming smooth and rich. Then fill the pig with this stuffing, bind with twigs, cover firmly with papyrus, and roast in the oven. [When the suckling pig is done] remove paper and twigs and serve.

VII-5

PORCELLUM LACTE PASTUM ELIXUM CALIDUM IURE FRIGIDO CRUDO APICIANO *Boiled Suckling Pig Fed on Milk, Served Hot with Apicius' Cold Uncooked Sauce* Throw into a mortar and bruise together pepper, lovage, coriander seed, mint, and rue. Pour stock over

VII-6

Leg of Pork with Calf's Brains and Sausage

VII-3

6 lb. leg of pork

Stuffing:
½ t. ground pepper
1 t. celery seed (or lovage)
1 t. oregano
2 T. pork or chicken stock
1 lb. chopped, browned calf's brains
2 raw eggs
2 c. bread crumbs
½ lb. pork sausage, cooked, or Myrtle Sausage (see p. 21)

In a mortar, grind together pepper, celery seed (or lovage), and oregano. Moisten with stock, and mix with chopped brains and bread crumbs. Bind with well beaten eggs, and combine with thinly sliced pieces of cooked pork or myrtle sausage.

Debone the pork, fill the opening with the mixture, and cover with foil or tie with string. Roast in a 350°F oven for 3 to 3½ hours or till done. Serve the stuffing with a sprinkling of pepper.

Roast Pork Stuffed with Bread and Honey

VII-5

3–5 lb. roast of pork
Stuffing:
½ t. pepper
2 T. honey
½ c. red wine
1 bay leaf
2 c. bread crumbs

Debone the pork roast.

In a saucepan, mix pepper, honey, red wine, and bay leaf. Bring to a boil, stirring occasionally. Remove the bay leaf, and add bread crumbs. Simmer gently until the stuffing is smooth. (Add more wine if required.) Fill the pork roast. Bind the openings with string and wrap the stuffed roast in foil. Roast in a 350°F oven, 35 minutes per pound.

Apicius' Cold Sauce for Roast Pork or Baked Ham

Sauce:
¼ t. ground pepper
½ t. celery seed (or lovage)
½ t. coriander
pinch of mint
pinch of rosemary (or rue)
¾ c. pork or chicken stock
1 T. honey
¼ c. red wine

Dry the cooked meat and serve with the following chilled sauce.

To make the sauce, in a mortar, grind together pepper, celery seed (or lovage), coriander, mint, and rosemary (or rue). Combine with stock, honey, and wine. Bring to a boil, then simmer slowly for 25 minutes to reduce. Chill, and serve with slices of meat.

VII-6

Vitellian Roast Pork with Onions

3–5 lb. choice pork roast

Seasoning:
1 t. salt
3 t. cumin

Prepare the pork in the manner of wild boar by wiping the meat, then sprinkling it with salt and cumin several hours before cooking. (See p. 189.)

Roast with onions, uncovered, in a 350°F oven, 35 minutes per pound.

VII-7

Sauce:
¼ t. ground pepper
1 t. celery seed (or lovage)
¾ c. stock
¼ c. red wine
1 T. butter or olive oil
4 onions
1 T. flour

For the sauce, in a mortar, grind together pepper and celery seed (or lovage). Combine with stock, wine, and butter or olive oil. When the meat is done, take it out of the oven, set aside, preserving the pan juices and onions. Now, to the roasting pan add the sauce and simmer for 20 minutes, stirring occasionally. Thicken with flour, and serve with slices of meat.

[these seasonings and] add honey, wine, and [more] stock. [Blend.] Now take the boiled suckling pig and, while still very hot, dry with a clean linen cloth. Pour [the cold sauce] over [the pig] and serve.

VII-7   PORCELLUM VITELLIANUM *Suckling Pig Vitellius* * Dress the pig as you would a wild boar. Sprinkle with salt and roast in the oven. [While it is cooking] put in a mortar, pepper and lovage. [Grind.] Moisten with stock and blend with wine and raisin wine. Boil in a saucepan with a drop of olive oil. Pour the sauce over the roast pig to allow the sauce to penetrate under the skin. [Serve.]

VII-8   PORCELLUM FLACCIANUM *Suckling Pig Flaccus* Season the pig as you would a wild boar. Sprinkle with salt and put [roast] in the oven. While it is cooking, throw into a mortar, pepper, lovage, caraway, celery seed, laser root, and fresh rue. Bruise [all of these seasonings together]. Pour stock over them and blend with wine and raisin wine. Heat this sauce in a pan with a little olive oil. [Boil and] thicken with starch. Coat all parts of the roast suckling pig [with this sauce]. Lastly, grind celery seed into a powder. Sprinkle [this over the meat] and serve.

VII-9   PORCELLUM LAUREATUM *Suckling Pig Crowned with Laurel* Bone the suckling pig and prepare it as you would for wine sauce. Cook [the seasoned suckling pig in the oven] until half done. Take enough green laurel, break it in half, and decorate the animal. [Finish] roasting in the oven. [For the sauce, first] bruise in a mortar, pepper, lovage, caraway, celery seed, laser root, and laurel berries. Moisten with stock and blend with wine and raisin wine. Heat in a pan with a little olive oil. Boil and thicken [with starch]. Serve the cooked pig, remove the laurel decoration, and coat with sauce all over.

VII-10   FRONTINIANUM PORCELLUM *Suckling Pig Frontinian* Bone, half cook, and prepare [the pig]. In a pan put stock, wine, and a bouquet garni of chives and aniseed. When half done, add boiled wine. Take the cooked suckling pig out of the pan and dry it. Then sprinkle with pepper and serve.

* For a description of the emperor Vitellius' dining habits, see p. 108.

Roast Pork in Celery Seed Sauce

3–5 lb. choice pork roast

Prepare the roast pork in the manner of wild boar   VII-8
by first wiping the meat, then sprinkling it with salt

Seasoning:
and cumin several hours before cooking. (See p.

1 t. salt
189.) Roast uncovered in a 350°F oven, 35 minutes

2–3 t. cumin
per pound.

Sauce:
For the sauce, grind together pepper, celery seed

¼ t. ground pepper
(or lovage), caraway, fennel, and rosemary (or rue).

1 t. celery seed (or lovage)
Blend with stock, red wine, and butter or olive oil.

pinch each of caraway and
Put the sauce in a pan, bring to a boil, then simmer

fennel
slowly for 25 minutes. Thicken with flour.

1 t. rosemary (or rue)
Remove the finished roast from the oven and

1 c. pork or chicken stock
sprinkle it with celery seed. Serve slices of meat with

¼ c. red wine
the sauce.

1 T. butter or olive oil

flour

1 t. celery seed, ground

Frontinian Pork with Anise and Chives

3–5 lb. choice pork roast

Marinate the pork roast in the wine marinade in-   VII-10
gredients for about 4 hours, turning the meat from

Marinade:
time to time. Then roast in a 350°F oven for 35 min-

½ c. red wine
utes per pound.

1 c. pork or chicken stock

½ t. ground pepper

2 T. celery seed (or lovage)

1 t. coriander

Sauce:
Remove roast from pan when done, and reserve pan

1 c. pork or chicken stock
juices. To these add the stock, chives, and aniseed,

¼ c. red wine
and simmer for 20 minutes. Then thicken with flour

2 T. chopped chives
and serve with slices of meat. If you wish, sprinkle

pinch of aniseed
with pepper.

flour

Roast Pork Crowned with Laurel

VII-9   *3–5 lb. choice pork roast*

Marinate the pork roast in the wine marinade in-gredients for about 4 hours, turning the meat from time to time. Then roast in a 350°F oven for 35 min-utes per pound.

Marinade:
½ c. red wine
1 c. pork or chicken stock
½ t. ground pepper
2 t. celery seed (or lovage)
1 t. coriander

Sauce:
¼ t. ground pepper
1 t. celery seed (or lovage)
pinch of caraway
pinch of fennel
4 juniper berries or 2 cloves,
crushed
¾ c. pork or chicken stock
¼ c. red wine
1 T. butter or olive oil
flour
laurel fronds

For the sauce, in a mortar, grind pepper, celery seed (or lovage), caraway, fennel, and juniper berries or cloves. Blend with stock, wine, and olive oil or but-ter. Bring to a boil, simmer slowly for 25 minutes, then thicken with flour. Plait laurel leaves into a crown and decorate the roast.

At the table, drench slices of pork with the sauce, and serve.

Marinated Pork Cooked in Two Wine Sauces

3–5 lb. choice pork roast

Marinade:
½ c. red wine
1 c. pork or chicken stock
½ t. ground pepper
2 T. celery seed (or lovage)
2 t. coriander

Marinate the pork roast in the wine marinade ingredients for about 4 hours, turning from time to time. Then roast in a 350°F oven for 35 minutes per pound.

When the roast has been half cooked, add the first sauce, basting the meat with it.

VII-II

First sauce:
2 T. olive oil or butter
¼ c. stock
¼ c. red wine
¼ c. water
1 T. chopped chives
1 t. coriander
¼ c. red wine

For this sauce, combine olive oil or butter, stock, red wine, water, chopped chives, and coriander, and add to the roast. After 1 hour, add more red wine.

Second sauce:
½ t. ground pepper
½ t. lovage (or celery seed)
pinch of caraway
½ t. celery seed
½ t. ginger
½ c. pork or chicken stock
¼ c. gravy from roasting pan
¼ c. sweet raisin wine or muscatel
flour
ground pepper

For the second sauce, grind together pepper, lovage (or celery seed), caraway, celery seed, and ginger. Combine with stock, gravy from the roast, and sweet wine. Bring this sauce to a boil, simmer slowly for 25 minutes to reduce, or thicken with flour. Place the meat on a serving platter and drench it with this sauce. Sprinkle with pepper and serve.

VII-11

PORCELLUM OENOCOCTUM *Suckling Pig Stewed in Wine*
Half cook and prepare [the pig]. Put in the pan, olive oil, stock, wine, water, and a bouquet of chives and coriander. When it is half cooked, add boiled wine for color. Put in a mortar, pepper, lovage, caraway, oregano, celery seed, and laser root. Mix. Pour stock [over this] and gravy [from the roasting pan]. Blend with wine and raisin wine. Pour [the sauce] into a pan and bring to the boil. When it boils, thicken with starch. Set the stewed suckling pig on a serving dish. Drench [in the sauce, and] sprinkle with pepper and serve.

> *This pig will make your Saturnalian dinner good,*
> *He once feasted under the oak trees with the foaming boars.*
>
> Martial, 14.70.

VII-12

PORCELLUM CELSINIANUM *Pork Celsinian* Prepare [the pig] and pour over the skin [a mixture of] pepper, rue, onion, and savory, and pour eggs into an ear. [Cook] in pepper, stock, and a little wine — about one-eighth of a pint. Then serve.

⟨This dish was possibly named in honor of Aulus Cornelius Celsus, who lived during the reign of Tiberius Caesar (14–37 A.D.). He was the author of many works but only his eight books on medicine have survived. He discussed at some length the importance of diet.

VII-13

PORCELLUM ASSUM *Roast Suckling Pig* Grind pepper, rue, savory, onion, the yolks of hard-boiled eggs, stock, wine, olive oil, and spiced wine. Boil. Serve the roast suckling pig on a mushroom dish,* drenched [with sauce].

VII-14

PORCELLUM HORTULANUM *Suckling Pig with Garden Vegetables* Bone by the throat [leaving the skin] like a bag. Fill with [these ingredients:] chicken forcemeat chopped finely, thrushes, figpecker birds, forcemeats made from the pig itself, Lucanian sausages, pitted dates, smoked-dried bulbs, shelled snails, mallows, beets, leeks, celery,

*A particularly fine serving dish.

Roast Suckling Pig with Garden Vegetables

10–12 lb. suckling pig

Dress the pig by removing organs and cleaning the interior.

VII-14

Stuffing:
1 c. cooked chicken meat, finely chopped
1 c. thinly sliced cooked pork sausage
½ c. pitted dates
1 large onion, finely chopped
1 c. chopped beets
2 c. chopped celery
1 small cabbage chopped
½ c. blanched almonds, whole
2 t. ground pepper
4–5 c. bread crumbs
3–4 raw eggs
(pork or chicken stock)

For the stuffing, combine chicken, sausage, chopped dates, chopped onion, beets, celery, cabbage, almonds, pepper, and bread crumbs. Add well beaten eggs to bind, and stock to moisten, if necessary. Stuff the pig. (If necessary increase the stuffing to suit the size of the animal.) Finish by securing the ear flaps with skewers.

Roast in a 350°F oven for 35 minutes per pound. An hour before it is done, put an apple in the pig's mouth.

Sauce:
¼ t. ground pepper
½ t. rosemary
1 c. pork or chicken stock
½ c. red wine
1 t. honey
2 T. butter
flour

For the sauce, grind together pepper and rosemary. Combine with stock, wine, honey, and butter. Heat the sauce and baste the pig frequently with the liquid. When the meat is cooked, simmer the pan drippings combined with the sauce, and thicken with flour. Serve with the roast pig as a gravy.

boiled cabbage, coriander, peppercorns, nuts, fifteen eggs, and stock seasoned with pepper sauce [and mixed with three eggs]. Sew up [the throat of the animal], brown, and put [the suckling pig] in the oven to roast. When done, cleave its back [from end to end] and pour over it a sauce [prepared from the following:] grind [together] pepper, rue, stock, raisin wine, honey, and a little oil. When it boils, thicken it with starch.

VII-15   IUS FRIGIDUM IN PORCELLUM [ELIXUM] ITA FACIES   *[Boiled]* *Suckling Pig in Cold Sauce* Grind pepper, caraway, anise, a little oregano, and pine nuts. [Over these ingredients] pour vinegar and fish-pickle. Add dates, honey, and prepared mustard. [Stir well.] Pour drops of olive oil [over the sauce], sprinkle with pepper, and serve [cold over boiled suckling pig].

VII-16   PORCELLUM TRAIANUM SIC FACIES *Suckling Pig Trajan* Bone and prepare as for *Suckling Pig Stewed in Wine*, and cure by hanging it in woodsmoke. Weigh the pig and put its weight in salt into a deep pan. Cook [the cured suckling pig] in the boiling [salted] water. [When done] dry and serve in place of fresh saltfish.

⟨Marcus Ulpius Trajanus was Roman Emperor, 98–112 A.D. He was renowned for his justice and benevolence as a ruler. The third and last of the three Roman authorities to bear the name Apicius lived during Trajan's reign, and the composition of *The Roman Cookery of Apicius* was, I believe, largely his work. This Apicius is said to have devised a way of sending fresh oysters to the Emperor when he was campaigning in Parthia many days march from the sea.

VII-17   IN PORCELLO LACTANTE *For Piglet* Use one ounce of pepper, half a pint of wine, better than one-eighth of a pint of the best olive oil, one-eighth of a pint of stock, and slightly less than one-eighth of a pint of vinegar.

Cold Condiment for Ham

1 medium cooked ham

Use a ham that is not heavily salted.

VII-15

Sauce:
½ t. ground pepper
pinch each of caraway and aniseed
½ t. oregano
2 T. pine nuts or almonds, finely chopped
1 T. cider vinegar
dash of fish-pickle (see p. 305)
1 t. anchovy paste
2 dates, finely chopped
1 t. honey
½ t. ground mustard
4 T. olive oil
ground pepper

In a mortar, grind together pepper, caraway, aniseed, and oregano. To this add chopped nuts, then moisten with vinegar and a little fish-pickle. Add chopped dates, honey, and mustard. Blend with olive oil, and add a sprinkling of pepper. Serve cold with cold ham slices.

Marinated Pork Chops

2 lbs. ¾" pork chops

Marinade:
½ c. red wine
½ c. chicken stock
2 t. cider vinegar
½ t. ground pepper
½ t. cumin

Marinate chops for 4 hours in wine marinade ingredients, turning from time to time. Then sauté in butter or olive oil till done.

VII-17

OF HARE

Among birds, the thrush, if I'm any sort of judge,
But among quadrupeds the foremost delicacy's the hare.

Martial, 13.16.

VIII-1   LEPOREM MADIDUM   *Soaked Hare*   Precook the hare briefly in water, then arrange it in a stewing dish. It should now be cooked in olive oil in the oven and, when nearly done, in another portion of olive oil. Then all parts of the hare should be coated with a sauce compounded of these ingredients written below: grind pepper, [lovage,] savory, onion, rue, celery seed, stock, laser, wine, and a little olive oil. Roll [the hare] several times [in this sauce so the meat may become thoroughly impregnated with the seasonings]. Cook thoroughly in the sauce [and serve].

VIII-2   ITEM ALIAM AD EUM IMPENSAM   *The Same Thing with Other Ingredients*   When it is nearly time to take out [the hare], grind pepper, dates, laser, raisins, boiled wine, stock, and olive oil. Pour, and when it has boiled, sprinkle with pepper and serve.

VIII-3   LEPOREM FARSUM   *Stuffed Hare*   [To make the stuffing, use] whole, [shelled] small nuts, almonds, chopped nuts or chestnuts, peppercorns, and hare forcemeats. Bind [these elements of the stuffing together] with raw eggs. [Stuff the hare,] roll it in pig's caul, and roast in the oven. This is the sauce recipe: [mix] rue, pepper to suit, onion, savory, dates, stock, boiled wine or spiced honeyed wine. Boil these ingredients for a long time [and stir] until they thicken, and then pour [over the roast hare]. The hare remains in this pepper, stock, and laser sauce.

VIII-4   IUS ALBUM IN ASSUM LEPOREM   *Roast Hare in White Sauce*   Take pepper, lovage, cumin, celery seed, and the yolk of a hard boiled egg. Mix well [in a mortar] and then combine into a ball. [Meanwhile] simmer stock, wine, olive oil, a little vinegar, and a chopped shallot in a saucepan. Now put the ball of seasoning [into the mixture] and stir with a sprig of oregano or savory. If necessary, thicken with starch. [Pour over the roast hare and serve.]

Rabbit or Hare in Onion Fennel Sauce

3 lb rabbit, or hare

Sauce:
olive oil or butter
½ t. ground pepper
½ t. lovage (or celery seed)
¼ t. savory
1 small onion, chopped
pinch of rosemary (or rue)
½ t. celery seed
1 c. chicken stock
¼ t. fennel
½ c. white wine
1 T. olive oil

Put the rabbit into a covered pan and braise gently   VIII-1
for ½ hour. Remove, wipe, and brush with oil or
butter. Cook covered, in a 350°F oven in a stewing
pot for 30 minutes. Then brush a second time with
oil or butter, and cook a further 30 minutes. Lastly,
uncover the pot and cook the rabbit for 30 minutes
in the following sauce.

In a mortar, grind together pepper, lovage (or celery seed), savory, chopped onion, rosemary (or
rue), and celery seed. Combine with stock, fennel,
wine, and olive oil. Add this sauce to the rabbit, and
cook 30 minutes, basting from time to time. Serve
the rabbit in its own gravy.

Braised Rabbit or Hare in a Sweet Wine Sauce

VIII-2

3 lb. rabbit, or hare
½ t. ground pepper
¼ c. dates, finely chopped
pinch of fennel
⅛ c. raisins
¼ c. boiled sweet wine (see
p. 306)
1 c. chicken stock
1 T. olive oil
ground pepper

Prepare and cook the rabbit according to the preceding recipe, but cook in the following sauce for the last 30 minutes. Combine pepper, chopped dates, fennel, raisins, wine, stock, and olive oil. Braise the rabbit in this sauce, basting from time to time. Serve with a sprinkling of pepper.

Stuffed Rabbit or Hare

VIII-3

3 lb. rabbit or hare
Stuffing:
¼ c. chopped almonds or
walnuts
¼ t. ground pepper
¾ c. pork sausage meat
1 raw egg
1 c. bread crumbs
Sauce:
pinch of rosemary (or rue)
½ t. ground pepper
1 small onion, finely chopped
½ t. savory
¼ c. dates, chopped
¾ c. chicken stock
¼ c. boiled red wine (see
p. 306) or Spiced Wine (see
p. 21)

Roast the stuffed rabbit in a 325°F oven in a covered pan for 1½ hours. Then uncover and finish cooking in the sauce.

To make the stuffing mix nuts with pepper, sausage meat, bread crumbs, well beaten egg to bind, and a little of the pan juices. Stuff the rabbit and tie with string or secure with skewers. Roast until done.

To make the sauce, grind together rosemary (or rue), pepper, and savory. Mix with chopped onion and dates, then combine with stock and wine.

Then, when rabbit has baked for 1½ hours, uncover it and finish it in this sauce for 30 minutes more, basting from time to time. Serve meat with the sauce thickened with flour.

Roast Rabbit or Hare in Thick Cumin Sauce

3 lb. rabbit or hare

Sauce:
¼ t. ground pepper
½ t. celery seed (or lovage)
¾ t. cumin
1 hard-boiled egg yolk
1 c. chicken stock
½ c. white wine
1 T. olive oil
1 t. wine vinegar or cider vinegar
¼ c. shallots or onion, chopped
1 t. oregano or 1 t. savory

Roast the rabbit in a 325°F oven in a covered pan for 1½ hours. Uncover, add the following sauce, and cook for about 30 minutes more, basting occasionally.

For the sauce, in a mortar, grind pepper, celery seed (or lovage), cumin, and the hard-boiled yolk. Mix well and form into a ball. In a saucepan, simmer stock, white wine, olive oil, vinegar, and shallots or onion. Add the ball of seasonings and stir in oregano or savory. Simmer to reduce for 15–30 minutes, and serve over the roast meat.

VIII-4

Rabbit Stuffed with Liver and Sausage

3 lb. rabbit
¼ t. ground pepper
1 t. oregano
½ t. cumin
¼ lb. rabbit liver, chopped
½ c. ground pork sausage meat
1 small onion, chopped
½ c. bread crumbs
1 raw egg yolk
t. cumin (for the skin of the rabbit)
3 T. butter

Clean the inside of the rabbit, and reserve the liver. To make the stuffing, grind together pepper, oregano, and cumin. Add to chopped liver, sausage meat, onion, and bread crumbs. Bind with well beaten egg yolk. Now, stuff the animal, and secure opening with string. Moisten the skin of the rabbit with butter and season with cumin.

Place in a greased roasting pan, and cook in a 300°F oven for 1½ hours, basting from time to time. (Very good served with new potatoes and gravy made from the pan juices. Though the Romans did not have potatoes, Apicius would have approved of this combination.)

VIII-5

VIII-5

ALITER IN LEPOREM EX SANGUINE ET IECINERE ET PULMON-
IBUS LEPORINIS MINUTAL *Hare's Blood, Liver, and Lung Ragout*
In a pan, cook stock, olive oil, reduced stock, finely chopped leek and
coriander, [and the blood] and chopped liver and lungs of the hare.
When they are cooked take a mortar and grind pepper, cumin,
coriander, laser root, mint, rue, and pennyroyal. Moisten [these
seasonings] with vinegar and add the liver and lungs of the hare. Grind.
Add honey and gravy, flavor with vinegar. Pour into a saucepan, and
put the very finely chopped lungs of the hare into the same saucepan.
Bring to the boil. When it has boiled, thicken with starch, sprinkle with
pepper, and serve.

VIII-6

ALITER LEPOREM EX SUO IURE *Hare Served in Its Own Gravy*
Clean, bone, and dress the hare and put it in a stewing pan. Add olive
oil, stock, reduced stock, coriander, anise, and a bouquet garni of chives.
While [the hare is] cooking, throw into a mortar, pepper, cumin, lovage,
coriander seed, laser root, dried onion, mint, rue, and celery seed. Bruise
[all of these seasonings together]. Moisten with stock. Add honey, juices
from the pan, boiled wine, and vinegar. Blend [carefully]. Bring this
sauce to the boil and then thicken with starch. Arrange the hare, drench
in sauce, sprinkle with pepper, and serve.

VIII-7

LEPOREM PASSENIANUM *Passenian Hare* Clean and bone the
hare. Extend the legs [of the animal] and suspend it in woodsmoke until
it colors. Then half cook [the cured hare]. Lift [out of the pan], sprinkle
with salt, and roast, basting in wine sauce. Throw into a mortar, pepper and lovage. Grind. Over [these seasonings] pour stock and blend
with wine and gravy [from the roast]. [Pour this mixture] into a pan
with a little olive oil, and bring to the boil. Thicken with starch. Pour
[this sauce] on the back of the roast hare. Sprinkle with pepper and
serve.

⟨This dish is named after either Passienus, an orator who died in
9 B.C., or Passennus Paulus, a Roman poet who wrote elegies in
the first century A.D.

Rabbit or Hare Served in Its Own Gravy

3 lb. rabbit or hare

Seasoning:
1 T. olive oil
1 c. chicken stock
¼ c. reduced chicken stock
2 t. chives
1 t. coriander
pinch of aniseed

In a stewing pot, put olive oil, stock, chives, coriander, and aniseed. Cut up rabbit into pieces and add to pot. Cover, bring to a boil, and cook rabbit for 1 hour over low heat.

VIII-6

Sauce:
¼ t. ground pepper
1 t. celery seed (or lovage)
½ t. cumin
½ t. coriander
pinch of fennel
1 t. mint
pinch of rosemary (or rue)
1 small onion, chopped
2 t. honey
½ c. stewing pan juices
½ c. boiled red wine (see p. 306)
1 t. white wine or cider vinegar
flour
pepper

For the sauce, in a mortar grind pepper, celery seed (or lovage), cumin, coriander seeds, fennel, mint, and a pinch of rosemary (or rue). Add onion, and combine with honey, liquid from the rabbit pan, boiled wine, and vinegar.

Uncover the rabbit, add the sauce to the stewing pan, and cook for a further 30 minutes. Thicken sauce with flour, and serve the meat drenched in sauce. Sprinkle with pepper at the table.

Rabbit or Hare with Wine Sauce

VIII-7

3 lb. rabbit or hare

Sauce:
½ t. ground pepper
1 t. celery seed (or lovage)
¾ c. chicken stock
¼ c. white wine
roasting pan juices
1 T. olive oil, or butter
flour
ground pepper

Roast the rabbit in a 325°F oven for 1½ hours or until tender, basting frequently with wine sauce to moisten the skin. To make the sauce, in a mortar, grind pepper and celery seed (or lovage). Add these to stock, wine, pan juices, and olive oil or butter. Heat and baste rabbit with the sauce. Before serving, thicken sauce with flour, then pour over the meat with a sprinkling of pepper.

Stuffed Rabbit or Hare with Wine Sauce

VIII-8

3 lb. rabbit or hare

Stuffing:
¾ c. pork sausage meat
¼ c. chopped almonds
1 c. bread crumbs
1 raw egg
chicken stock

1½ wine sauce (see p. 306)

For the stuffing, combine pork sausage, meat, almonds, bread crumbs, and well beaten egg. Add a touch of chicken stock, and stuff the rabbit. Secure opening with string or skewers, and roast in a 325°F oven for 1½ hours. Baste frequently with wine sauce, and serve the roast with 1 cup of the heated wine sauce at the table.

Richly Stuffed Rabbit or Hare with Wine Sauce

3 lb. rabbit or hare

Stuffing:
½ t. ground pepper
1 t. celery seed (or lovage)
1 t. oregano
2 T. chicken stock
½ c. cooked chicken livers,
chopped
¼ c. cooked calf's brains,
chopped
½ c. cooked chicken, chopped
1 raw egg

butter

Sauce:
¼ t. ground pepper
1 t. celery seed (or lovage)
1 c. chicken stock
½ c. white wine
¼ c. pan juices
flour
ground pepper

For the stuffing, in a mortar, grind together pepper, VIII-9 celery seed (or lovage), and oregano. Add stock. Mix. Now add chicken livers, calf's brains, and chicken. Mix with well beaten egg. Stuff the rabbit with this mixture, and secure opening with string or skewers. Roast in a 325°F oven for 1½ hours, basting frequently with wine sauce or butter.

For the sauce, combine pepper, celery seed (or lovage), stock, and wine. Add juices from the roasting pan. Bring the sauce to a boil, simmer for 25 minutes, and thicken with flour. Serve sauce at the table with the roast, and sprinkle with pepper.

VIII-8

LEPOREM ISICIATUM *Hare Forcemeat* Spice the forcemeat with the same sauce [as above]. Combine with nuts that have steeped [in must]. [Stuff.] Cover [the opening] with caul or paper, bring the edges together and secure with twigs.

VIII-9

LEPOREM FARSILEM *Stuffed Hare* Clean and dress the hare and place it in a square roasting pan. In a mortar, grind pepper, lovage, and oregano. Pour stock [over these seasonings]. Add cooked chicken livers, cooked brains, and chopped meats. Then blend with three raw eggs and [more] stock. [Stuff the hare and] cover the opening with caul and paper and bind with twigs. Lightly roast the hare over a slow fire. In a mortar, bruise pepper and lovage. Blend these seasonings with a little stock and wine and juices from the roasting pan. Boil and thicken the sauce with starch. Pour over the lightly roasted hare. [Cook in the sauce until done.] Sprinkle with pepper and serve.

> *You deny the hare was cooked and demand a whip.*
> *Rufus, you'd rather carve your cook than carve your hare.*
>
> Martial, 3.94.

VIII-10

ALITER LEPOREM ELIXUM *Boiled Hare* [Prepare the boiled hare and] arrange [on a serving dish]. Add olive oil, stock, vinegar, raisin wine, chopped onion, fresh rue, and finely chopped thyme, the serving dish.

VIII-11

LEPORIS CONDITURA *Seasoning for Hare* [In a mortar] grind pepper, rue, shallots, and the [chopped] liver of the hare. [Blend with] stock, boiled wine, raisin wine, and a little olive oil. Boil [the sauce] and thicken with starch.

VIII-12

LEPOREM PIPERE SICCO SPARSUM *Peppered Hare* Prepare the hare as you would Tarpeian kid. Before cooking, dress and sew up. Marinate in pepper, rue, savory, onion, a little thyme, and stock. Then put it in the oven. Cook, and scatter all over it the following sauce: half an ounce of pepper, rue, onion, savory, four [chopped] dates, raisins, sauce colored over the heat, wine, olive oil, stock, and

Thyme Sauce for Braised Rabbit or Hare

3 lb. braised rabbit or hare

Sauce:
3–4 medium onions, sliced
2 T. olive oil
¼ c. chicken stock
1 t. white wine vinegar or
cider vinegar
¼ c. white wine
¼ t. rosemary (or rue)
1 t. ground thyme
flour

Sauté onion in olive oil. Add stock, vinegar, wine, VIII-10 rosemary (or rue), and thyme. Simmer for 10–15 minutes, then thicken with flour, and pour over the cooked rabbit. Serve.

Seasoned Liver Sauce for Rabbit or Hare

VIII-11   *3 lb. braised rabbit or hare*

Sauce:
½ t. ground pepper
pinch of rosemary (or rue)
1 c. chicken stock
¼ c. shallots or onion
¼ c. cooked chicken livers,
chopped
½ c. white wine
1 T. olive oil or butter

In a mortar, grind together pepper and rosemary (or rue). Add stock, chopped shallots or onion, the chopped liver, wine, and olive oil. Bring to a boil, then reduce for 25 minutes, and serve over rabbit.

Marinated and Basted Rabbit or Hare

VIII-12   *3 lb. rabbit or hare*
Marinade:
2 t. peppercorns
½ t. rosemary (or rue)
1 t. savory
2 onions, chopped
1 t. thyme
2 c. chicken stock

Marinate rabbit pieces 8 hours in a covered dish with pepper, rosemary (or rue), savory, onions, thyme, and stock. Baste occasionally.

Sauce:
½ t. ground pepper
pinch of rosemary (or rue)
½ t. savory
3 small whole onions
¼ c. dates, chopped, or raisins
½ c. white wine
1 T. olive oil or butter
2 c. chicken stock
(flour)
ground pepper

Combine pepper, rosemary (or rue), savory, onions, dates or raisins, wine, olive oil or butter, and stock in a stewing pan. To this sauce, add the marinated meat, and cook on the stove for 1 hour, or until tender, stirring from time to time to distribute the seasonings. When done, thicken the sauce with flour, if you wish. Serve with the meat, and add a sprinkling of pepper.

Well Seasoned Rabbit or Hare

3 lb. rabbit or hare

Braise the rabbit in a 325°F oven for 1½ hours in the following seasonings.

VIII-13

Seasoning:
½ c. boiled white wine (see p. 306) or must
½ c. chicken stock
1 t. ground mustard seed
pinch of aniseed
2 whole leeks
½ c. water

For the seasonings, combine wine, stock, mustard, aniseed, and leeks. Stir occasionally and make sure the leeks remain covered with liquid.

Sauce:
½ t. ground pepper
½ t. savory
one onion ring
4 dates, chopped
4 plums (or damsons), sliced
¼ c. white wine
½ c. chicken stock
¼ c. boiled wine (see p. 306)
1 T. olive oil or butter
(flour)
(pepper)

For the sauce, grind together pepper and savory, and add these to onion, dates, plums (or damsons), wine, stock, and olive oil or butter. Bring the mixture to a boil, then simmer slowly for 25 minutes. Thicken with flour, if you wish. Serve the sauce with the rabbit and leeks. Sprinkle with pepper if you wish.

boiled wine. Baste [the hare] frequently [as it cooks] so that it may absorb all the sauce. Afterwards, sprinkle [the hare] with [dry] pepper and serve on a round dish.

VIII-13   ALITER LEPOREM CONDITUM *Seasoned Hare* Cook [the hare] in wine, stock, water, a little mustard, anise, and whole leeks. When it is cooked, prepare [a sauce by combining] pepper, savory, an onion ring, dates, two damsons, wine, stock, boiled wine, and a little olive oil. [Blend and put into a saucepan.] Thicken with starch, boil for a little while, and bind [all together] with starch. Place the seasoned, cooked hare in a dish and drench [in sauce].

> *Whenever you sell me a hare, Gellia, you say:*
>   *"Marcus, you'll be handsome for seven days."*
> *If you aren't mocking me, my love, if you really believe that*
>   *story,*
> *You've never eaten hare.*
>
>   Martial, 5.29.

DORMICE

IX   GLIRES *Dormice* Stuff with pork forcemeat, minced dormice from all its parts, pepper, nuts, laser, and stock. Stitch up [the openings] and put [the stuffed dormice] on a tile [and roast] in the oven, or bake them, stuffed, in a clay oven.

  ⟨Dormice (*Myoxi avellanarii*) are hibernating rodents who resemble both mice and squirrels. The Romans regarded them as a delicacy and served them at the "gustatio," or hors d'oeuvre, course.

BOOK VIII OF APICIUS,
QUADRUPEDS, IS
— ENDED —

The Sea

OF LOBSTERS

In winter lobsters seek out sunny coasts, but in summer they withdraw into the shade of the sea. All members of this [bloodless] class are afflicted by winter but become fat in the autumn and spring, and even more so at the full moon since by night the moon makes them mellow by the warmth of its gleams.

Pliny, 9.50.

I-1   IUS IN LOCUSTA ET CAMMARI *Sauce for Lobster and Crayfish* Brown chopped pallacanian onions...Add pepper, lovage, caraway, cumin, a date, honey, vinegar, wine, fish stock, oil, and boiled new wine. Add mustard to the sauce while it is still boiling.

I-2   LOCUSTAS ASSAS SIC FACIES *Roast Lobsters* Open the lobsters, as is customary, and then leave them in their shells. Pour pepper sauce and coriander sauce over them, [cover] and roast on a gridiron. When they become dry, pour more sauce over the gridiron. Repeat this as often as necessary until they are roasted well and then serve.

I-3   LOCUSTA ELIXA CUM CUMINATO *Boiled Lobster with Cumin Sauce* Pepper, lovage, parsley, dried mint, more of cumin, honey, vinegar, and fish stock. If you like, add spikenard and cinnamon.

I-4   ALITER LOCUSTA *Lobster* Make lobster-tail forcemeats this way. Remove the harmful flesh. Boil [thoroughly] and chop into small pieces. Then shape into forcemeats with stock and pepper, and eggs.

I-5   IN LOCUSTA ELIXA *[Sauce] for Boiled Lobster* Pepper, cumin, rue, honey, vinegar, fish stock, and olive oil.

I-6   ALITER IN LOCUSTA *[Sauce] for Lobster* Pepper, lovage, cumin, mint, rue, nuts, honey, vinegar, fish stock, and wine.

OF RAY

II-1   IN TORPEDINE *Of Ray* Grind pepper, rue, and a small dried onion. Add honey, fish stock, some raisin wine, a little wine, and drops of good quality olive oil. Taste, and add a little olive oil if necessary. When [the sauce] has begun to boil, thicken with starch. [Pour over the cooked ray and serve.]

Spiced Sauce for Lobster or Crab

2½ lbs. lobster or crab meat
2 T. chopped onion or
shallots
2 t. olive oil or butter
¼ t. ground pepper
1 t. celery seed (or lovage)
pinch of caraway
¼ t. cumin
¼ c. dates, chopped
1 t. honey
1 t. white wine vinegar or
cider vinegar
½ c. white wine
⅔ c. shellfish stock
2 t. olive oil
⅓ c. boiled white wine
pinch of mustard seed

First brown onion or shallots in olive oil or butter. I-I
Grind together pepper, celery seed (or lovage), caraway, cumin, and dates. Add to the cooked shallots
or onion. Blend with honey, vinegar, wine, fish
stock, olive oil, and boiled wine. Bring to a boil, and
add mustard. Reduce for 25–30 minutes, and serve
hot over the lobster or crabmeat.

Lobster Baked in Two Sauces

2½–3 lb. lobster
Pepper sauce:
1 T. mild fish-pickle to each
generous dash pepper
Coriander sauce:
1 t. coriander
pinch of aniseed
½ t. oregano
¼ t. ground pepper
1 t. honey
¼ c. white wine
¾ c. lobster stock
2 t. olive oil
1 t. white or cider vinegar

Plunge the lobster in boiling water for 3 minutes, I-2
then split the lobster in two along its length. Season,
to taste, with the pepper sauce, and then the coriander sauce below, and bake.

For the coriander sauce, grind together coriander,
aniseed, oregano, and pepper. Combine with honey,
wine, fish stock, olive oil, and vinegar. Heat to a
boil, then simmer slowly for 5 minutes.

After seasoning the lobster with this sauce, bake
for 25–30 minutes in a 325°F oven or over coals,
basting with olive oil or butter. Add more olive oil
as required to avoid drying out the flesh of the lobster. Serve.

Boiled Lobster or Crab with Thick Cumin Sauc

1-3   one 2½–3 lb. lobster, or 7–8 small crabs

Boil the lobster or crabs for 25 minutes and reserv stock.

Sauce:
¼ t. ground pepper
1 t. celery seed (or lovage)
1 t. parsley
1 t. mint
1 t. honey
¼ t. cumin
1 t. white or cider vinegar
1 c. fish stock
1 bay or spikenard leaf
(dash of cinnamon)

For the sauce, grind together pepper, celery see (or lovage), parsley, mint, and cumin. Add honey vinegar, and fish stock (to cover). Add bay leaf (o spikenard), and heat to a boil, then simmer to re duce the sauce for 25 minutes. Strain out bay leaf and serve sauce as seasoning for the shelled lobste or crab pieces.

If you like, add a dash of cinnamon in the last fiv minutes to the simmering sauce.

Simple Sauce for Boiled Lobsters or Crabs

1-5   2½–3 lb. lobster, or 7–8 small crabs

Boil lobster or crabs for 25 minutes and reserv stock.

Sauce:
¼ t. cumin
pinch of rosemary (or rue)
1 t. honey
3 t. olive oil or butter
½ c. lobster stock

Combine cumin with rosemary (or rue), honey olive oil or butter, and lobster stock. Bring to a boil pour over lobster or crabs, and serve together. O serve over the shelled meats.

Sauce for Boiled Lobster

2½–3 lb. lobster

Boil lobster for 25 minutes and reserve stock.

1-6

Sauce:
½ t. ground pepper
1 t. celery seed (or lovage)
¼ t. cumin
1 t. mint or
pinch of rosemary (or rue)
¼ c. pine nuts or blanched
almonds, chopped
1 t. honey
2 t. white or cider vinegar
1 c. lobster stock
½ c. white wine

In a mortar, grind together pepper, celery seed (or lovage), cumin, mint, and rosemary (or rue). Add to nuts, then blend with honey, vinegar, stock, and white wine. Bring to a boil, then simmer to reduce for 25 minutes. Serve with shelled lobster meat.

II-2   IN TORPEDINE ELIXA *[Sauce] for Boiled Ray* Pepper, lovage, parsley, mint, oregano, egg yolk, honey, fish stock, raisin wine, wine, and olive oil. If you like, add mustard and vinegar. If you wish [to serve the ray] in a hot sauce, add raisins.

OF SQUID

III-1   IN LOLLIGINE IN PATINA *A Pan of Squid* Mix pepper, rue, a little honey, stock, boiled wine, and drops of olive oil.

III-2   IN LOLLIGINE FARSILI *Stuffed Squid* Pepper, lovage, coriander, celery seed, egg yolk, honey, vinegar, stock, wine, and olive oil. Thicken.

OF CUTTLEFISH

IV-1   IN SEPIA FARSILI *[Sauce] for Stuffed Cuttlefish* [Mix] pepper, lovage, celery seed, caraway, honey, fish stock, wine, and cooking seasonings. Simmer and then open the cuttlefish and pour [the sauce inside].

IV-2   SIC FARCIES EAM SEPIAM COCTAM *Stuffed and Cooked Cuttlefish* Grind cooked brains, with the membranes removed, and pepper. Mix this with a fitting number of raw eggs, peppercorns, and small forcemeats. [Stuff the cuttlefish] and stitch up [the openings]. Cook thoroughly in a pan of boiling water so that the ingredients can set.

IV-3   SEPIAS ELIXAS A BALINEO *Boiled Cuttlefish from the Tank* Put them in cold [water] with pepper, laser [root], stock, and small nuts. You may add eggs and other seasonings as you wish.

IV-4   ALITER SEPIAS *Cuttlefish* [Make the sauce with] pepper, lovage, cumin, green coriander, dried mint, egg yolk, honey, stock, wine, vinegar, and a little olive oil. When [the sauce] has boiled, thicken with starch.

OF OCTOPUS

V   IN POLYPO *Of Octopus* Serve with pepper, fish stock, and laser, and serve.

Rosemary Sauce for Poached Skate

½ lb. skate

Poach the wings of the skate in water or fish stock II-I
till done.

Sauce:
½ t. ground pepper
pinch of rosemary (or rue)
1 medium onion,
finely chopped
1 t. honey
¾ c. fish stock
¼ c. white wine
olive oil
(flour)

To make the sauce, grind together pepper and rosemary (or rue). Add to onion, and blend with honey, stock, wine, and olive oil to taste. Bring the sauce to a boil, then simmer for 25 minutes to reduce. (Or, if desired, thicken with flour). Pour over each serving of the poached fish, and serve.

Sharp Sauce for Poached Skate

½ lb. skate

Prepare fish as in previous recipe.

Sauce:
½ t. ground pepper
1 t. celery seed (or lovage)
½ t. oregano
2 t. fresh parsley
3 fresh mint leaves
1 t. honey
1 c. fish stock
¼ c. white wine
2 T. olive oil or butter
(dash of mustard seed)
(1 t. white or cider vinegar)
(¼ c. raisins)

In a mortar, grind together pepper, celery seed (or II-2
lovage), and oregano. Add chopped parsley and
mint. Blend with honey, stock, white wine, and
olive oil or butter. (If you like, add mustard and vinegar, and, for a livelier flavor, raisins.) Bring to a
boil, then simmer to reduce for 25–30 minutes, and
serve over each portion of the poached skate.

Sautéed Squid in Wine Sauce

III-1

1 lb. squid, fresh or canned*
2 T. olive oil
½ t. ground pepper
¼ t. rosemary (or rue)
1 t. honey
1 c. fish stock
¼ c. white wine
(flour)

Clean squid, cut up, and sauté the pieces in olive o
then finish in the sauce for 40 minutes over lo
heat.

For the sauce, grind together pepper, rosema
(or rue). Add honey, stock, and wine. Bring to
boil, then pour over the pan of squid, and coc
slowly together.

If desired, add flour at the end to make a thi
sauce.

*Canned squid may be used without alteration. (Dri
squid must be well soaked before use, and even then is i
ferior to fresh or canned squid.)

Sausage Stuffed Squid

III-2

2 lbs. squid

Clean the squid and cut off the tentacles.

Stuffing:
2 T. olive oil
½ c. finely chopped
pork sausage meat
½ t. ground pepper
1 t. lovage (or celery seed)
½ t. coriander
½ t. celery seed
1 egg yolk

To make the stuffing, cut up tentacles very finel
and fry in olive oil. Mix together with sausage mea
Season with pepper, lovage (or celery seed), cor
ander, and celery seed. Bind with well beaten egg
Fill each squid with stuffing and secure wit
toothpicks. Cook gently in the following wine sauc
for 30 minutes.

Sauce:
1 t. honey
1 t. white or cider vinegar
1 c. fish stock
½ c. white wine
2 T. olive oil

For the sauce, combine honey, vinegar, stock, wine
and olive oil, cook squid with it, and serve togethe

Sauce for Stuffed Squid or Cuttlefish

2 lbs. cooked stuffed squid (see next recipe)

Sauce:
1/4 t. ground pepper
1/2 t. lovage (or celery seed)
1/2 t. celery seed
pinch of caraway
1 t. honey
3/4 c. beef stock
1/4 c. white wine

In a mortar, grind together pepper, lovage (or celery IV-1
seed), celery seed, and caraway. Mix with honey,
stock, and white wine. Bring to a boil, then simmer
for 25 minutes to reduce. Pour over the sliced,
stuffed squid, and serve.

This sauce may also be used with the *Sausage
Stuffed Squid* above.

Squid or Cuttlefish Stuffed with Brains

2 lbs. squid
2 T. olive oil
1/4 lb. calf's brains
butter
peppercorns
1/2 c. finely chopped
pork sausage
1 raw egg
1/2 t. ground pepper
pinch of fennel

Clean squid, cut off tentacles, and chop them very IV-2
finely. Fry the pieces in olive oil. Next, brown calf's
brains in butter, and chop very finely. Mix tentacles
and brains together with pork sausage. Bind with
well beaten egg, and season with pepper. Stuff the
squid and secure each with toothpicks. Cover with
water seasoned with fennel, and cook 1 hour over
low heat.

OF OYSTERS

I'm just arrived from Baiae
 An oyster drunk from Lake Lucrine:
But wanton though I am
 I still can crave your noble sauce.

Martial, 13.82.

VI   IN OSTREIS   *Of Oysters*   [Season with] pepper, lovage, egg yolk,
vinegar, stock, olive oil, and wine. If you wish, add honey.

The First Oyster Ponds

The first oyster ponds were devised by Sergius Orata at Baiae,
during the career of Lucius Crassus, before the Marsian War
[Social War, 90–88 B.C.]. *Orata invented these vivaria not to*
satisfy his gluttony, but his avarice. He obtained a great profit by
his own ingenuity, for he was also the first to invent shower baths.
He used to adorn the country houses he sold with them. This man
first judged the flavor of the oysters of the Lucrine Lake to be the
best, for the same species of aquatic animals can be of better quality
in one place than in another. This is the case with wolffish in the
Tiber river between the two bridges, Ravenna's turbot, the moray
eel in Sicily, the sturgeon of Rhodes, and also with other kinds —
not to continue my judgement of seafood to its conclusion. The
coasts of Britain were not yet supplying oysters when Orata made
the Lucrine variety famous. Afterwards, however, it was considered
worth the price to fetch oysters from Brundisium at the end of
Italy. To avoid disputes between the two delicacies, in modern times
the Lucrine Lake has contrived to satisfy the hunger caused by the
long transportation from Brundisium.

Pliny, 9.79.

Thick Sauce for Squid or Cuttlefish

2 lbs. cooked squid

Sauce:
½ t. ground pepper
½ t. celery seed (or lovage)
½ t. coriander
½ t. mint
1 raw egg yolk
1 t. honey
¾ c. fish stock
¼ c. white wine
1 t. white or cider vinegar
2 t. olive oil or butter

To make the sauce, grind together pepper, celery IV-4 seed (or lovage), coriander, and mint. Mix with honey, stock, white wine, vinegar, and olive oil. Heat and carefully stir in well beaten egg yolk. Bring to a boil and simmer slowly to thicken. Serve with boiled or sautéed squid. If you wish, thicken the sauce further with flour before serving.

Seasoned Octopus

2 lbs. octopus meat
1 t. salt
3 T. fish-pickle (see p. 305)
½ t. ground pepper
¼ t. fennel

Clean octopus. Pound meat to tenderize, then cut v body and tentacles into small pieces and cook till tender in salted water.

Combine fish-pickle, pepper, and fennel, and season the cooked meat with the mixture before serving.

Oyster Stew with Wine

3 c. shelled oysters
½ t. ground pepper
1 t. celery seed (or lovage)
1 t. white or cider vinegar
2 t. olive oil or butter
½ c. white wine
1½ c. oyster stock
2 raw egg yolks
1 T. flour
(honey)

Put oysters into a stewing pan, and season with pep- vi per, celery seed (or lovage), vinegar, olive oil or butter, white wine, and strained oyster stock. Simmer for 20 minutes, stirring from time to time. At the end, beat the yolks, mix with flour, and add liquid from the oyster stew to make a smooth paste. Add to the stew, thicken, and serve.

If you wish, add a little honey to sweeten.

OF ALL KINDS OF SHELLFISH

VII

IN OMNE GENUS CONCHYLIORUM *For All Kinds of Shellfish*
[Prepare them with] pepper, lovage, parsley, dried mint, a goodly
quantity of cumin, honey, stock and if you wish, add some cinnamon
and spikenard.

OF SEA URCHINS

Demetrius of Scepsis says that a Spartan once went to a feast and
sea urchins were placed on his table. He picked one up, not
understanding which part was edible, nor turning to his dinner
companions for advice. At once, he put it into his mouth intending
to tear it to pieces, shell and all. When he found the sea urchin
difficult to chew and couldn't understand the reason for its
sharpness, he declared, "Bloody food, I won't be weak now and give
it up but I'll never take another."

Athenaeus, 3.91.

VIII-1

IN ECHINO *Of Sea Urchin* Take a fresh saucepan [and pour
into it] a little olive oil, stock, sweet wine, and finely ground pepper.
Boil. Then add some [sauce] to each sea urchin. [Cook them over a
slow fire.] Stirring repeatedly, allow to boil three times. Spinkle with
pepper and serve.

VIII-2

ALITER IN ECHINO *[Sauce] for Sea Urchin* Use pepper, a little
costmary, dried mint, honey wine, stock, and Indian spikenard and bay
leaf.

VIII-3

ALITER IN ECHINO *Sea Urchin* Put the sea urchins alone in
hot water only, cook, then lift them out and arrange them in a small
pan. Now add bayleaf, pepper, honey, stock, a little olive oil, and eggs
to thicken [the mixture]. Cook [the sea urchins and the sauce] in the
thermospodium. Sprinkle with pepper and serve.

The hedgehog of the sea has a shell that's sharp
And only your bleeding fingers can touch the softness
that lie beneath

Martial, 13.86.

Cumin Sauce for All Kinds of Shellfish

½ t. ground pepper
¼ t. celery seed (or lovage)
½ t. fresh parsley
½ t. fresh mint
cumin, to taste
1 c. shellfish liquid
1 t. honey
1 t. white or cider vinegar
(pinch of bay leaf)
(dash of cinnamon)
(flour)

In a mortar, grind together pepper, celery seed (or VII
lovage), and cumin to taste. Add finely chopped
parsley and mint. Mix with shellfish liquid, honey,
and vinegar. (If you like, also add crushed bay leaf
and cinnamon.) Bring to a boil, then simmer 25 minutes to reduce.

This sauce can be used as a court bouillon in the
preparation of oysters, cockles, scallops, or mussels.
For use with clams, thicken with flour, if you wish.

Sea Urchins Cooked in Wine Sauce

20–30 sea urchins
Sauce:
2 t. olive oil
1 c. fish stock
2 T. sweet white wine
dash of ground pepper

In a pan, combine olive oil, stock, and wine. Add a VIII-1
very small quantity of pepper. Bring this sauce to a
boil, then simmer.

Meanwhile, remove the edible parts (the ovaries)
of the sea urchins, and add them to the sauce. Simmer gently for 5 minutes. When cooked, remove
from the sauce, sprinkle with pepper, and serve.

Herb Sauce for Sea Urchins

20–30 sea urchins
Sauce:
pinch each of costmary (or
mint), pepper, and mint
2 T. sweet white wine (or
mead)
1 c. fish stock
pinch of spikenard, or
bay leaf, crushed

Combine costmary (or mint), sweet wine (or mead), VIII-2
pepper, mint, fish stock, and spikenard or bay leaf.
Heat the sauce, and cook the sea urchins as in the
preceding recipe (Sea Urchins Cooked in Wine Sauce).

VIII-4   IN ECHINO SALSO *Salted Sea Urchins* [Cook] the salted sea urchins with the finest quality fish stock, and season with boiled wine and pepper. Serve.

VIII-5   ALITER [*Sea Urchin*] Mix the salted sea urchins with the best fish stock, and they will appear to be fresh, so that they can be eaten as one comes out of the bath.

OF MUSSELS

IX   IN MITULIS *Of Mussels* [Mix the cooking] stock [of the mussels], chopped chives, cumin, raisin wine, savory, and wine. Blend this sauce with water and cook the mussels in it [immediately].

OF SARDINES, TUNNYFISH FRY, AND MULLET

X-1   IN SARDIS *Of Sardines* Stuffed sardines should be made thus. Remove the bones. Combine pennyroyal, cumin, peppercorns, mint, nuts, and honey. Fill up [the sardines with this stuffing], tie them, and then roll in papyrus leaf and set them in a covered pan in the steam from the fire. Season with olive oil, boiled wine, and fish-pickle.

X-2   SARDA ITA FIT *Sardines* The sardines are cooked and boned [and stuffed]. [To make the stuffing] mix pepper, lovage, thyme, oregano, rue, dates, and honey. Put [the cooked,] stuffed [sardines] in a small dish and decorate with sliced hard-boiled eggs. [Add a dressing of] a little wine, vinegar, boiled wine, and fresh olive oil.

X-3   IUS IN SARDA *Sauce for Sardines* Pepper, oregano, mint, onion, a little vinegar, and olive oil.

X-4   IUS IN SARDA *Sauce for Sardines* Pepper, lovage, dried mint, cooked onion, honey, vinegar, and olive oil. Pour over [the sardines and] sprinkle with sliced hard-boiled eggs.

X-5   IUS IN CORDULA ASSA *Sauce for Baked Tunnyfish Fry* Pepper, lovage, celery seed, mint, rue, dates, honey, vinegar, wine, and olive oil. This [preparation] may also be used with sardines.

X-6   IUS IN MUGILE SALSO *Sauce for Salted Grey Mullet* Pepper, lovage, cumin, onions, mint, rue, smooth-shelled nuts, dates, honey, vinegar, mustard, and olive oil.

Sea Urchins in Thick Sauce

20–30 sea urchins
1 small bay leaf
¼ t. ground pepper
1 t. honey
1 c. sea urchin or fish stock
1 raw egg yolk
(pepper)

Simmer the sea urchins in water for 5 minutes. VIII-3 Drain, reserve liquid, and put them in a fresh pan.

For the sauce, combine bay leaf, pepper, honey, and stock. Heat, simmer for 10 minutes, remove bay leaf, and thicken with well beaten egg.

Serve the sea urchins in the sauce, with a sprinkling of pepper if you wish.

Mussels in Savory Wine

4 c. mussels in the shell

Sauce:
1 c. mussel stock, strained
2 T. chopped chives
¼ t. cumin
½ t. savory
¼ c. white wine

Clean the mussels and cook them until the shells IX open. Drain and reserve stock.

For the sauce, combine the stock, chives, cumin to taste, savory, and white wine. Add to the mussels, and simmer together for 15 minutes before serving.

Stuffed Sardines

10 fresh sardines

Stuffing:
…ch of pennyroyal (or mint)
⅛ t. cumin
1½ t. mint
¼ c. finely chopped almonds or other nuts
2 t. honey
foil or greaseproof paper
½ c. water
½ c. fish-pickle (see p. 305)

Open the sardines and remove the backbones. X-1

To make the stuffing, combine pennyroyal (or mint) cumin, pepper, mint, and nuts. Bind with honey. Fill the sardines with this stuffing, and wrap in foil or greaseproof paper. Steam gently in water in a covered steamer for 30 minutes. Serve with fish-pickle.

Sweet, Stuffed Sardines with Eggs

x-2

10 fresh sardines

Stuffing:
¼ t. ground pepper
½ t. celery seed (or lovage)
¼ t. thyme
¼ t. oregano
pinch of rosemary (or rue)
¼ c. finely chopped dates
1 t. honey
eggs, hard-boiled

½ c. fish-pickle (see p. 305)

Open the sardines and remove the backbone

To make the stuffing, combine pepper, celery see (or lovage), thyme, oregano, rosemary (or rue), ar dates. Bind with honey. Then stuff sardines ar steam, as in the preceding recipe (Stuffed Sardines

When done, unwrap the sardines and arrang them on a serving dish. Decorate with sliced egg and serve with fish-pickle.

Onion Dressing for Cold Sardines

x-3

¼ t. ground pepper
⅛ t. cumin
¼ t. oregano
1 mint leaf, finely chopped
2 T. chopped onion
1 t. dried onion
¾ c. olive oil or salad oil
3 T. white wine or
cider vinegar

In a mortar, grind together pepper, cumin, an oregano. Add to mint, onion, oil, and vinegar.

Serve as a dressing with chilled, baked, or steame sardines.

Alternatively, place canned sardines in a colande and wash gently in cold water. Serve with the dres ing, as an appetizer.

Sweet Dressing for Cold Sardines

x-4

¼ t. ground pepper
⅛ t. cumin
¼ t. celery seed (or lovage)
1–2 t. liquid honey
1 hard-boiled egg, chopped

Make the dressing as above, but substitute celer seed (or lovage) for the oregano and add honey to taste.

Garnish cold sardines with a sprinkling of chop ped hard-boiled egg, and pour a little dressing ove them.

Date Sauce for Baked Tuna or Sardines

1 lb. tuna or sardines

Sauce:
¼ t. ground pepper
1 t. lovage (or celery seed)
2 t. celery seed
1 t. mint
pinch of rosemary (or rue)
2 T. dates, finely chopped
1 t. honey
1 t. white wine vinegar or cider vinegar
¼ c. white wine
2 T. olive oil
1 c. fish stock

In a mortar, grind together pepper, lovage (or celery   x-5
seed), celery seed, mint, and a pinch of rosemary
(or rue). Add to dates. Blend with honey, vinegar,
white wine, olive oil, and stock. Bring to a boil, simmer for 25 minutes to reduce, and serve with chilled
fish.

Alternatively, make a cold dressing using 1 c. of
olive oil, ¼ c. of vinegar, 2 T. white wine, and the
chopped dates and seasonings.

Sweet Cumin Dressing for Cold Fish Fillets

2 lbs. cooked cold fish fillets

Dressing:
¼ t. ground pepper
1 t. celery seed (or lovage)
¼–½ t. cumin to taste
1 fresh mint leaf
pinch of rosemary (or rue)
2 T. chopped onion
1 T. finely chopped almonds
1 T. finely chopped dates
1 t. liquid honey
3 T. white wine vinegar or cider vinegar
⅛ t. ground mustard
⅓ c. olive oil

In a mortar, grind together pepper, celery seed (or   x-6
lovage), cumin, chopped mint, and rosemary (or
rue). Combine with onion, almonds, dates, honey,
vinegar, mustard, and olive oil.

Serve chilled with cold fish fillets or in fish salads.

Sweet Oregano Dressing for Cold Fish Fillets

x-7   *2 lbs. cooked, cold fish fillets*

Dressing:
¼ t. ground pepper
½ t. oregano
dash mustard seed (or colewort)
1 mint leaf
pinch of rosemary (or rue)
1 T. finely chopped almonds
1 T. finely chopped dates
1 t. liquid honey
⅓ c. olive oil
3 T. white wine vinegar or cider vinegar
⅛ t. ground mustard

In a mortar, grind together pepper, oregano, mustard seed (or colewort), mint, and rosemary (or rue). Add almonds and dates, and blend with honey, olive oil, vinegar, and mustard.

Chill and serve with cold fish fillets or in fish salads.

Onion Lovage Dressing for Cold Tuna

x-8   *1 lb. canned tuna or cooked, cold fish fillets*

Dressing:
¼ t. ground pepper
1 t. celery seed (or lovage)
¼ t. cumin
1 mint leaf
pinch of rosemary (or rue)
3 t. chopped onion
1 T. finely chopped almonds
1 T. finely chopped dates
1 t. liquid honey
2 T. white wine vinegar or cider vinegar
⅛ t. ground mustard
⅓ c. olive oil

In a mortar, grind pepper, celery seed (or lovage), cumin, mint, and rosemary (or rue). Add to onion, almonds and dates, and blend with honey, vinegar, mustard, and olive oil.

Chill and serve with cold tuna, cold cooked fillets, or in a fish salad.

Almond and Wine Dressing for Cold Fish

1 lb. cooked, cold fish fillets
⅛ t. cumin
¼ t. ground pepper
1 T. boiled white wine (see
p. 306)
2 T. finely chopped almonds
2 T. white wine vinegar or
cider vinegar
⅓ c. olive oil

In a mortar, grind together cumin and pepper. Add   x-10
to almonds, and mix with wine, vinegar, and olive
oil.

Serve with cold fish fillets, or in fish salads.

Baian Oysters in Spiced Broth

2 c. very small or
chopped oysters
2 c. mussels
½ c. sea urchins
c. roasted almonds, chopped
8 T. shellfish liquid
pinch of rosemary (or rue)
1 c. chopped celery
½ t. ground pepper
1 t. coriander
¼ c. boiled white wine (see
p. 306)
fish stock
3 T. finely chopped dates
2 T. olive oil

Combine oysters, mussels, the edible parts of sea   xi
urchins (the ovaries), and almonds. Put these ingredients into a deep pot and add shellfish liquid. Season with rosemary (or rue), celery, pepper, coriander, boiled white wine, sufficient stock to cover,
dates, and olive oil. Cook over low heat for 40 minutes in the covered pan.

X-7   ALITER IUS IN MUGILE SALSO *Another Sauce for Salted Grey Mullet* Pepper, oregano, colewort, mint, rue, smooth-shelled nuts, dates, honey, olive oil, vinegar, and mustard.

X-8   IUS IN SILURO IN PELAMYDE ET IN THYNNO SALSIS *Sauce for Salted Sheatfish, Young Tunnyfish, and Tunnyfish Over a Year Old* Pepper, lovage, cumin, onion, mint, rue, smooth-shelled nuts, dates, honey, vinegar, mustard, and olive oil.

X-9   IUS IN MULLO TARICHO *Sauce for Salted Red Mullet* Pepper, rue, onion, dates, mustard. Mix [these ingredients] with chopped sea urchin and add olive oil. Pour this [sauce] over the fried or baked fish.

X-10   SALSUM SINE SALSO *Saltfish without Saltfish* Cook and chop the liver of a hare, of a kid, of a lamb, or of a chicken, [and season it] with pepper, fish stock, or salt. Add olive oil. If you wish, shape [the cooked liver] in a mold into the form of a fish. Add fresh olive oil above [and serve].[1]

X-11   ALITER VICE SALSI *Another Substitute for Saltfish* Grind cumin, pepper, and fish stock. Add a little raisin wine or boiled wine and mix [these ingredients] with a large quantity of chopped nuts. Blend well, and then pour over the salted [livers]. Sprinkle a few drops of olive oil over [the dish], and then serve.

X-12   ALITER SALSUM SINE SALSO *Saltfish without Saltfish* Take five fingers' worth of cumin, half of this quantity of pepper, and one washed clove of garlic. Mix these ingredients well. Pour stock over them. Sprinkle with a few drops of olive oil. This will restore an upset stomach exceedingly well and help digestion.

BAIAN STEW

XI   EMBRACTUM BAIANUM *Baian Stew* Into a cooking pot, put chopped oysters, mussels, and [sea] nettles. Add chopped, roasted nuts, rue, celery, pepper, coriander, cumin, raisin wine, fish stock, dates, and olive oil. [Simmer and serve.]

BOOK IX OF APICIUS, THE SEA, IS
ENDED

The Fisherman

This Book of *The Roman Cookery of Apicius* is devoted entirely to fish sauces. There are very few instructions for their preparation, but common sense suggests that in the case of baked or fried fish dishes, the sauces were to be cooked separately from the fish. The simplicity and spareness of this Book suggests that it is a translation of another (probably Greek) work on cookery, one that was concerned only with fish sauces, and which assumed common knowledge of cooking methods on the part of its readers.

OF FISH

1-1   IUS DIABOTANON IN PISCE FRIXO   *An Herb Sauce for Fried Fish*   Take whatever fish you like, gut it, wash and fry it. [In a mortar] grind pepper, cumin, coriander seed, laser root, oregano, and rue. Blend. Pour vinegar [over these seasonings and then] add dates, honey, boiled wine, olive oil, and fish stock. Blend and pour into a cooking pot. Heat until [the sauce] has boiled. Pour [this sauce] over the fried fish. Sprinkle with pepper and serve.

1-2   IUS IN PISCE ELIXO   *Sauce for Poached Fish*   Pepper, lovage, cumin, shallot, oregano, nuts, dates, honey, vinegar, fish stock, mustard, and a little olive oil. This sauce [should be served] hot. If you like, add raisins.

1-3   ALITER IN PISCE ELIXO   *[Sauce] for Poached Fish*   Mix pepper, lovage, fresh coriander, savory, onion, the yolks of boiled eggs, raisin wine, vinegar, olive oil, and fish stock.

1-4   IUS IN PISCE ELIXO   *Sauce for Poached Fish*[1]   [Wash and] gut the fish carefully. Then put salt and coriander seed in a mortar and grind well. Roll the fish in this [seasoning]. Put the fish into a shallow pan. Cover and seal with gypsum. Cook in the oven. When the fish is cooked, lift it out [onto a platter]. Sprinkle with the sharpest vinegar and serve.

1-5   ALITER IUS IN PISCE ELIXO   *Sauce for Poached Fish*   When you have gutted the fish, put it into a frying pan. Add [coriander] seed, water, and fresh anise. When [the fish is] cooked, sprinkle with vinegar and serve.

Herb Sauce for Fried Fish

2 lbs. fried fish fillets

Sauce:
¼ t. ground pepper
⅛ t. cumin
¼ t. coriander
pinch of fennel
pinch of rosemary (or rue)
1 t. white or cider vinegar
3 dates, finely chopped
(1 t. honey)
⅓ c. white wine
2 t. olive oil or butter
⅔ c. fish stock

In a mortar, grind pepper, cumin, coriander seeds, I-I fennel, and rosemary (or rue). Moisten these seasonings with vinegar. Combine with dates, (honey, if you wish,) white wine, olive oil, and stock. Bring the mixture to a boil, and simmer for 25 minutes to reduce.

Pour over the fried fish, and serve with a sprinkling of pepper.

Sauce for Poached Fish Fillets

2 lbs. poached fish fillets

Sauce:
¼ t. ground pepper
1 t. celery seed (or lovage)
½ t. oregano
1 small onion, chopped
¼ c. pine nuts or
almonds, chopped
3 dates, finely chopped
1 t. honey
1 t. white wine vinegar or
cider vinegar
⅛ t. ground mustard
1 t. olive oil or butter
1½ c. fish stock
(raisins)

In a mortar, grind together pepper, celery seed (or I-2 lovage), and oregano. Mix with onion, nuts, and dates. Combine with honey, vinegar, mustard, olive oil or butter, and stock. Bring to a boil and simmer for 25 minutes to reduce.

Add raisins to the sauce ingredients, if you wish, and serve over poached fillets.

Egg Sauce for Poached Fish

1-3

2 lbs. poached fish fillets

Sauce:

¼ t. ground pepper

1 t. celery seed (or lovage)

½ t. coriander

¼ t. savory

2 T. chopped onion

3 hard-boiled egg yolks, chopped

½ c. white wine

1 t. white wine vinegar or cider vinegar

1 T. olive oil or butter

1 c. fish stock

In a mortar, grind pepper, celery seed (or lovage), coriander, and savory. Add to onion. Combine with the egg yolks, wine, vinegar, olive oil or butter, and stock. Bring to a boil and simmer for 25 minutes to reduce.

Fish Steamed with Coriander

1-4

2 lbs. fish fillets

½ t. salt

1 t. coriander

sharp white vinegar

In a mortar, grind salt and coriander seeds. Sprinkle these seasonings over the fish fillets. Roll the fish (so coriander remains on the fish) and secure each fillet with toothpicks. Cook in a little water in a covered pan in a 300°F oven for 30 minutes. Serve fillets on a platter with a sprinkling of vinegar.

Fish Poached with Anise

1-5

2 lbs. fish fillets

water

1 t. coriander seed

pinch of aniseed

sharp white vinegar

Put the fish fillets in a frying pan. Barely cover with water, and season with coriander and aniseed. Bring to a boil and simmer for about 10 minutes. Discard liquid and serve fillets with a sprinkling of vinegar.

Oregano Plum Sauce for Fish

2 lbs. fish fillets

Sauce:
½ t. ground pepper
1 t. lovage (or celery seed)
¼ t. cumin
½ t. oregano
½ t. celery seed
2 T. chopped onion
3 pitted damsons or plums, thinly sliced
1 t. honey or 2 T. mead
1 t. white wine vinegar or cider vinegar
½ c. white wine
1 T. olive oil or butter
1 c. fish stock

In a mortar, grind pepper, lovage (or celery seed), cumin, oregano, and celery seed. Mix with onion, damsons or plums, then add honey or mead, vinegar, white wine, olive oil or butter, and fish stock. Heat to a boil and simmer gently for 25 minutes to reduce. Then serve with the cooked fillets.   1-6

Alexandrine Wine Sauce for Fish

2 lbs. fish fillets

Sauce:
¼ t. ground pepper
1 t. celery seed (or lovage)
½ t. coriander
¼ c. dark raisins
¼ c. white wine
1 T. olive oil or butter
1 c. fish stock

In a mortar, grind pepper, celery seed (or lovage), and coriander. Combine with raisins, and blend with wine, olive oil or butter, and fish stock. Heat to a boil, and simmer gently for 25 minutes to reduce. Then serve with the cooked fillets.   1-7

I-6   IUS ALEXANDRINUM IN PISCE ASSO *Alexandrine Sauce for Baked Fish* [Make the sauce from these ingredients:] pepper, dried onion, lovage, cumin, oregano, celery seed, pitted damsons, honey wine, vinegar, fish stock, boiled wine, and olive oil. Cook.

    ❡This and the two succeeding sauces were named for the ancient inhabitants of Alexandria in Egypt. Alexandria was the great emporium for the spice trade between the Orient and the western Mediterranean.

I-7   ALITER IUS ALEXANDRINUM IN PISCE ASSO *Another Alexandrine Sauce for Baked Fish* [Blend] pepper, lovage, green coriander, pitted raisins, wine, fish stock, and olive oil. Cook.

I-8   ALITER IUS ALEXANDRINUM IN PISCE ASSO *Another Alexandrine Sauce for Baked Fish* [Make with] pepper, lovage, green coriander, onion, pitted damsons, raisin wine, fish stock, vinegar, and olive oil. Cook.

I-9   IUS IN GONGRO ASSO *Sauce for Baked Conger Eel* Pepper, lovage, fried cumin, oregano, dried onion, yolks of hard-boiled eggs, wine, honey wine, vinegar, fish stock, and boiled wine. Cook.

I-10   IUS IN CORNUTAM *Sauce for Horned Fish* Pepper, lovage, oregano, onion, pitted raisins, wine, honey, vinegar, fish stock, and olive oil. Cook.

    ❡The horned fish is probably the *Scorpaena porcus*, a species of scorpion fish, or rascasse.

I-11   IUS IN MULLOS ASSOS *Sauce for Baked Red Mullet* Pepper, lovage, rue, honey, nuts, vinegar, wine, fish stock, and a little olive oil. Heat [this sauce] and pour over [the baked red mullet].

This tiny mullet insults my golden plate.

Martial, 14.97.

Alexandrine Plum Sauce for Baked Fish

2 lbs. baked fish fillets

Sauce:
¼ t. ground pepper
1 t. celery seed (or lovage)
½ t. coriander
2 T. chopped onion
6 pitted damsons or plums,
sliced (or ¼ c. raisins)
¼ c. sweet white wine
1 t. white wine vinegar or
cider vinegar
1 T. olive oil or butter
1 c. fish stock

In a mortar, grind together pepper, celery seed (or lovage), and coriander. Add to onion. Combine with damsons, plums (or raisins), and mix with wine, vinegar, olive oil or butter, and fish stock. Heat to a boil and simmer gently for 25 minutes to reduce.

Serve with baked fish fillets.

I-8

Egg Sauce for Baked Eel

2 lbs. baked eel

Sauce:
½ t. ground pepper
1 t. celery seed (or lovage)
¼ t. cumin
½ t. oregano
2 T. chopped onion
¼ c. white wine
1 t. honey or 2 T. mead
1 c. fish stock
1 t. white wine vinegar or
cider vinegar
3 hard-boiled eggs, chopped

In a mortar, grind together pepper, celery seed (or lovage), cumin, and oregano. Then blend with onion, wine, honey or mead, fish stock, and vinegar to taste. Bring to a boil, then simmer gently for 25 minutes to reduce.

Pour sauce over pieces of baked eel, and garnish with chopped eggs.

I-9

Raisin Sauce for Poached Fish

I-10

2 lbs. poached fish fillets

Sauce:
½ t. ground pepper
1 t. celery seed (or lovage)
½ t. oregano
1 T. chopped onion
¼ c. dark raisins
¼ c. white wine
1 t. honey
1 t. white wine vinegar or
cider vinegar
½ c. fish stock
1 T. olive oil or butter

In a mortar, grind pepper, celery seed (or lovage), and oregano. Combine with onion and raisins, and blend with wine, honey, vinegar, fish stock, and olive oil or butter.

Poach the fish fillets with the sauce for 10 minutes, and serve in the sauce.

The red mullet used by Apicius can either be baked or fried whole in olive oil with a coating of flour.

Nut Sauce for Baked Trout or Red Mullet

I-11

3 lbs. whole baked trout or
red mullet

Sauce:
½ t. ground pepper
1 t. celery seed (or lovage)
pinch of rosemary (or rue)
1 t. honey
¼ c. almonds, chopped
1 t. white wine vinegar or
cider vinegar
2 T. white wine
¾ c. fish stock
1 t. olive oil or butter

In a mortar, grind pepper, celery seed (or lovage), and rosemary (or rue). Combine with honey, nuts, vinegar, wine, fish stock, and olive oil or butter. Heat to a boil and simmer gently 25 minutes to reduce.

Serve with baked trout or red mullet.

Honey Mint Sauce for Baked Trout or Mullet

3 lbs. whole baked trout or
red mullet

Sauce:
pinch of rosemary (or rue)
1 t. mint
½ t. coriander
pinch of fennel seed
½ t. ground pepper
1 t. celery seed (or lovage)
2 t. honey
1 c. fish stock
1 t. olive oil
3 T. white wine

In a mortar, grind rosemary (or rue), mint, coriander, fennel seed, pepper, and celery seed (or lovage). Combine with honey, fish stock, olive oil, and white wine. Heat to a boil, then simmer gently for 25 minutes to reduce.

Serve with baked trout or red mullet.

1-12

⟨When the city of Rome was at the zenith of her power in the first century A.D., the mullet held pride of place at the tables of the very rich. Their pursuit of this luxury can only be described as an obsession.

Calliodorus, yesterday you sold a slave for 1,200 sesterces
To dine well once.
But you didn't eat well: the 4 lb mullet you bought
Was the spectacle, the chief dish of your dinner.
I cried out to you: "This is not a fish, you bastard, it's not:
It's a man, Calliodorus, you've been eating a man."

Martial, 10.31.

When the craze for red mullet threatened to undermine the economic health of the city, Tiberius Caesar imposed a sumptuary tax on its sale in the markets, and this excellent fish once again assumed its proper place.

1-12   ALITER IUS IN MULLOS ASSOS *Another Sauce for Baked Red Mullet* Take rue, mint, coriander, fennel. [Make sure that these herbs are] all fresh. Add pepper, lovage, honey, fish stock, and a little olive oil.

1-13   IUS IN PELAMYDE ASSA *Sauce for Baked Young Tunnyfish* [Mix] pepper, lovage, oregano, green coriander, onion, pitted raisins, raisin wine, vinegar, fish stock, boiled wine, and olive oil. Cook. If you wish, add some honey. This sauce may also be served with poached [tunnyfish].

1-14   IUS IN PERCAM *Sauce for Perch* Pepper, lovage, fried cumin, onion, pitted damsons, wine, honey wine, vinegar, olive oil, and boiled wine. Cook.

1-15   IUS IN PISCE RUBELLIONE *Sauce for Redfish* Pepper, lovage, caraway, wild thyme, celery seed, dried onion, wine, raisin wine, vinegar, fish stock, and olive oil. Thicken with cornstarch.

For the Mediterranean tunnyfish North American cooks may substitute the Californian tunny or tuna. The immature tuna is not commonly available in North America, but canned tuna can be used in its place. It should be drained, moistened with a little melted butter, seasoned with coriander, and then baked in foil. The hot sauce is then poured over the cooked tuna at the table.

Onion Raisin Sauce for Baked Tuna

1 lb. baked tuna

Sauce:
¼ t. ground pepper
½ t. coriander
1 t. celery seed (or lovage)
½ t. oregano
1 t. white wine vinegar or cider vinegar
2 T. olive oil or butter
2 T. boiled white wine (see p. 306)
2 T. sweet raisin wine or muscatel
1 c. fish stock
2 T. chopped onion
¼ c. dark raisins

I-13

In a mortar, grind together pepper, coriander, celery seed (or lovage), and oregano. Blend with vinegar, olive oil, boiled wine, sweet wine, and fish stock. Add onion and raisins. Heat to a boil, then simmer gently for 25 minutes to reduce.

Pour the cooked sauce over baked tuna.

This sauce, served with baked, canned tuna and a thick slice of French bread and butter, makes an exciting lunch.

Wine Sauce for Poached Perch

I-14

2–3 lbs. poached perch

Sauce:
¼ t. ground pepper
1 t. celery seed (or lovage)
¼ t. cumin
1 t. chopped onion
3 pitted damsons or plums,
thinly sliced
¼ c. white wine
1 t. white or cider vinegar
1 T. olive oil or butter
2 T. boiled wine (see
p. 306)
1 c. fish stock
(2 T. mead or 1 t. honey)

In a mortar, grind together pepper, celery seed (or lovage), and cumin. Combine with onion and sliced plums. Mix with white wine, mead or honey, vinegar, olive oil or butter, boiled wine, fish stock, and, if you wish, mead or honey.

Bring to a boil, then simmer gently for 25 minutes to reduce.

Serve the sauce over each portion of poached fish.

Caraway Sauce for Baked Salmon

I-15

2 lbs. baked salmon

Sauce:
¼ t. ground pepper
1 t. lovage (or celery seed)
½ t. thyme
½ t. celery seed
pinch of caraway
1 T. chopped onion
¼ c. white wine
1 t. white wine vinegar or
cider vinegar
1 T. olive oil or butter
1 c. fish stock
flour

In a mortar, grind together pepper, lovage (or celery seed), thyme, and celery seed. Add caraway and onion. Mix with white wine, vinegar, olive oil or butter, and fish stock. Bring to a boil, simmer gently for 20 minutes, then thicken with flour.

Serve the sauce over each portion of salmon.

OF MORAY EEL

Gaius Hirrius was the first to invent separate fish ponds for
rearing morays. He contributed 6,000 morays to the banquets at
which the dictator Julius Caesar celebrated his triumphs, but as a
loan, since he was unwilling to exchange them for a price or indeed
for any other kind of payment. When he sold his smallish country
seat, he received 4,000,000 sesterces largely on the strength of his
fish ponds. It was after this that a passion for individual fishes
began to seize certain people. At Bacolo, in the district of Baiae, the
orator Hortensius kept a fish pond in which there was a moray he
so prized that it is widely believed he shed tears at its death. In the
same country house, Antonia, the wife of Drusus, put earrings on
a moray she loved, and some people longed to see Bacolo because of
its famous fish.

Pliny, 9.81.

IUS IN MURENA ASSA *Sauce for Broiled Moray Eel* [Combine]   11-1
pepper, lovage, savory, saffron after its oil has been extracted, onions,
pitted damsons, wine, honey wine, vinegar, fish stock, boiled wine, and
olive oil. Cook.

ALITER IUS IN MURENA ASSA *Another Sauce for Broiled Moray*   11-2
Eel [Combine] pepper, lovage, damsons, wine, honey wine, vinegar,
fish stock, boiled wine, and olive oil. Cook.

ALITER IUS IN MURENA ASSA *Another Sauce for Broiled Eel*   11-3
[Combine] pepper, lovage, mountain catmint, coriander seed, onion,
pine nuts, honey, vinegar, fish stock, and olive oil. Cook.

ALITER IUS IN MURENA ELIXA *Sauce for Poached Moray Eel*   11-4
[Combine] pepper, lovage, anise, celery seed, Syrian sumach, dates,
honey, vinegar, fish stock, olive oil, mustard, and boiled wine.

ALITER IUS IN MURENA ELIXA *Another Sauce for Poached*   11-5
Moray Eel [Combine] pepper, lovage, caraway, celery seed, coriander,
dried mint, pine nuts, rue, honey, vinegar, wine, fish stock, and a little
olive oil. Simmer and thicken with starch.

Saffron Wine Sauce for Poached Eels

II-I

2 lbs. poached eels

Sauce:
½ t. ground pepper
1 t. celery seed (or lovage)
½ t. savory
pinch of saffron
1 T. chopped onion
3 pitted damsons or plums,
thinly sliced
¼ c. white wine
2 t. white wine vinegar or
cider vinegar
1 c. fish stock
1 T. olive oil

In a mortar, grind together pepper, celery seed (or lovage), savory, and saffron. Add onion and sliced plums. Mix with white wine, vinegar, fish stock, and olive oil. Bring to a boil, then simmer gently for 25 minutes to reduce.

Serve the sauce with slices of poached eel.

Plum Sauce for Poached Eels

II-2

2 lbs. poached eels

Sauce:
½ t. ground pepper
½ t. celery seed (or lovage)
3 pitted damsons or plums,
thinly sliced
¼ c. white wine
2 t. white wine vinegar or
cider vinegar
1 c. fish stock
1 T. olive oil

In a mortar, grind together pepper and celery seed (or lovage). Mix with sliced plums, wine, vinegar, stock, and olive oil.

Bring to a boil, then simmer gently for 25 minutes to reduce.

Serve the sauce with slices of poached eel.

Onion Nut Sauce for Poached Eels

2 lbs. poached eels
¼ t. ground pepper
½ t. celery seed (or lovage)
1 t. mint
10 coriander seeds
1 T. chopped onion
¼ c. pine nuts or chopped almonds
1 t. honey
2 t. white wine vinegar or cider vinegar
1 c. fish stock
1 T. olive oil

In a mortar, grind together pepper, celery seed (or lovage), mint, and coriander. Add onion and nuts, and mix with honey, vinegar, fish stock, and olive oil. Bring to a boil, then simmer gently for 25 minutes to reduce. Serve the sauce over slices of poached eel.

II-3

Anise Sauce for Poached Eels

2 lbs. poached eels

Sauce:
¼ t. ground pepper
1 t. celery seed (or lovage)
pinch of aniseed
⅛ t. ground mustard
½ t. celery seed
3 dates, finely chopped
1 t. honey
2 t. white wine vinegar or cider vinegar
1 c. fish stock
1 T. olive oil or butter
¼ c. white wine

In a mortar, grind together pepper, lovage (or celery seed), mustard, and celery seed. Combine with aniseed and dates. Mix with honey, vinegar, fish stock, olive oil, and wine.

Bring to a boil, then simmer gently for 25 minutes to reduce.

Serve the sauce over slices of poached eel.

II-4

II-6   IUS IN MURENA ELIXA *Sauce for Poached Moray Eel* [Combine] pepper, lovage, caraway, cumin, nuts, dates, mustard, honey, vinegar, fish stock, olive oil, and boiled wine. [Simmer.]

II-7   IUS IN LACERTOS ELIXOS *Sauce for Poached Lizard Fish* [Combine] pepper, lovage, cumin, green rue, onions, honey, vinegar, fish stock, and a little olive oil. After [these ingredients] have been brought to the boil, thicken [the sauce] with starch.

II-8   IUS IN PISCE ELIXO *Sauce for Poached Fish* [Combine] pepper, lovage, parsley, oregano, dried onion, honey, vinegar, fish stock, wine, and a little olive oil. When [the sauce] has been brought to the boil, thicken it with starch and serve [the poached fish] on a platter.

II-9   IUS IN PISCE ASSO *Sauce for Baked Fish* [Combine] pepper, lovage, thyme, green coriander, honey, vinegar, fish stock, wine, olive oil, and boiled wine. Simmer [these ingredients] and stir them with a sprig of rue. Thicken with starch [and pour over the baked fish].

II-10   IUS IN THYNNO *Sauce for Tunnyfish* [Combine] pepper, cumin, thyme, coriander, onion, raisins, vinegar, honey, wine, fish stock, and olive oil. Simmer [these ingredients] and thicken with starch.

II-11   IUS IN THYNNO ELIXO *Sauce for Poached Tunnyfish* [Grind] pepper, lovage, thyme, and seasonings used for *Country Sauce*. Add onions, dates, honey, vinegar, fish stock, olive oil, and mustard.

II-12   IUS IN DENTICE ASSO *Sauce for Baked Bream* [Combine] pepper, lovage, coriander, mint, dried rue, cooked quince-apples, honey, wine, fish stock, and olive oil. Simmer, thicken [the sauce] with starch [and pour over the baked bream].

The Preparation of Mediterranean Tunny

These fish are cut in pieces and the neck and belly are most valued; and the throat, too, as long as it is fresh, although even then it will give rise to severe belching. All of the remaining flesh is preserved in salt: these pieces are called melandrya because they resemble splinters of oak. Of these, the cheapest are those next to the tail because they lack fat, and the most excellent parts are next to the throat; but in other fish the parts around the tail are most sought in the market.

Pliny, II.18.

Cumin Sauce for Poached Fish Fillets

2 lbs. poached fish fillets

Sauce:
⅛ t. ground pepper
1 t. celery seed (or lovage)
½ t. cumin
pinch of rosemary (or rue)
1 T. chopped onion
1 t. honey
1 t. white wine vinegar or cider vinegar
1 c. fish stock
1 T. olive oil
(flour)

In a mortar, grind together pepper, celery seed (or 11-7 lovage), cumin, and rosemary (or rue). Add to onion, and blend with honey, vinegar, stock, and olive oil. Bring the sauce to a boil, and simmer gently for 25 minutes to reduce. Thicken with flour, if you wish, and serve over cooked fillets.

Parsley Sauce for Poached Fish Fillets

2 lbs. poached fish fillets

Sauce:
¼ t. ground pepper
1 t. celery seed (or lovage)
4 T. fresh parsley, finely chopped
1 t. oregano
1 T. chopped onion
1 t. honey
1 c. fish stock
2 T. white wine
1 T. olive oil
(flour)

In a mortar, grind together pepper, celery seed (or 11-8 lovage), parsley, and oregano. Add to onion, and combine with honey, stock, wine, and olive oil. Bring the sauce to a boil, then simmer gently for 25 minutes to reduce. Thicken with flour, if you wish, and serve over poached fillets.

Thyme Sauce for Poached Fish Fillets

II-9

2 lbs. poached fish fillets

Sauce:
½ t. ground pepper
1 t. celery seed (or lovage)
¾ t. thyme
¼ t. coriander
1 t. honey
1 t. white wine vinegar or
cider vinegar
1 c. fish stock
¼ c. white wine
pinch of crushed rosemary (or
sage)
(flour)

In a mortar, grind together pepper, celery seed (or lovage), thyme, and coriander. Combine with honey, vinegar, stock, and wine. Heat these ingredients to a boil, adding a pinch of rosemary or, if you prefer, sage, then simmer for 25 minutes to reduce.

Thicken with flour, if you wish, and serve over cooked fillets.

Coriander Sauce for Canned Tuna

II-10

1 lb. canned tuna

Sauce:
¼ t. ground pepper
¼ t. cumin
½ t. thyme
½ t. coriander
1 T. chopped onion
2 T. dark raisins
1 t. honey
¼ c. white wine
2 T. olive oil
¾ c. fish stock
(flour)

In a mortar, grind together pepper, cumin, thyme, and coriander. Add to onion and raisins, and mix with honey, white wine, olive oil, and stock. Heat to a boil and simmer gently for 25 minutes to reduce. Thicken with flour, if you wish, and serve with canned tuna.

Date and Thyme Sauce for Poached Tuna

1 lb. poached tuna

Sauce:
¼ t. ground pepper
½ t. celery seed (or lovage)
½ t. thyme
1 T. chopped onion
2 dates, finely chopped
1 t. honey
1 t. white wine vinegar or cider vinegar
2 t. olive oil
⅛ t. ground mustard
1 c. fish stock

In a mortar, grind together pepper, celery seed (or lovage), thyme, and mustard. Combine with onion, chopped dates, honey, vinegar, olive oil, and stock. Bring to a boil, then simmer gently for 25 minutes to reduce.

Serve with the cooked fish.

II-11

Pear or Quince Sauce for Baked Bluegill

2–3 lb. baked bluegill

Sauce:
¼ t. ground pepper
½ t. celery seed (or lovage)
¼ t. coriander
1 t. mint
pinch of rosemary (or rue)
¼ c. diced, cooked pear or quince
1 t. honey
½ c. white wine
1 T. olive oil
2 c. fish stock

In a mortar, grind together pepper, celery seed (or lovage), coriander, mint, and rosemary (or rue). Combine with pear or quince, honey, wine, olive oil, and stock. Bring to a boil, then simmer gently for 25 minutes to reduce.

Serve with the baked fish.

II-12

Rosemary-Mint Sauce for Poached Bluegill

II-13

2–3 lb. poached bluegill

Sauce:
½ t. ground pepper
pinch of aniseed
¼ t. cumin
½ t. thyme
1 t. fresh or dried mint
pinch of rosemary (or rue)
1 t. honey
1 t. white wine vinegar or
cider vinegar
½ c. white wine
1 T. olive oil
1 c. fish stock
(flour)

In a mortar, grind together pepper, aniseed, cumin thyme, mint, and rosemary (or rue). Combine with honey, vinegar, white wine, olive oil, and stock Bring to a boil and simmer gently to reduce for minutes.

Thicken with flour, if you wish, and serve with the poached fish.

Thick Myrtle Berry Sauce for Poached Bluegill

II-14

2–3 lb. poached bluegill

Sauce:
¼ t. ground pepper
½ t. celery seed (or lovage)
½ t. oregano
pinch of rosemary (or rue)
1 t. myrtle berries
½ t. mint
pinch of caraway
1 t. honey
1 t. white or cider vinegar
1 T. olive oil
½ c. white wine
2 c. fish stock
2 raw egg yolks

In a mortar, grind together pepper, celery seed (o lovage), oregano, rosemary (or rue), myrtle berrie and mint. Add caraway, and combine with honey vinegar, olive oil, wine, and stock. Bring to a boi simmer gently for 25 minutes, then thicken wit well beaten yolks.

Serve with the poached fish.

Celery Mint Sauce for Poached Bluegill

2–3 lbs. poached bluegill

Sauce:
½ t. ground pepper
½ t. coriander
½ t. mint
¼ c. chopped celery
1 T. chopped onion
2 T. dark raisins
1 t. honey
1 t. white or cider vinegar
1 T. olive oil
¼ c. white wine
1 c. fish stock

In a mortar, grind together pepper, coriander, and mint. Mix with celery, onion, raisins, honey, vinegar, olive oil, white wine, and stock. Bring to a boil, then simmer gently for 25 minutes to reduce. Serve with the poached fish.

11-15

Caraway Date Sauce for Poached Fish Fillets

2 lbs. poached fish fillets

Sauce:
½ t. ground pepper
pinch of caraway
⅛ t. ground mustard
1 T. fresh parsley
¼ c. dates, finely chopped
1 t. honey
¾ c. fish stock
1 t. white or cider vinegar
1 T. olive oil
¼ c. white boiled wine (see
wine sauce (see p. 306)

In a mortar, grind together pepper, caraway, mustard, and chopped parsley. Blend with dates, honey, stock, vinegar, olive oil, and wine. Bring to a boil, then simmer gently for 25 minutes to reduce. Serve with the poached fish.

11-16

11-13   IUS IN DENTICE ELIXO *Sauce for Poached Bream* [Combine] pepper, anise, cumin, thyme, mint, green rue, honey, vinegar, fish stock, wine, and a little olive oil. Simmer and thicken with starch.

11-14   IUS IN PISCE AURATA *Sauce for Gilthead Bream* [Combine] pepper, lovage, caraway, oregano, rue berry, mint, myrtle berry, egg yolk, honey, vinegar, olive oil, wine, and fish stock. Heat [these ingredients] and so serve.

11-15   IUS IN PISCE AURATA ASSA *Sauce for Baked Gilthead Bream* [Combine] pepper, coriander, dried mint, celery seed, onion, raisins, honey, vinegar, wine, fish stock, and olive oil.

11-16   IUS IN SCORPIONE ELIXO *Sauce for Poached Scorpion Fish [the Lesser Weaver]* [Combine] pepper, caraway, parsley, dates, honey, vinegar, fish stock, mustard, olive oil, and boiled wine.

⟪ The scorpion fish, or lesser weaver, was served on the sign of the scorpion as part of the *Foods of the Zodiac* dish at Trimalchio's famous dinner in the *Satyricon* (see p. xix).

11-17   IN PISCE OENOGARUM *Wine Sauce for Fish* Grind pepper and rue. Mix with honey, raisin wine, fish stock, and wine boiled down one-third, and simmer over the gentlest of fires.

11-18   IN PISCE OENOGARUM *Wine Sauce for Fish* Make [the sauce in exactly the same manner] as above. When it has [very slowly] been brought to the boil, thicken with starch.

OF EEL

III-1   IUS IN ANGUILLA *Sauce for Eels* [Combine] pepper, lovage, celery seed, anise, Syrian sumach, dates, honey, vinegar, fish stock, olive oil, mustard, and boiled wine. [Heat and pour over the prepared eels.]

III-2   IUS IN ANGUILLA *Sauce for Eels* [Combine] pepper, lovage, Syrian sumach, dried mint, rue berries, the yolks of hard-boiled eggs, honey wine, vinegar, fish stock, and olive oil. Cook.

—— BOOK X IS ENDED ——

THE EXCERPTS OF APICIUS
BY THE ILLUSTRIOUS
VINIDARIUS

ℂ Of the "illustrious" Vinidarius nothing is known except the excerpts he made from Apicius' work in the late fourth or early fifth centuries A.D. Enough differences appear in this book to suggest that Vinidarius was using a different, or an imperfect, version of the text used in translating the preceeding ten Books of the *Roman Cookery of Apicius*. The "Excerpts" are thus of historical as well as culinary interest.

A LIST OF CONDIMENTS WHICH SHOULD BE IN THE HOUSE SO THAT NO SEASONING MAY BE ABSENT

Saffron, pepper, ginger, laser, bay leaf, myrtle berry, costmary, cloves, Indian spikenard, cardamon, spikenard.

Of seeds: poppy, rue seed, rue berry, laurel berry, aniseed, celery seed, fennel seed, lovage seed, colewort seed, coriander seed, cumin, parsley, dill, caraway, sesame.

Of dry seasonings: laser roots, mint, Italian catmint, sage, cypress, oregano, juniper, onion, gentian roots, thyme, coriander, pellitory, citrus [leaves], parsnip, shallots, rush roots, pennyroyal, cyperus, garlic, pulse, marjoram, elecampane, silphium, cardamon.

Of liquids: honey, new wine reduced one-third by boiling, new wine reduced one-half by boiling, pepper sauce, raisin wine.

Of nuts: larger nuts, pine nuts, almonds, filberts.

Of dried fruits: damsons, dates, raisins, pomegranates. Store all of these in a dry place lest they lose their smell and effect.

I-I CACCABINAM MINOREM *Small Casserole* Take a selection of cooked garden vegetables and arrange them in a dish. [Strew] chicken parts among them, if you like. Season with stock and olive oil. Boil. Grind a little pepper and bay leaf in a mortar and combine this with an egg and press [into the casserole].

I-2 ALIAS TRITURA UNDE PERFUNDES CACCABINAM *The Ground Seasonings Which You Pour into the Small Casserole* Grind a sufficient quantity of bay leaf with one part clove and ¼ part laurel berries and the [tender] middle [leaves] of a boiled cabbage and coriander leaves. Dilute with the juice [of the cabbage] and steam in hot ashes. And before you pour it over the small casserole, pour over spiced wine and so use.

II CACCABINAM FUSILEM *A Liquid Casserole* Arrange variously [in a casserole] mallows, leeks, beets or boiled stalks, thrushes and chicken forcemeats, and choice cuts of pork or chicken and other tender meats which you have on hand. [In a mortar] grind pepper and lovage. [Blend] with two measures of aged wine, one measure of stock,

Vegetable and Chicken Casserole

2–3 lbs. chicken
large stalk of broccoli, sliced
1 c. whole mushrooms
1 c. carrots, sliced
½ c. peas
½ t. ground coriander
1 t. ground pepper
1 bay leaf
1 t. thyme
2 t. celery seed (or lovage)
2 c. chicken stock
2 raw egg yolks

Simmer the chicken in water for about 2½ hours. I-I
Then cut up, skin, and bone it, and put the meats in
a large casserole. Add broccoli, mushrooms, carrots,
and peas. Season with coriander, ground pepper,
bay leaf, thyme, and celery seed (or lovage). Take
well beaten egg yolks and combine with stock. Pour
over the casserole, cover it, and cook in a 350°F
oven for 30–40 minutes.

Chicken, Pork, and Vegetables in Custard

½ lb. cooked chicken, sliced
½ lb. cooked pork, sliced
½ c. peas
large stalk of broccoli, sliced
2 heads of leeks, chopped
1 c. whole small beets
1 c. green beans, sliced
1 t. ground pepper
2 t. celery seed (or lovage)
1 t. thyme
½ t. sage
½ t. coriander
2 T. butter
¼ c. white wine
1 T. honey
1½ c. chicken stock
2 c. milk
2 raw egg yolks

Arrange the meats and vegetables in layers in a II
greased casserole. In a mortar, grind together pepper, celery seed (or lovage), thyme, sage, and coriander. Melt butter and blend with wine, honey, and
stock. Scald the milk. Beat the yolks and add the
milk little by little to the eggs. Then mix with the
wine sauce. Now add the seasonings and stir well.
Heat over low heat, stirring till partly thickened.
Then pour the custard over the casserole, and bake,
uncovered, in a 350°F oven for 45 minutes to 1 hour,
or until the custard has set.

one measure of honey, and some olive oil. Taste, stir, and combine. Pour the sauce into a saucepan and heat moderately. When done, mix eggs in a pint of milk and add this into the sauce. Pour over the casserole, and serve as soon as it has set.

III   OFELLAS GARATAS *Hors D'oeuvres Made with Fish-pickle* Put pieces of meat into a frying pan. Add a measure of fish-pickle, similarly [a measure] of olive oil, some honey, and fry.

IV   OFELLAS ASSAS *Roast Hors D'oeuvres* Prepare the roasted morsels of choice meat carefully and put them in a frying pan. Fry in wine sauce. Afterwards, serve in the very same wine sauce and sprinkle with pepper.

V   ALITER OFELLAS *Another Hors D'oeuvre* Fry the pieces of meat in fish-pickle. When hot, smear [each] with honey, and serve.

VI   OFELLAS GARATON *Hors D'oeuvres Made with Fish-pickle* Take laser, ginger, and cardamon, and mix one-eighth of a pint of stock with all of these ground seasonings. Cook the pieces of meat in this [sauce].

The Poet Martial's Lament

Full glasses of Setine strained through snow,*
When shall I drink you again, without my doctor saying no?

                                                    Martial, 6.86.

*Setine wine, like many other great classical Italian wines, was strained through snow both to cool it and to dilute its strength.

Meat Hors D'oeuvres with Fish-pickle

lb. choice cooked beef, pork,
lamb, or kid
2 T. olive oil
¼ c. fish-pickle (see p. 305)
¼ c. liquid honey

Cut thinly sliced meat into 1 inch squares, and sauté III
on each side in olive oil. Brush each piece with honey, and season with ½ teaspoon fish-pickle.

These hors d'oeuvres are excellent served on
squares of toast.

Roast Meat Morsels in Wine Sauce

2 lb. choice roast beef, pork,
lamb, or kid

Sauce:
½ c. red wine
½ c. beef stock
pinch of rosemary
1 t. celery seed (or lovage)
½ t. coriander
⅛ t. basil
1 t. honey

Thinly slice roast meat, and cut into 1 inch squares. IV
Combine wine and beef stock, and season with rosemary, celery seed (or lovage), coriander, and basil.
Add honey. Bring to a boil, then simmer the morsels of meat in it for 15 minutes.

Serve the pieces of meat in a little of the sauce,
with a sprinkling of pepper.

Spiced Roast Meat Hors D'oeuvres

2 lb. choice roast beef, pork,
lamb, or kid

Sauce:
¼ t. ginger
pinch of cardamon
pinch of fennel
¼ c. beef stock
2 T. olive oil

Take cooked meat and slice into thin 1 inch squares. VI
In a mortar, grind together ginger, cardamon, and
fennel. Moisten each slice with stock, and season
with the spices. Sauté briefly in olive oil in a very
hot frying pan.

VII   PISCES SCORPIONES RAPULTOS   *Scorpion Fish [Lesser Weaver]*
with Turnips Half cook [the scorpion fish] in fish-pickle and olive oil.
Remove from the pan. Take boiled turnips while still wet and chop
very finely. Press the moisture out of them with your hands. Coat the
scorpion fish with the turnip paste and boil in a lot of olive oil. When
boiled, grind cumin and half a laurel berry in a mortar. [Blend with
honey, wine, stock, and a little olive oil]. Add saffron for color. [Boil
and] thicken with rice [flour]. Pour [the sauce over the scorpion fish]
and serve. Add a little vinegar.

VIII   PISCES FRIXOS CUIUSCUMQUE GENERIS SIC FACIES   *Fried
Fish of Whatever Kind* [In a mortar] grind pepper, coriander seed, laser
roots, oregano, rue, and dates. Moisten with vinegar, olive oil, and
stock. Add boiled wine. Blend all these and put them into a pan and
bring to the boil. When hot, pour over the [fried] fish. Sprinkle with
pepper and serve.

IX   ITEM PISCES FRIXOS   *Fried Fish in the Same Manner*   [In a mor-
tar] grind pepper, lovage, laurel berry, and coriander. Blend with
honey, stock, wine, and raisin wine or boiled wine. Cook over a slow
fire. Thicken the sauce with rice [flour], [pour over the fried fish] and
serve.

X   PISCES ASSOS   *Baked Fish*   [In a mortar] grind pepper, lovage,
savory, and dried onion. Moisten [these seasonings] with vinegar. Add
dates, anise, egg yolks, honey, vinegar, stock, olive oil, and boiled
wine. Blend all of these into one mixture, [heat, and] pour over [baked
fish].

XI   PISCES ZOMOTEGANON[1]   *Stewed Fish*   Fry the fish [in their
own juices and add these seasonings:] grind pepper, lovage, rue, green
herbs and dried onion, olive oil, and fish-pickle. Serve.

XII   SARDAS SIC FACIES   *Sardines*   In a mortar, grind pepper, lovage
seed, oregano, dried onion, and hard-boiled egg yolks. Blend with vinegar and olive oil, and pour [over the sardines].

*Young trout, the smallest of little fish, whether baked or fried, suit
the fastidious.*

Anthimus, 44.

Fish Fillets with Turnips in Saffron Sauce

2 lbs. fish fillets
1 c. fish stock
1 T. olive oil
6 medium turnips

Sauce:
½ t. cumin
a few crushed laurel berries,
or ¼ t. ground pepper
¼ c. white wine
1 t. honey
¾ c. fish stock
1 T. olive oil or butter
1 T. flour
pinch of saffron
white wine vinegar or
cider vinegar

To make this dish, peel turnips, and cook until soft. VII
Mash them, and spread the paste on a serving platter. Take fish fillets and poach them lightly in stock
and a little olive oil. Place the cooked fillets on top of
the mashed turnips, season with the saffron sauce
below, and serve with a sprinkling of pepper.

For the sauce, grind together cumin and laurel
berries or pepper. Combine with white wine, honey, stock, and olive oil or butter. Bring to a boil,
simmer for 25 minutes, and thicken with flour. Add
saffron for color. Pour the sauce over the cooked
fillets and serve with a sprinkling of vinegar.

(Although this sauce is excellent, fish fillets coated
in turnip paste and deep fried are satisfying in themselves.)

Date Sauce for Fried or Poached Fish Fillets

2 lbs. fried fish or poached
fillets

Sauce:
¼ t. ground pepper
½ t. coriander
pinch of fennel
½ t. oregano
pinch of rosemary (or rue)
2 dates, finely chopped
1 t. white wine vinegar or
cider vinegar
1 t. olive oil
¾ c. fish stock
¼ c. boiled white wine

In a mortar, grind together pepper, coriander, fen- VIII
nel, oregano, rosemary (or rue). Add to chopped
dates. Moisten with vinegar and olive oil, and combine with stock and boiled wine. Bring to a boil and
simmer for 25 minutes to reduce.

Serve with cooked fish and a sprinkling of pepper.

Coriander Sauce for Fried or Poached Fish

IX 2 lbs. fried or poached fish
fillets

Sauce:
¼ t. ground pepper
1 t. celery seed (or lovage)
½ t. coriander
1 t. honey
¼ c. white wine
¾ c. fish stock
1 whole bay leaf
flour

In a mortar, grind together pepper, celery seed, (or lovage), and coriander. Blend with honey, white wine, and fish stock. Add bay leaf. Bring to a boil and simmer gently for 25 minutes. Remove bay leaf and thicken with flour.

Pour over cooked fish, and serve.

Aniseed Sauce for Baked Salmon

X 2-3 lbs. salmon, baked

Sauce:
¼ t. ground pepper
1 t. celery seed (or lovage)
½ t. savory
2 T. chopped onion
2 t. white or cider vinegar
2 dates, finely chopped
pinch of aniseed
1 t. honey
1 c. fish stock
2 t. olive oil or butter
¼ c. boiled white wine (see
p. 306)
1 raw egg yolk

In a mortar, grind together pepper, celery seed (or lovage), and savory. Add to onion. Moisten these seasonings with vinegar. Combine with chopped dates, aniseed, honey, fish stock, olive oil, and boiled white wine. Bring to a boil, then simmer for 15 minutes, and thicken with well beaten egg yolk.

Serve over portions of baked salmon.

Spiced Fish Stew

2 lbs. fish fillets or steaks
2 c. water
½ t. ground pepper
2 t. celery seed (or lovage)
½ t. thyme
½ t. rosemary (or rue)
2 T. chopped onion
2 t. butter or olive oil
2 T. fish-pickle (see p. 305)

Cover the fish in water and cook for 10–15 minutes. XI
Pour off the liquid and reserve. In a mortar, grind
together pepper, celery seed (or lovage), and rosemary (or rue). Add to onion, olive oil, and fish-
pickle. Combine with the reserved stewing liquid,
and pour back over the stewed fish. Cook together
over low heat for 5 minutes, then serve.

Dressing for Cold Sardines

8 oz. plain canned sardines

Dressing:
¼ t. ground pepper
1 t. celery seed (or lovage)
½ t. oregano
2 T. chopped onion
hard-boiled egg yolks, finely chopped
3 T. white wine vinegar or cider vinegar
½ c. olive oil

In a mortar, grind together pepper, celery seed (or XII
lovage), and oregano. Add to onion. Combine with
egg yolks, vinegar, and olive oil. Chill. Serve with
the sardines after they have been drained and rinsed
in cold water.

XIII PISCES ZOMOTEGANON¹ *Stewed Fish* Wash the blood from the fresh fish you wish [to cook] and put them into a stewing pan. Add olive oil, fish stock, wine, and a bouquet garni of chives and coriander. Cook. Grind pepper, oregano, lovage, and the bouquet garni which you have stewed. Moisten with gravy from the pan. [Pour over the fish and] thicken [with eggs]. When it has set, sprinkle with pepper and serve.

XIV MULLOS ANETHATOS SIC FACIES *Red Mullets with Aniseed* Scale and wash the fish. Arrange them in a stewing pan. Add olive oil, fish stock, wine, [aniseed,] and a bouquet of chives and coriander. Cook. [Meanwhile] put pepper in a mortar, bruise them, and add olive oil and measures of wine and raisin wine. Blend. Pour into a saucepan and heat. Thicken the sauce with starch and pour it over the pan of [cooked] fish. Sprinkle with pepper [and serve].

XV ALITER MULLOS *Red Mullets* Scale and wash the fish. Arrange them in a stewing pan. Add olive oil, fish stock and wine, and, during the cooking, a bouquet of chives and coriander. Cook. [In a mortar] grind peppercorns, lovage, and oregano. Add gravy from the stewing pan and blend with [wine and] raisin wine. Heat [this sauce] in a pan until it boils and then thicken with starch. Afterwards, pour [the sauce] over the dish, sprinkle with pepper, and serve.

XVI MURENAM AUT ANGUILLAS VEL MULLOS SIC FACIES *Moray Eels and [Common] Eels or Mullets* Clean [the eels] and arrange them in a stewing pan, carefully. In a mortar, grind pepper, lovage, oregano, mint, dried onion, wine, a half measure of fish stock, a third part of honey, and a spoonful of boiled wine. [The eels] should be wholly covered with this sauce so that there is some sauce left on them when they are cooked.

XVII LOCUSTA ET SCILLAS *Lobster and Prawns* [In a mortar] grind pepper, lovage, and celery seed. Add vinegar, stock, and egg yolks. Mix together, pour over, and serve.

XVIII IN PISCIBUS ELIXIS *Of Poached Fish* [In a mortar] grind pepper, lovage, celery seed, and oregano. Pour vinegar [over the seasonings]. Add pine nuts, sufficient dates, honey, vinegar, fish stock, and mustard. Blend [cook] and use [as a sauce for poached fish].

Fish Stewed in Seasoned Wine

2 lbs. uncooked fish fillets or steaks
1 c. fish stock
1 c. boiled white wine (see p. 306)
1 T. olive oil
2 heads of leeks, sliced
1 t. coriander
½ t. ground pepper
1–2 t. celery seed (or lovage)
2 raw egg yolks

Chop fillets into pieces, and put into a stewing pot. XIII
Add stock, boiled wine, olive oil, leeks, coriander,
pepper, and celery seed (or lovage). Bring to a boil
and simmer for 10–15 minutes. Then thicken the
liquid by adding the well beaten egg yolks, little by
little.

Serve with a sprinkling of pepper.

Mullet Stewed with Aniseed

Prepare fish and liquid as in *Fish Stewed in Seasoned* XIV
Wine, above, adding a pinch of aniseed. In the
sauce, omit oregano and celery seed (or lovage), and
add 1 teaspoon white or cider vinegar.

Trout in Thickened Wine Sauce

XV

2 lbs. trout
1 t. olive oil
3 T. fish-pickle (see p. 305)
1 T. white wine
2 T. chives, finely chopped
½ t. coriander

Clean the insides of the fish, and season with a mixture of olive oil, fish-pickle, white wine, chives, and coriander. Then sauté trout, till done, in olive oil or butter.

Sauce:
¼ t. ground pepper
½ t. mint
½ t. thyme
a pinch of aniseed
2 t. olive oil or butter
1 t. white wine vinegar or cider vinegar
1 T. sweet white wine or muscatel
1 c. fish stock
flour

For the sauce, grind together pepper, mint, and thyme. Add aniseed. Combine with olive oil or butter, vinegar, sweet wine, and stock. Bring to a boil, then simmer for 25 minutes, and thicken with flour. Serve over the hot, cooked trout.

Eels Poached in Sweet Sauce

XVI

2 lbs. eels

Sauce:
¼ t. ground pepper
1 t. celery seed (or lovage)
½ t. oregano
½ t. mint
2 T. chopped onion
1 t. honey
¼ c. boiled white wine (see p. 306)
1 c. fish stock

Arrange pieces of eel in a stewing pan. In a mortar, grind together pepper, celery seed (or lovage), oregano, and mint. Add to onion. Blend with honey, boiled wine, and stock, and pour into the pan with the eels. Bring sauce to a boil and simmer over low heat for 30 minutes, or until done.

Celery Seed Sauce for Lobsters or Prawns

2 c. cooked shellfish meats

Sauce:
¼ t. ground pepper
2 t. lovage (or celery seed)
1 t. white wine vinegar or
cider vinegar
1 c. shellfish liquid
1 raw egg yolk

In a mortar, grind together pepper and celery seed (or lovage). Combine with vinegar and liquid from the boiled shellfish. Bring to a boil and simmer for 25 minutes. Then add well beaten egg yolk little by little to thicken.

Serve with cooked lobster or prawns.

XVII

Nut Sauce for Poached Fish Fillets

2 lbs. poached fish fillets

Sauce:
¼ t. ground pepper
1 t. lovage (or celery seed)
1 t. celery seed
½ t. oregano
1 t. white wine vinegar or
cider vinegar
¼ c. pine nuts, chopped, or
almonds, thinly sliced
2 dates, finely chopped
1 t. honey
1 c. fish stock
1 t. white or cider vinegar
¼ t. ground mustard
vinegar

In a mortar, grind together pepper, lovage (or celery seed), celery seed, and oregano. Moisten these seasonings with vinegar, and combine with nuts, dates, honey, fish stock, vinegar, and mustard. Bring to a boil, then simmer to reduce for 25 minutes.

Pour over poached fish and serve with a sprinkling of vinegar.

XVIII

XIX   PATINA SOLEARUM EX OVIS *A Dish of Sole with Eggs* Scale, clean, and arrange [the soles] in a pan. Add fish-pickle, olive oil, wine, a bouquet of chives and coriander seed. Cook. [In a mortar] grind a little pepper and oregano. Pour gravy from the pan and add ten raw eggs. Blend [these ingredients] so that the texture is smooth. Now pour this mixture over the soles and cook over a slow fire. When [the sauce] has thickened, sprinkle with pepper and serve.

XX   PORCELLUM CORIANDRATUM *Suckling Pig Coriander* Roast the suckling pig well. In a mortar, grind pepper, anise, oregano, and green coriander. Blend with honey, wine, stock, olive oil, vinegar, and boiled wine. Heat all together, and then pour [the sauce over the roast suckling pig]. Sprinkle with raisins, pine nuts, and chopped onion. Serve.

XXI   PORCELLUM OENOCOCTUM *Suckling Pig Stewed in Wine* Dress the suckling pig and cook in olive oil and stock. While it is cooking, add pepper, rue, laurel berry, stock, raisin wine or boiled wine, and aged wine into a mortar. Grind these together and blend. [Now take the suckling pig and] set it in a bronze dish. [Pour the wine sauce over it and simmer.]

XXII   [UNTITLED] [*Thick Sauce for Suckling Pig*] Cook the suckling pig thoroughly in the same sauce. Take [the pig] out [of the pan]. Thicken the sauce with starch, pour into a vessel, and serve [with the cooked suckling pig].

XXIII   PORCELLUM THYMO SPARSUM *Suckling Pig Sprinkled with Thyme* Boil a suckling pig that has been slaughtered on the previous day and steeped in a mixture of cold water, salt, and aniseed in order to blanch it. Then [pound in a mortar] green herbs, thyme, a little pennyroyal, hard-boiled eggs, and finely chopped onion. [Place the suckling pig in a roasting pan and] sprinkle all [these seasonings] on top. Now mix one-half pint of stock and one measure each of olive oil and raisin wine. [Add to the roasting pan.] [Cook] and serve.

XXIV   PORCELLUM OXYZOMUM *Suckling Pig in Sour Sauce* Clean and dress a suckling pig and put it in a sauce made thus: In a mortar, grind fifty peppercorns. Add sufficient honey, three dried onions, coriander which may be green or dried, half a pint of stock, one pint of

Fillet of Sole Omelette

1 lb. fillets of sole
2 T. olive oil or butter
2–3 T. fish-pickle (see p. 305)
1 T. chives, chopped
½ t. coriander
¼ t. ground pepper
½ t. oregano
4 raw eggs
½ c. milk

Put olive oil or butter in a baking pan, and arrange XIX fillets of sole in it. Season with fish-pickle, chives, and coriander. Cook in oven for 10 minutes at 300°F. Meanwhile, in a mortar, grind pepper and oregano. Combine juices from the pan of fillets, with well beaten eggs, and milk. Blend and pour into a greased frying pan, and add the fish. Cook the omelette until it is firm, sprinkle with pepper, and serve.

Roast Pork

4 lb. pork roast or suckling pig
1 t. cumin

Sprinkle the roast with cumin, and roast uncovered XX for 2½ hours in a 325°F oven.

Sauce:
½ t. ground pepper
1 t. oregano
1½ t. coriander
pinch of aniseed
1 T. honey
¼ c. red wine
1 c. beef or chicken stock
2 t. olive oil or butter
1 t. wine vinegar or cider vinegar
¼ c. red boiled wine (see p. 306)
¼ c. dark raisins
flour
¼ c. almonds, chopped
1 small onion, finely chopped
¼ c. coconut, finely chopped

For the sauce, in a mortar, grind together pepper, oregano, and coriander. Add aniseed, and combine with honey, red wine, stock, olive oil or butter, vinegar, and boiled wine. After 2½ hours, pierce the roast here and there with a fork to release some of the juices into the pan. Add the prepared sauce to the pan, and baste from time to time for a further ½ hour. Thicken sauce with flour, and serve with slices of pork. Garnish with raisins, almonds, chopped onion, and coconut. (Although the Romans did not have the coconut, it makes a splendid addition to the garnish.)

olive oil, and half a pint of water. Blend these ingredients and pour [the sauce] into a roasting pan. [Carefully prepare the suckling pig] and put it in the sauce. [Cook.] When the sauce begins to boil, stir frequently so that it may thicken. If the sauce begins to diminish, add half a pint of water. Cook the pig thoroughly [in the sauce] and serve.

XXV   PORCELLUM LASARATUM   *Suckling Pig Seasoned with Laser*   In a mortar, grind pepper, lovage, and caraway, and mix with a pinch of cumin, fresh laser, and laser root. Moisten [these seasonings] with vinegar. Add pine nuts, dates, honey, vinegar, stock, and prepared mustard. Blend all [these ingredients] with olive oil and pour [over the suckling pig].

XXVI   PORCELLUM IUSCELLATUM   *Sauce for Suckling Pig*   Put in a mortar and bruise pepper, lovage or aniseed, coriander, rue, and laurel berry. Pour stock, a leek, a little raisin wine or honey, a little wine, and some olive oil. When the sauce is cooked, thicken with starch.

XXVII   AGNUM SIMPLICEM   *Plain Lamb*   Skin the lamb, remove the choice cuts, and wash them carefully. Put them in a pan. Add olive oil, stock, wine, leeks, and chopped coriander. When the sauce begins to boil, stir frequently and serve.

XXVIII   HAEDUM LASARATUM   *Kid Seasoned with Laser*   Wash the intestines of the kid scrupulously and then fill them with [a mixture of] pepper, stock, laser, and olive oil. Put them back inside the kid and carefully sew up [the opening]. Roast them together with the kid, and when cooked, add [and grind] in a mortar, rue and laurel berry. Take the drained kid [from the pan and set it on a platter]. [Mix the rue and laurel berry] into the juices [in the roasting pan], [simmer and] pour this gravy [over the kid], and serve.

XXIX   TURDOS [APONCOMENOS]   *Thrushes [Seasoned by the Throat]*   Grind pepper, laser, and laurel berry. Mix cumin [with these seasonings and add] fish-pickle. Fill the thrushes with the seasonings, by the throat, and sew up [the openings] with thread. Now cook [the seasoned thrushes] in a sauce prepared from olive oil, salt, water, aniseed, and the heads of leeks.

Pork Roast Stewed in Wine

4 lb. choice loin roast or
suckling pig
1 c. pork, beef, or
chicken stock
2 T. olive oil or butter

Roast the pork or suckling pig, uncovered, in a   xxi
325°F oven for 2½ hours, basting with a mixture of
stock and olive oil or butter.

Sauce:
½ t. ground pepper
3 cloves (or laurel berries)
½ c. pork, beef, or
chicken stock
¼ c. sweet raisin wine or
muscatel
¼ c. aged red wine
flour

For the sauce, in a mortar, grind the pepper, and
cloves (or laurel berries), and combine with stock,
sweet wine, and red wine. Bring this sauce to a boil,
then pour over roast, and cook together for another 30 minutes, basting occasionally. Strain out
the cloves, and thicken the sauce with flour before
serving.

Roast Pork with Thyme

4 lb. pork roast
1 t. thyme

Take the roast and sprinkle it with thyme. Roast,   xxiii
uncovered, in a 325°F oven for 2½ hours.

Sauce:
1 t. fresh chervil, chopped
½ t. mint
1 t. celery seed (or lovage)
1 t. thyme
nch of pennyroyal (or mint)
1 onion, finely chopped
1 c. pork, beef, or
chicken stock
2 t. olive oil or butter
¼ c. red wine
flour
1 onion, finely chopped
3 hard-boiled eggs, chopped

Meanwhile, for the sauce, finely chop chervil, and
combine with mint, celery seed (or lovage), thyme,
and pennyroyal (or mint). Mix these herbs with
onion, stock, olive oil or butter, and wine. Bring to
a boil, then pour over the roast. Cook for a further
½ hour, basting occasionally. Then thicken sauce
with flour.

Serve slices of meat with a little of the sauce and a
garnish of chopped hard-boiled eggs and onion.

Roast Pork in Onion Coriander Sauce

XXIV

4 lb. pork roast

Sauce:
1 T. honey
3 large onions, chopped
2 t. coriander
1 c. pork, beef, or
chicken stock
2 T. olive oil or butter
ground pepper

Roast meat, uncovered, in a 325°F oven for 2½ hours.

Meanwhile, for the sauce, mix honey, chopped onions, coriander, stock, and olive oil or butter. Pour this sauce into the pan with the meat and mix it with pan juices. Cook together for a further ½ hour. Serve slices of meat with the sauce and a sprinkling of pepper.

Roast Pork or Suckling Pig in Cumin Sauce

XXV

4 lb. pork roast
1 t. cumin

Sauce:
½ t. ground pepper
1 t. celery seed (or lovage)
½ t. cumin
¼ t. fennel
1 t. white wine vinegar or
cider vinegar
pinch of caraway
¼ c. pine nuts or almonds,
chopped
¼ c. dates, chopped
1 T. honey
1½ c. pork, beef, or
chicken stock
⅛ t. ground mustard
2 t. olive oil or butter
flour
ground pepper

Sprinkle cumin over the roast and cook, uncovered, in a 325°F oven for 2½ hours.

For the sauce, in a mortar, grind pepper, celery seed (or lovage), cumin, and fennel. Combine with vinegar, and add caraway, nuts, chopped dates, honey, stock seasoned with mustard, and olive oil or butter. Bring this sauce to a boil, add roasting pan juices, and simmer for 20 minutes. Thicken with flour and serve with a sprinkling of pepper.

Sweet Aniseed Sauce for Pork Roast

4 lb. pork roast

Sauce:
¼ t. ground pepper
1 t. celery seed (or lovage)
¼ t. rosemary (or rue)
pinch of aniseed
2 cloves or laurel berries
*1 c. pork, beef, or
chicken stock*
1 head of leek, thinly sliced
*¼ c. sweet white wine, or
muscatel, or 1 T. honey*
¼ c. red wine
2 t. olive oil or butter
flour

In a mortar, grind together pepper, celery seed XXVI (or lovage), and rosemary (or rue). Add aniseed and cloves or laurel berries. Combine with stock, sliced leek, sweet wine or honey, red wine, and olive oil or butter. Bring the sauce to a boil, simmer for 25 minutes, then remove cloves.

Thicken with flour, and serve with slices of roast pork.

Lamb Chops in a Simple Sauce

2 lbs. lamb chops
2 T. olive oil

Sauce:
2 heads of leeks, sliced
½ c. beef or chicken stock
¼ c. red wine
1½ t. coriander
1 t. mint
ground pepper

In a pan, brown lamb chops in olive oil. Add sliced XXVII leeks, stock, red wine, coriander, and mint. Cook the lamb in this sauce for about 30 minutes, stirring repeatedly.

Serve in the sauce with a sprinkling of pepper.

Roast Kid Stuffed with Ginger Sausage

XXVIII

8–10 lb. kid
½ t. ground pepper
½–1 t. ginger
2 t. celery seed (or lovage)
½ t. cumin
2 T. olive oil or butter
1 c. finely ground pork or beef
1 c. calf's liver, chopped
1 T. butter
1 raw egg
2 c. bread crumbs
beef or chicken stock
four 8" sausage casings

Prepare the kid for roasting. For the stuffing, make sausages by filling casings with the following ingredients.

In a mortar, grind together pepper, ginger, celery seed (or lovage), and cumin. Add to olive oil or butter. Combine with ground meats, and calf's liver browned in butter. Bind the mixture with the well beaten egg and bread crumbs. Moisten with stock as required, before stuffing into sausage casings. Simmer the sausages in a little water in a covered pan for 20 minutes.

Stuff the kid with the cooked sausage, and roast in a 325°F oven for 4–5 hours.

(Serve with a sauce from Book VIII.)

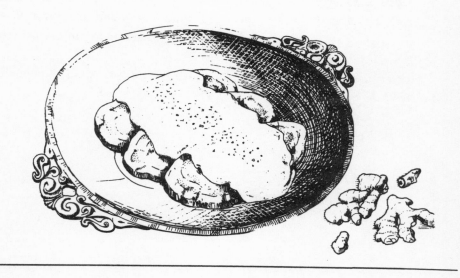

Stuffed Cornish Hens in Wine Gravy

*2 cornish hens or 1 small
roasting chicken*

In a mortar, grind together pepper, ginger, cloves   XXIX
(or juniper berries), and cumin. Add to fish-pickle,
chicken livers, and ground pork. Bind with bread
crumbs and well beaten egg. Stuff the birds with this
mixture, and roast in oven till done.

Seasoning:
¼ t. ground pepper
½ t. ginger
3 cloves (or juniper berries)
½ t. cumin
1 T. fish-pickle (see p. 305)
*½ c. cooked chicken livers,
chopped*
¼ lb. ground pork
1 c. bread crumbs
1 raw egg

Gravy:
heads of leeks, finely chopped
1 t. celery seed (or lovage)
½ t. oregano
1 c. chicken stock
¼ c. white wine
*2 T. finely chopped dates or
dark raisins*
2 T. olive oil or butter
salt
flour

Make the gravy by combining leeks, celery seed (or
lovage), oregano, stock, wine, dates or raisins, and
salt, to taste. Add pan juices, bring to a boil, simmer
slowly for 20 minutes, and thicken with flour.

XXX   TURTURES   *Turtledoves*   Open [the turtledoves and] clean them carefully. Grind pepper, laser, and a little stock. Pour this over the turtledoves themselves until they have absorbed all they can, and roast.

XXXI   IUS IN PERDICES   *Sauce for Partridges*   In a mortar, grind pepper, celery, mint, and rue. Moisten with vinegar. Add dates, honey, vinegar, stock, and olive oil. Cook together and serve.

Trimalchio Serves Dessert to His Sated Guests

Our trials would have had no limit if the dessert courses had not been carried into the dining room: pastry thrushes stuffed with raisins and almonds followed by quince-apples transfixed with thorns to resemble sea urchins. Even this we could have endured had not the strangest dish of all been served next — so strange that we would have preferred to die of starvation rather than submit our stomachs to more rich food. For we thought the dish placed in front of us was a fattened goose surrounded by fish and every kind of bird. "Friends," said Trimalchio, "whatever you see served here was made from the flesh of a single animal. . . . may my patrimony swell and not my waist if my cook didn't make everything out of a pig. The man couldn't be more valuable. If you like he can make a fish out of a sow's belly, a wood pigeon out of a bacon, a turtledove out of a ham, or a chicken from the pig's knuckle. And because he's got such an apt mind I bought him a present in Rome: carving knives made of the Norican [Austrian] steel." Trimalchio ordered the knives brought instantly to the dining room and then sat marvelling at them. He even gave us leave to test the edges on our cheeks.

Petronius, 69–70.

THE LIST OF DISHES IS ENDED

APPENDIX I

ROMAN WEIGHTS AND MEASURES

In this table are the weights and measures used by Apicius in his book. The Roman pound, or libra, was equal to 0.721 of a modern pound, or approximately 11.5 ounces. It was, however, divided into only 12 ounces, whereas ours is divided into 16. Accordingly, the Roman ounce and our ounce are very close in weight and can be used interchangeably (one Roman ounce = .96 of a modern ounce). Similarly, the Roman pint measure, or sextarius, was equal to 1.2 pints (.96 imperial pints), or 19.2 fluid ounces. The following simple rule will allow you to use Apicius' weights and measures without doing violence to his recipes: regard Roman ounces and pints as modern, but reduce the modern pound weight by ¼ to correspond to the Roman pound.

Roman weights:	*Modern equivalents:*
libra (1 Roman pound)	¾ pound
semilibra ½ pound	6 ounces
unica (1 Roman ounce)	.96 ounce
scripulum (a scruple: $\frac{1}{24}$ ounce)	a dash
six scruples	approximately 1 teaspoonful
sextarius (1 Roman pint)	14.75 fluid ounces
hemina (½ pint)	7.4 fluid ounces
quartarius (¼ pint)	3.7 fluid ounces
acetabulum ($\frac{1}{8}$ pint)	3 Tablespoons
cyathus ($\frac{1}{12}$ pint)	1½ Tablespoons (sometimes meaning a "measure")
coclearum ("snail's shellful")	1 teaspoonful
coclearum dimidium	½ teaspoonful

APPENDIX II

LIST OF SUBSTITUTIONS

These substitutions may be made without doing violence to the authenticity of the Roman recipes.

For:	*Use:*
alecost	mint
chervil	aniseed
colewort	mustard seed
costmary	mint
cyperus root	ginger
Damascus plums	damsons
Egyptian bean root	taro root, potato
Egyptian beans	broad beans
elecampane	aniseed
fish-pickle	See p. 305.
hyssop	mint
laser	fennel or ginger (see recipes)
laurel berries (with fish)	peppercorns
laurel berries (with meat)	cloves or juniper berries
lovage	celery seed or dried celery leaves
mastic	cinnamon, pistachio nut extract, ground pistachios
myrtle berries (with fish)	peppercorns
myrtle berries (with meat)	cloves or juniper berries
pellitory	chamomile
pennyroyal	mint
rocket	mustard seed
rue	rosemary
rue berries	peppercorns
savory	oregano
silphium	fennel or ginger (see recipes)
spelt	fine flour
spikenard, Indian spikenard, European nard	bay leaf

APPENDIX III

SPECIAL INGREDIENTS

Mild Fish pickle

(Use both as a seasoning and as a relish)

3 ounces, drained and washed, canned tuna or salmon, or unsalted sardines or unsalted anchovies
2 t. white wine
1 T. vinegar
½ t. mustard seed
½ t. oregano
½ t. celery seed (or lovage)
1 T. olive oil
½ t. honey
pinch of basil
¼ t. thyme
1 mint leaf, finely chopped

In a mixing bowl, thoroughly combine all ingredients. This fish-pickle may be stored in the refrigerator in a glass jar for up to 2 weeks, and should then be replaced.

Hot Fish-pickle

(Use both as a seasoning and as a relish)

3 ounces, drained and washed, canned tuna or salmon, or unsalted sardines or unsalted anchovies
1 T. white wine
1 T. vinegar
1 T. olive oil
1 small clove of garlic, crushed
¼ t. pepper
2 t. parsley
¼ t. rosemary, ground
¼ t. sage
1 mint leaf, finely chopped
pinch of basil

In a mixing bowl, thoroughly combine all ingredients. This fish-pickle may be stored in the refrigerator in a glass jar for up to 2 weeks, and should then be replaced.

Special Ingredients—*continued*

Boiled Wine

Whenever boiled wine is indicated as an ingredient, the required quantity is obtained by bringing double the amount to a boil and simmering it till it is reduced to ½ its volume.

Example: To obtain ½ cup of boiled wine, boil 1 cup till it is reduced by half.

Wine Sauce

Combine equal parts of wine and an appropriate stock, with olive oil or butter added, to taste.

FOOTNOTES

Book One

1. This recipe is remarkable not only for its subject, wormwood, but also for its geography. Camerinum (Camerino) was a town in the mountainous region of Umbria. Pontica meant, in general, the regions bordering the Black Sea, and in particular a Roman province on the southeast coast of the Black Sea between Bithynia and Armenia, whose king, the famous Mithridates, was defeated by Pompey in 66 B.C. Thebes was, respectively, a Boeotian city in Greece, the setting of Sophocles' play *Oedipus Tyrannus*, and an ancient capital of Egypt.
2. Cyperus is possibly carex of the order cyperaceae, also known as bluegrass or sedge. Carex is a hardy grass that typically grows on the margins of ponds and can be distinguished from other grasses by the absence of joints on the stem.

Book Three

1. Though recorded among vegetable recipes, this formula rightfully belongs in Book I with the other remedies for an upset stomach. The measurements in this preparation are Apician. (See Appendix I: Roman Weights and Measures.)
2. The Latin word "sphondyli" has two meanings in Apicius' work. In the recipes in this Book, a member of the carrot family is meant; whereas in Book IX, sphondyli refers to mussels. Possibly the ancients cultivated the species *Heracleum sphondylium*, or cow parsnip. The modern cook may substitute any edible variety of cultivated parsnip for the recipes contained in this section.

Book Four

1. The word Alexandrine when used as an adjective by Apicius implied "expensive" or "best quality." Alexandria itself was the great port of arrival for spices from India and China.

2. The beccafico is a small bird of the family Sylviadae and resembles the nightingale in appearance. It was regarded as a delicacy by both Greeks and Romans and, indeed, is still prized in Italy. "Beccafico" and the Latin "ficedula" both literally mean figpecker. In the autumn, beccafico birds fatten themselves on figs and were snared for the richness of their meat. The bird is migrant and changes its plumage at the beginning of winter. Pliny (10.44) called it "melancoryphus," or "blackcap."

3. This sentence seems more appropriate for the next recipe than for this one.

4. The word I have interpreted as lizard fish is "lagitis." The reading "lagidis" (grouse) is unlikely since the recipes in this section of Book IV deal with fish dishes. For the same reason, "laridis" (salt pork/bacon) must be excluded since the recipe still would be without its fish. The lizard fish is also mentioned in Book X. It appears from Martial (2.27) that the lizard fish, like the Mediterranean tuna, was salted and then brought to Rome. Apicius was very fond of dishes which combine fish and meats. In this case calf's brains is used.

5. With minor differences, this recipe is a duplicate of a recipe on p. 74.

6. In the case of this recipe, the Apician measurements are eccentric, possibly because of anonymous tinkerings with the manuscripts throughout their long history.

7. The variety of serviceberry given a wine taste by Pliny is the medlar (*Mespilus germanica*), and the other varieties are probably fruits of the mountain ash or rowan tree.

8. Nettles are among the "greens" described earlier in this section.

9. The reference in the recipe to another part of the book is unusual and was not made by Apicius, but by an anonymous Roman or mediaeval transcriber.

10. I believe that the Romans were accustomed to eating a variety of sweet citron similar in taste to the *Medica limetta*, or sweet lime. Thus Apicius describes his citron ragout as "dulce" (sweet) and places it between recipes for Matian apples and apricots. Pliny (23.105) advises that citrons should be eaten with vinegar, an impossibility with a strong acid citrus fruit. Today candied citron peel can be bought to use with cakes and confectionery.

Book Five

1. This recipe is nearly identical to *Pottage Julian*. The only significant difference is that unmixed (thicker) wine is specified. (See Introd., p. xxvii.)

2. See note 2 for Book III, above.

3. Strictly speaking, the Latin word "conchicla" refers to beans cooked in their pods, the ancestors of the modern French or string beans. Apicius appears to have used the word in the larger sense of "legumes in the pod."

4. The reference to Commodus is by far the latest reference to a living person in the pages of *The Roman Cookery of Apicius*, and could not have been written by the last Apicius, who lived during the reign of Trajan (98–117 A.D.). Perhaps the recipe was given its title by a chef unfortunate enough to be in the service of the insane Commodus.

5. This recipe is identical to *Barley Soup with Meat*. See p. 95.

6. This recipe is identical to *Vegetable and Lentil Soup*. See p. 95.

Book Seven

1. These directions in the text were transcribed in reverse, no doubt by a mediaeval copyist whose thoughts were on his dinner and not on the manuscript.
2. The Latin word "sumen" can refer both to the udder and the belly.
3. This section, Roasts, actually belongs in Book VIII, Quadrupeds, and not among the "costly recipes" of Book VII. The five recipes below are to be used with neck of mutton, beef pot roasts, and rump roasts.
4. An unknown hand has added the following words to the manuscript of *The Roman Cookery of Apicius:* "Varro says that onions boiled in water 'seek the mouth of Venus,' and so are put on the table at wedding feasts seasoned with colewort juice and pepper."
5. The Latin of this section is larded with ambiguity. Strictly speaking, "boleti" refers to the *Boletus edulis* mushroom, but Pliny uses the word to include all mushrooms, whether poisonous or not.

Book Nine

1. This and the following two recipes are not, strictly speaking, to do with fish and perhaps were added by an unknown hand after Apicius' death. The first two employ a culinary subterfuge to present hare, kid, or chicken livers in the shape of a fish. The third is medicinal, and resembles the preparations in Book I for aiding the digestion.

Book Ten

1. The Latin title of this recipe is "Sauce for poached fish," which is obviously incorrect. "Fish steamed in its own jueces" is much more appropriate

The Excerpts of Apicius

1. In the original Latin, the title of this recipe reads *Pisces Oenoteganon.* The word *oenoteganon,* however, does not appear in any of the ancient texts, and it is much more likely that the intended word was *zomoteganon* and was transcribed incorrectly. *Zomoteganon* appears earlier, in Book IV, in the recipe *Patina Zomoteganon,* and implies that the fish is to be stewed in its own juices.

ANNOTATIONS TO ILLUSTRATIONS

PAGE

1. This bronze disk, found in Pompeii, was used to call slaves.
1. A Greek stone frieze showing the harvesting of grapes.
5. A bronze dipper, found in Pompeii, which may have been used to ladle wine.
6. Part of a bronze scale, with the counterweight in the image of the god Mercury.
12. Though *situlae* were generally used for drawing water, this one of silver, found in France, was probably ornamental and an expression of wealth.

7. This silver gilt *cantharus*, used for drinking wine, was found in Pompeii. It is decorated with a relief of cranes, a bird eaten by the wealthy for its status value, rather than its flavor.

8. This Graeco-Roman bowl is similar to bronze pieces found in Pompeii. It was possibly used as a serving dish in the dining room.

3. A first century bronze saucepan, found in Pompeii, with a decorated handle.

4. A first century pottery bowl, found in Pompeii.

6. A bronze strainer, found in Pompeii, possibly used in the straining of legumes.

9. A bronze *cista* (box) from the first century B.C., used for stowing a variety of things, including foods.

1. A bell-shaped pottery bowl of a common design, from Pompeii.

3. A silver egg dish, possibly used to serve eggs during the dessert courses.

9. A first century ceramic bowl, found in Pompeii.

4. This piece, with its elaborate fluted shape and decorated handle was probably used for serving dessert foods such as eggs, snails, small pastries, and quince apples.

9. A typical first century ceramic serving bowl.

9. These *pithoi* are very large and ancient storage jars for olive oil, made of clay. Found at Knossos in Crete.

06. A first century, Pompeiian, ceramic bowl.

6. A first century copper *caccabus* used as a cooking pot, stewing pot, and all-purpose saucepan.

21. A bronze, elaborately decorated *thermospodium* from first century Pompeii. Fuelled by charcoal, it was probably used to keep liquids warm, while the deep tray was for fuel storage.

47. From a Roman wall painting, an upper class girl of Pompeii, holding a stylus and, probably, waxen tablets.

57. First century clay *amphorae*, found in Pompeii. Used for storing and carrying a wide variety of foods, such as olive oil, fish-pickle, and wines. They were sealed with pitch and stopped with cork and gypsum.

64. A first century Roman glass wine flask. Used to serve wine or for pouring oils used in the baths.

70. A bronze *askos*, (pitcher) shaped like a wineskin. A utilitarian vessel, probably used to pour liquids at the table or in the kitchen.

35. A first century silver dish on a silver stand, found in Pompeii, possibly used for fish-pickle.

87. A second century mosaic detail of a hunting scene. Mosaics were a common form of decoration in the Roman dining rooms of Apicius' day.

93. A first century silver jug and saucepan, or dipper, found in Pompeii.

00. A first century ceramic bowl, found in Pompeii.

20. A first century colored glass goblet, found near Vesuvius. A typical drinking cup used in the dining room. The silver spoon from the same area was the utensil commonly used for eating, in the absence of forks. The cook or another servant cut up the foods into small pieces before they were served.

227. A first century pottery jug, found in Pompeii, possibly used as a warming or servin vessel.
235. A first century *caccabus*, or cook pot, found in Pompeii.
239. A first century Pompeian mosaic in the shape of a crab.
243. A first century pottery bowl, from Pompeii. Possibly used for serving sauces. Th bronze ladle is from the same area.
267. A first century silver bowl from the Vesuvius area, possibly used to serve nuts.
281. A first century Roman frieze showing a cutlery vendor.
289. A first century pottery bowl, possibly used as a mortar or mixing bowl.
291. A first century cooking pot, from Pompeii, possibly used for cooking ragouts an soups.

BIBLIOGRAPHY

Anthimus. *De Observatio Ciborum*. Text, commentary, and glossary, with a study of th Latinity. Edited by Shirley Howard Weber. Leidin: E.J. Brill, Ltd., 1924.

Apicius. *De Re Coquinaria*. Edited by M.E. Milham. Leipzig: Teubner, 1969. This is th best Latin text of *De Re Coquinaria*..

Apicius. *De Re Coquinaria*. Edited by Barbara Flower and Elisabeth Rosenbaum as *Tl Roman Cookery Book*. London: Harrap, 1958. A Latin-English text principally of scholarl interest.

Apicius. *De Re Coquinaria*. Edited by Joseph Dommers Vehling as *Cookery and Dining i Imperial Rome*. Chicago: Walter M. Hill, 1936; republished by Dover, 1977. The text almost unreadable, but the "review," or introduction, contains a number of interestir speculations concerning the identity of Apicius and the art of ancient cookery.

Apicius. *L'Art Culinaire*. Texte établi, traduit, et commenté par Jacques André. Pari L'Association Guillaume Budé, 1974.

Athenaeus. *The Deipnosophists*. 7 vols. Loeb Classical Library. London: Heinemann, 196r

Bardswell, F. *The Herb Garden*. London: A & C Black, 1930.

Bury, J. B., and Meiggs, R. *A History of Greece to the Death of Alexander the Great*. Fourt Edition. New York: St. Martin's Press, 1975.

Cato. "De Agri Cultura," *De Re Rustica*. Edited by W. D. Hooper and H. B. Ash. Loe Classical Library. London: Heinemann, 1954.

Catullus. *Carmina*. Edited by R. A. Mynors. Oxford: Oxford University Press, 1967.

Clausen, W. V., ed. *Persi et Iuuenalis Saturae*. Oxford: Oxford University Press, 1966.

Columella. *On Agriculture*. Edited by Harrison Boyd Ash. Cambridge, Mass: Harvar University Press, 1955.

Columella, Cato, Varro, Palladius. *De Re Rustica*. Paris: Robert Stephen, 1543.

Cyril, Ray. *The Wines of Italy*. London: Octopus, 1966.

Davidson, Alan. *Mediterranean Seafood*. London: Penguin, 1972. Of use in the identificatio of certain fish in Books IX and X of Apicius and in its account of contemporary Medite ranean seafood recipes.

Florus. *Epitome Rerum Romanarum.* Edited by Jo Georgii Graevii. Amsterdam: Henry Wetstein, 1692.

Gibbon, Edward. *The History of the Decline and Fall of the Roman Empire.* 12 vol. London: Cadell & Davies, 1807.

Herodotus. *Histories.* Third Edition. Edited by Charles Hyde. Oxford: Oxford University Press, 1908.

Hieatt, C., and Butler, S. *Pleyn Delit: Medieval Cookery for Modern Cooks.* Toronto: University of Toronto Press, 1976.

Hirth, F. *China and the Roman Orient.* New York: Paragon, 1966.

Horace. *Odes.* Edited by P. E. Page. London: MacMillan, 1964.

Juvenal. *The Sixteen Satires.* Translated, with an introduction and notes by Peter Green. Harmondsworth, Middlesex, England: Penguin, 1967.

Luce, J. V. *The End of Atlantis.* St. Albans: Paladin, 1975.

Lust, John. *The Herb Book.* New York: Bantam, 1979.

Martial. *Epigrams.* 2 vol. Loeb Classical Library. London: Heinemann, 1943.

Martialis, Q. Gargilii. *De Hortis.* Edited by Innocenzo Mazzini. Bologna: Pàtron Editore, 1978.

Montagne, Prosper. *The New Larousse Gastronomique: The Encyclopedia of Food, Wine and Cooking.* Edited by Charlotte Turgeon. New York: Crown Publishers, 1977.

Parry, J. H. *An Illustrated History of Men, Ships and the Sea in the Fifteenth and Sixteenth Centuries.* New York: Dial, 1974.

Petronius. *Satyricon.* Loeb Classical Library, London: Heinemann, 1956.

Pliny. *Natural History.* Vols. I–X. Loeb Classical Library. London: Heinemann, 1963. On the subjects of foods and wines Pliny and Petronius are highly entertaining.

Rhys, Ernest, ed. *Atlas of Ancient and Modern Geography.* Everyman Library. London: Dent.

Rose, H. J. *A Handbook of Greek Mythology.* London: Methuen, 1964.

Seneca. *Ad Lucilium Epistulae Morales.* 2 Vols. Oxford Classical Texts Ser. Oxford: Oxford University Press, 1965.

Smith, Henry. *The Master Book of Poultry and Game.* London: Spring Books, 1950.

Soper, Musia, ed. *Encyclopedia of European Cooking.* London: Spring Books, 1962.

Soyer, Alexis. *The Pantropheon, or A History of Food and Its Preparation in Ancient Times.* London Simpkin, Marshall, 1853. Reprint. Paddington Press, 1977.

Suetonius. *Lives of the Caesars.* 2 Vols. Loeb Classical Library. Cambridge, Mass.: Harvard University Press.

Tarn, W. W. *The Greeks in Bactria and India.* Second Edition. Cambridge: Cambridge University Press, 1951.

Theophrastus. *Inquiry into Plants.* 2 vols. Loeb Classical Library. London: Heinemann, 1961.

Trypanis, Constantine A., ed. *Penguin Book of Greek Verse.* London: Penguin, 1971.

Varro. *De Re Rustica.* Edited by W. D. Hooper and H. B. Ash. Loeb Classical Library. London: Heinemann, 1954.

Virgil. *Opera.* Edited by R. A. Mynors. Oxford: Oxford University Press, 1969.

Warmington, E. H. *The Commerce Between the Roman Empire and India,* London: Curzon Press, 1974.

Younger, William. *Gods, Men and Wine.* Cleveland: World Publishing Company, 1966.

INDEX